WHY THE DALAI LAMA MATTERS

HIS ACT OF TRUTH AS THE SOLUTION FOR CHINA, TIBET, AND THE WORLD

ROBERT THURMAN

ATRIA PAPERBACK
New York London Toronto Sydney

BEYOND WORDS
Hillsboro, Oregon

ATRIA PAPERBACK
A Division of Simon & Schuster, Inc.
1230 Avenue of the Americas
New York, NY 10020

BEYOND WORDS
20827 N.W. Cornell Road, Suite 500
Hillsboro, Oregon 97124-9808
503-531-8700 / 503-531-8773 fax
www.beyondword.com

Managing editor: Lindsay S. Brown
Editor: Julie Steigerwaldt
Copyeditor: Ali McCart
Proofreader: Gretchen Stelter
Illustrations: Robert Beer
Design: Sara E. Blum and Devon Smith
Composition: William H. Brunson Typography Services

First Atria Books/Beyond Words trade paperback edition May 2011

ATRIA PAPERBACK and colophon are trademarks of Simon & Schuster, Inc. Beyond Words Publishing is a division of Simon & Schuster, Inc.

For more information about special discounts for bulk purchases, please contact Simon & Schuster Special Sales at 1-866-506-1949 or business@simonandschuster.com.

The Simon & Schuster Speakers Bureau can bring authors to your live event. For more information or to book an event, contact the Simon & Schuster Speakers Bureau at 1-866-248-3049 or visit our website at www.simonspeakers.com.

Manufactured in the United States of America

10 9 8 7 6 5 4 3 2 1

The Library of Congress has cataloged the hardcover edition as follows:

Thurman, Robert A. F.
    Why the Dalai Lama matters : his act of truth as the solution for China, Tibet, and the world / by Robert Thurman.
        p. cm.
        1. Bstan-'dzin-rgya-mtsho, Dalai Lama XIV, 1935– 2. Buddhism—China—Tibet. 3. Central-local government relations—China—Tibet. 4. Tibet (China)—History—Autonomy and independence movements.   I. Title.
    BQ7935.B777T48   2008
    294.3'923092—dc22
                                                                        2008008529
ISBN: 978-1-58270-220-9 (hc)
ISBN: 978-1-58270-221-6 (pbk)
ISBN: 978-1-4165-9196-2 (ebook)

The corporate mission of Beyond Words Publishing, Inc.: *Inspire to Integrity*

DEDICATION

To the brave people of Tibet (Böd Kawajen) and their leader, His Holiness the Great Fourteenth Dalai Lama—I dedicate this humble effort to help their heroic efforts for their own freedom, for the freedom of their neighbors in four directions, in China, India, the Turkestans, and the Mongolias, and for the peace of our world. May the truth prevail!

CONTENTS

ACKNOWLEDGMENTS

There are many who have helped me with this fated book, but none have been more helpful than my old friend Barbara Dills with her Lakota determination and sense of justice, and her hi-tech communication insights. For inspiration, I thank Marc and Lynne Benioff, Joost Elffers, Fred Doner, and Roland Comtois. Cynthia Black and Richard Cohn of Beyond Words caught the vision and made it happen. They deserve my most heartfelt thanks. I also deeply thank Judith Curr for her clear and decisive support; Lindsay Brown and Sara Blum for their patient perseverance and creativity; Annie Bien, William Meyers, Leslie Kriesel, Julie Steigerwaldt, Marie Hix, and Ali McCart for their skillful and perspicacious editorial help; Tsering Wangyal Shawa, the Norbulingka Institute, Steve Marshall and Suzette Cooke for their creation of the all-important maps that tell the story; William Bushell, Ph.D., for his research into high-altitude physiology and genetics; Suzanne van Drunick, Ph.D., Tingjun Zhang, Ph.D., and Oliver Frauenfeld, Ph.D., from the Cooperative Institute for Research in Environment Sciences (CIRES) at the University of Colorado, for research on climate change on the Tibetan Plateau; and among photographers who love Tibet, the late and much lamented Galen Rowell as well as Steve McCurry, Sonam Zoksang, Nina Schroeder, Don Farber, Joseph Gottwald, Martin Gray, and Rajiv Mehrotra. I am grateful to the Office of His Holiness the Dalai Lama in Dharamsala, to the helpful staff members of the Office of Information of the Tibetan Government in Exile, to the Tibet Environmental Watch website, to the Norbulingka Institute in Dharamsala, and to the staff of Tibet House US in New York. Finally, I live in constant gratitude to my wife, Nena, and all my children, grandchildren, and my great-granddaughter.

"The problem of Tibet is very complicated. It is intrinsically linked with many issues: politics, the nature of society, law, human rights, religion, culture, the identity of a people, the economy and the state of the natural environment. Consequently, a comprehensive approach must be adopted to resolve this problem that takes into account the benefits to all parties involved, rather than one party alone."

His Holiness the Fourteenth Dalai Lama Tenzin Gyatso
Speech on the forty-ninth anniversary of the
Tibetan National Uprising Day

Introduction

Everyone tends to like the Dalai Lama, even when they don't think they will. The question is, "Why?" Traveling the world as an author and professor, and talking with all kinds of people, I have seen the way individuals everywhere have embraced His Holiness the Dalai Lama and almost universally granted him a huge degree of moral authority. In an era marked by a pervasive sense of hopelessness and discouragement about the state of things—despite all our advances in science and culture—it is a humble Buddhist monk from the remote highlands of Tibet who inspires optimism for the future.

I have witnessed this strange phenomenon time and again over the years whenever the Dalai Lama appears in public, as well as in private meetings with noted scientists, dignitaries, and heads-of-state. Even secular materialists flock to the wisdom of this man, recognized by his own followers to be the incarnation of a divine being. People of every background and faith perk up when they recall his presence, impact, and meaning. And they feel a huge weight lifted from them when they meet him or hear his teachings. It certainly isn't because of his Buddhist practice, since many who admire him are nonbelievers or followers of other religions. The Dalai Lama is a dynamic person, but he is neither theatrical nor glamorous. He's also been called a dreamer, an idealist, and unrealistic in his prescriptions for world peace, nonviolence, demilitarization, and happiness through sharing and justice.

People like him so much because, despite the state of our world and the ongoing oppression of his people, the Dalai Lama sees that all is possible—even the good, the true, and the beautiful. And yet, despite his extraordinary popularity in all corners and his repeated and sincere attempts at reconciliation with the Chinese leadership, he remains living in exile after half a century of repressive Chinese rule in Tibet. And again we must ask, "Why?"

This book is a response to the questions above, offering many more reasons why people like him—and why our admiration should be even greater. It also describes what the Dalai Lama could accomplish for China, Tibet, and the world if he were allowed to do so. Should people choose to follow his practical advice about ethics and society, astonishing benefits await. I outline simple, practical steps that the leadership of China could take, showing how easily they could cease making an enemy of a good friend and accept him as a key ally in winning the goodwill and cooperation of the Tibetan people. And I suggest what specific benefits he could confer upon them, as they work together toward a positive future for China and Tibet, giving to both sides what they really need.

I provide here a vision of what things would look like if his country were restored to his people and himself, and if they were allowed to freely manage it as an autonomous region within China, for the benefit of China and the entire world. My claims are grounded by the Dalai Lama's own words. His speeches from various solemn settings can seem so simple and direct that people tend not to fully appreciate their weight. Elucidating them here will help to underscore their profound implications in ways that he is too humble to do himself.

The Dalai Lama's wish and vision for humanity are absolutely right and reliable, realistic and not far-fetched, helpful and not harmful. And he has been living his act of truth for the last sixty years, as you'll see throughout this book. I present to you his exemplary act of truth and the implications of his wise words as the key to solving the problem of China and Tibet and, indeed, flowing away from the planetary crisis into which we are plunging headlong.

I am not saying he so presents himself—not at all. He never makes such claims about himself. He never seeks to impose his views on others, except as his good advice may emerge in dialogue. He prefers to listen to people and engage with their ideas. Actually, he is altogether too humble.

As a former monk and nearly lifelong Buddhist, I have known the Dalai Lama for over four decades and have studied under him for many years. But this book is *not* a collaboration with him; I ground many of my thoughts in his published words, but he is not responsible for my conclusions and expressions. It is my own vision of how he can and should be better understood, his wisdom and compassion more actively deployed to solve our planet-wide problems. I am not telling him what to do either. He already does everything that I describe him as doing and probably more on subtler planes than I can perceive. The goal of this book is precisely to let people know more clearly and thoroughly all that he does. If more people recognize the amazing service he provides, they will magnify his efforts to the degree needed to get the job done. I mean really get it done—not just go through the motions, all the while constricted by the thought that, while it's nice to imagine goodness winning out in the end, it's really not possible.

Here we are all together in the soup. Hope is essential for the quality of our being—and for our potential saving of the world—for the sake of our children and children's children. We must envision positive outcomes and work for them with all our might, whether we succeed or not. As the Dalai Lama often says, we must try with all our might and never give up. Then, even if we fail, we will have less regret, having done our best.

Anything is possible, anytime, anywhere, any way.

YOU ARE THE REVOLUTION

It's time for a global revolution. Not just a different regime here and there, an election of different leaders, a war won or lost (always lost by all sides nowadays)—these will not suffice at this critical moment in our interwoven human lives. The pace of positive change has to match the pace of the clearly apparent devastation. It has to be revolutionary, and it must involve us all.

Luckily, a revolution has been going on for almost three thousand years. I call it an *inner revolution,* a revolution in human consciousness. It is not a religious movement, though it can seem to be, depending on how you think of religion. It is spiritual but also material—fully evolutionary. It falls to us humans to realize our true destiny, achieve our unique creative potential, become gentle, transcend our prejudices and delusions, realize our immortality, become conscious evolvers, love one another, and be brave enough to seize our human right to supreme, natural bliss.

World leaders, no matter how misguided they have been, caught in the grip of the attitudes and habits of military-industrial savagery, must join the humblest people in advancing this revolution. This is not the kind of "hot" revolution that violently topples oppressive leaders only to replace them with even more violent revolutionary ones. This is a non-violent revolution, a "cool" revolution. This revolution begins within each person who wants to know what it's all about, who is not satisfied with being told he or she can't know, but must just believe this or that, and that common sense is unreliable. It continues to gather strength as people gain some new insight into their true condition, and through that insight, feel so much better about things that they become less tolerant of their own and others' habitual misery. The revolution becomes visible in society when such people become activated through the energy of joy and compassion, in that they won't take no for an answer, they become determined to make things better, they make cheerful but powerful waves that stir up positive change around them. And the revolution succeeds when the actual patterns of courtesy and custom between people, and even the structures of governance, become more oriented toward freedom and fulfillment of individuals.

The supreme leader of this revolution alive today is the Dalai Lama. He is the true leader of world leaders, just as Shakyamuni Buddha was thousands of years ago. Believed to be a perfectly enlightened person, he grew up a prince of India but left his throne to investigate life and death to the ultimate degree. He was finally overjoyed when he discovered the true nature of reality and proceeded to teach hundreds of thousands of people for forty-five years, founding the Buddhist movement with still over a billion followers today, if those under communism are counted.

I have always acknowledged Shakyamuni Buddha and the Dalai Lama for their revolutionary leadership, at the two ends of the 2,600-year-old ongoing inner revolution. Shakyamuni the Buddha founded the inner revolution in our world around the middle of the first millennium BCE, with the great planetary energy of the Axial Age, the time of most of the world's great teachers, including Pythagoras, Socrates, Isaiah, Zoroaster, Yajnavalkya, Confucius, and Lao Tzu. His profound insight into the selflessness and relativity of all persons and things released from his heart a great flood of universal love for beings, enabled him to understand the processes of human evolution and history in detail, and empowered him to become an amazingly competent world teacher. He preceded Einstein with his insight of total relativity, and he preceded the revolutionaries of the Western Enlightenment in setting the ideals for all civilized communities of individualism, gentleness, wisdom education, altruism, and egalitarianism. His teachings resonate in perfect harmony with all the great Axial Age teachers of all the known streams of literate culture, and we have all now reached together the moment on the planet when we either implement these ideals more fully or perish from the failure to do so.

Indeed, it might seem that we have failed to live up to the moral prescriptions of all the greats, but for the heroic example of the Dalai Lama and a few like him. He is a Prince of Peace and Philosopher King of Tibet, by which I mean that he walks successfully in the path of loving meekness so powerfully pointed out and exemplified by Jesus, while also fulfilling the ideals of Plato in action. He is the champion of the Buddha's wisdom, deep, vast, and exquisite for his carrying on Shakyamuni's scientific teaching of the ultimate freedom of voidness, his religious teaching of the vast art of compassionate action, and his psychological teaching of the power of beauty to liberate. The Dalai Lama calls himself a simple Shakya monk, but he is also Shakyamuni's devoted heir. He reaches out to all humans, nonreligious as well as followers of every kind of religion, as the upholder of the common human religion of kindness, embracing all, regardless of belief system, in the church of life in the rite of human kindness.

He is also a scientist, an explorer of the sciences of mind, spirit, society, and nature. He relentlessly pursues absolute truth for its own sake, and yet combines his discoveries with moral restraint and altruistic creativity. He has that mysterious ability to bring hope and boundless positivity when all seems doomed, leading people to wonder how he can be such a dynamo of positive energy when he and his people have suffered so terribly for half a century. He received the Nobel Peace Prize as a living exemplar of the path first made politically effective by Mahatma Gandhi, and so doing has made peace the path as well as thus the realistic goal. According to Buddhist science, he has mastered the death and rebirth process to continue his work unimpeded even by death. His followers believe that he lives again and again to continue the inner revolution, effective for all beings, believers or nonbelievers, through all world religions and all world sciences. Though many of us, with our one-life worldview, will not easily understand how Buddhist science considers reincarnation realistic, we can understand how powerful this sense of the continuous presence of a savior being is for those who do accept its plausibility.

The central force of this cool revolution today is the Dalai Lama. When I say he is the key to solving our problems, I do not mean that he is going to tell us all what to do. He would tell us that we ourselves will know what to do when we consult our deepest wisdom and feel our common human kindness. It does not mean we are going to have to believe in him, in some religious sense, since he tells us that we must think critically about what everyone says, including what we say to ourselves, and come to understand things on our own.

WHY YOU SHOULD CARE

Some people may think, "Tibet is on the other side of the world—why should I care about what is happening there? Whether Tibet is independent, autonomous, or a Chinese territory, what does it matter?" We should care because China's actions have implications for the entire world. As human beings, it's impossible not to care when you know of the appalling manner in which the Tibetans are being treated. To illustrate, I'd like to tell you about a day in the life of one Tibetan.

Sonam Choden is a farmer in the Tibet countryside. In addition to tilling his field of barley, he used to let his animals graze in the plentiful grasslands. But ever since the Chinese government began providing financial incentives for Chinese to settle in Tibet, that way of life has become impossible. Ever since he can remember, he has been heavily taxed by the Chinese government, but he could still manage. Recently, though, since the best lands are now given to Chinese settlers, there is no more open land left for Sonam and his animals. He has had to give up his way of life and look for work in the town.

Each morning after waking, Sonam fixes himself breakfast, like his wife, Dolma, used to do before she was imprisoned three years ago. Her crime was waving a Tibetan flag in a peaceful demonstration. Sonam is not allowed to visit her—is not even sure where she is imprisoned—and doesn't know when or if she will be released. His father was imprisoned in the 1960s for his political incorrectness, sent to a labor camp, and never heard from again. Sonam's mother died soon after, when Sonam was still young. Sonam bravely faced the future, married Dolma, and tried to begin anew during the 1980s. Now he has lost his wife. He tries not to think about the stories he's heard about the torture, starvation, and abuse of women that occurs in the prisons and labor camps.

After breakfast, Sonam sets off looking for a way to make a living. Work is scarce, and although just a few miles away the Chinese are damming one of the region's vital rivers to build an enormous hydroelectric dam to tap into Tibet's hydropower, Sonam cannot get work there as the jobs are open only to Chinese.

In town, Sonam nods to an old friend, Benba Tsering. Benba was one of hundreds of Tibetans sent away to China by the government here for "education" in the 1970s. He came back to the town and took up a position in the Chinese administration. Sonam and Benba used to celebrate Tibetan holidays together, but ever since Benba has returned, Sonam doesn't have the same trust for his friend that he used to. Plenty of his family have been imprisoned after speaking plainly to people who were really spies for the Chinese. Now Sonam feels it's safer to pretend to be pro-Chinese and hide his real views. Unfortunately, this means suppressing his very deep Tibetan-ness.

The nearby town that used to be filled with his people speaking his language is now inundated with Chinese settlers. Sonam is a minority here, in his own country. It is now afternoon and the children are done with school for the day. He sees his twelve-year-old nephew, who greets him in Chinese. He asks his nephew why he isn't being taught in Tibetan, and his nephew explains that if he wants a job after school the only way he can get one is if he speaks Chinese. Tibetan isn't taught at all, he explains to his uncle.

Sonam shakes his head as he makes his way back home. As the sun sets, he passes a monastery that had long ago been destroyed by the Chinese. After he and other local people had done partial reconstruction, they invited monks to move there, and some distance away they also reconstructed a small nunnery. After a while, some of the nuns were imprisoned for going to Lhasa and chanting "Long Live the Dalai Lama" in a peaceful demonstration, and the authorities came and closed the nunnery and sent the remaining nuns home. Some of the monks in the monastery were also expelled; Sonam doesn't know their fate. He knows this monastery will never again be rebuilt, as the Chinese have banned all further reconstruction on monasteries, and this village has exceeded the Chinese-enforced limit on the number of monks and nuns.

Back at home, loneliness overcomes Sonam and he wishes he and his wife had at least had a child when they had the chance. His wife had been coerced into sterilization by the Chinese authorities as part of their birth control campaign especially targeting Tibetan women. He could chant some Tibetan Buddhist prayers to comfort himself, but he fears his neighbors will hear the verses that call upon the compassion of his lamas, especially Tenzin Gyatso, the Dalai Lama. Instead he closes his eyes, turns his prayer wheel, and silently murmurs the mantra of the bodhisattva of universal compassion, "OM MANI PEYME HUM," and hopes that someday soon things will be better.

This is why we should care; it isn't just about something happening half a world away but what it means to be human, truly part of the global community. What is happening in Tibet represents much more than a simple political, environmental, or religious conflict. It matters deeply that we stand up for what is right and act now to achieve this peaceful future that directly affects each and every one of us, Tibetan or not.

A WORLD WAR WE CAN AVOID

Tibet's problem is China's problem and Asia's problem and therefore our global, individual problem—yours and mine. As an overview of Tibet's situation, it's important to briefly describe its recent history and the problems facing its people. Tibet is the nation of people who share a common language, culture, and ethnic identity and inhabit the Tibetan high plateau, the largest and highest such plateau, as large as all of Western Europe, with average altitude between two and three miles. Its indigenous name is actually Böd, which you'll see used now and then in this book. It has been an independent country like France or Switzerland for more than two thousand years (this current year is the Tibetan Royal Year 2135).

Due to the artificial isolation imposed on it throughout the nineteenth-century "great game" between the British, Russian, and Manchu empires, it came into the modern period relatively unknown, except for strange stories of magic and mystery swirling about it in the modern imagination. Therefore, in 1949–1951, when the newly triumphant Chinese Communist regime under Mao Zedong invaded Tibet, the world community was puzzled and paralyzed by cold war politics. The Chinese subsequently annexed Tibet after splitting it into twelve parts, destroyed its religion and culture, plundered its accumulated wealth, ravaged its natural resources, and killed or enslaved its population.

The Dalai Lama and around eighty thousand followers managed to escape to India in 1959, where they were sheltered and allowed to create the Tibetan Government in Exile, as a recompense for the fact that Pandit Nehru, out of perceived political expediency, did not tell the world what he knew about the independence of Tibet and the illegality of the Chinese invasion. For the last forty-nine years, the Dalai Lama and the Tibetan refugees, now numbering several hundred thousand worldwide, have continued the long process of keeping their culture and religion alive in exile and bringing the plight of their compatriots to the world's attention. At the same time, the Tibetan exiles have had a huge impact on the world through sharing their remarkable knowledge of the human mind and heart, cultivated over 1,300 years since the Buddhist movement found shelter in Tibet from the Western invasions of India that brought down devastating persecution on the Buddhist communities there.

The people of the world now know more widely the story of Tibet and its severe plight, and the Dalai Lama personally may be the most popular person in the entire world, far more so than any political leader. However, the world's governments, anxious for business with China and dreaming of access to the billion-plus person market, all pretend that Tibet is China's internal matter and so do not speak up officially, though they may deplore China's human rights violations in general, including those perpetrated in Tibet. So Tibet is still abandoned after almost sixty years of genocidal oppression and colonization, and it seems clear that its condition will not improve until the world system changes and international law and global ethics have real meaning.

In addition, this deadlock between Tibet and China stands at the cusp of an enormous global crisis in the making, which arises with the emergence of the Chinese nation into a world power in the modern sense. At the moment, the Europeans, Japanese, and Americans are working with China based on their wish to exploit it economically, as they did militarily in colonial days, using China as a source of cheap labor and wishing to use its potential market. But now China is emerging not as a mere labor pool and someday market for export goods but as a world competitor and perhaps conqueror, economically, technologically, culturally, and very soon, militarily. Within our human psyches hides an age-old dark and dank pool of racism and mistrust that goes both ways. This crisis could result in a real World War III, another irreconcilable "clash of civilizations," as the neocon historian Huntington has labeled it, ending in a nuclear world war that would ruin the northern hemisphere for a century—at the very least.

This is a World War we do not want to have. And here the Tibetans can be a miraculous bridge between the Chinese and the rest of the world if the Chinese could address and overcome their racist and frankly genocidal attitude toward the Tibetans, similar to the white Europeans' former attitude toward the Native Americans, and see them as valuable in themselves. The Dalai Lama is very much the keystone for this diplomatic effort, having received the Nobel Peace Prize from the Scandinavians and the Congressional Gold Medal of Honor from the US Congress and president, and numerous other awards and honors from many nations and all types of people.

Despite all of these accolades and recognition, the Chinese government—and those supposed realists in geopolitics who support it—depicts the Dalai Lama as the problem. They think he is the enemy, blocking their program to eradicate Tibetans and Tibetan culture, so as to keep possession of Tibet as if it were legitimate, as if it had always been a part of China. Quite simply, the Dalai Lama's presence and activities embarrass the leaders of China. He is visible, living testimony to the illegitimacy of their claims of sovereignty and the atrocity of their colonial aims in Tibet, and so unmasks their imperialist ambitions for the rest of Asia and indeed the world.

In order to make China appear unified and to substantiate their erroneous historical claims, the Chinese government has sought for 60 years to dominate both the land and its people in a futile effort to shape it to China's image and turn the Tibetans into Chinese. The government of China has used the same tactics employed by colonial powers the world over, including brutal repression of religious freedom, cultural expression, and language, and the implementation of programs of resettlement, intermarriage, forced sterilization, and the destruction of cultural identity.

Violent suppression, censorship, and disparaging propaganda about the Dalai Lama leaves most Chinese citizens uninformed about what is happening to Tibet. However, some brave and prominent Chinese intellectuals have circulated petitions decrying what they call a "one sided" portrayal of the crackdown in Tibet, asking the government to engage in direct dialogue with the Dalai Lama. Similar calls to the Chinese leadership to conduct good-faith meetings with the Dalai Lama are increasing from leaders in Europe, the US, and elsewhere.

But it is clear that the powers-that-be in China are hallucinating, projecting their own shadows upon his sunny persona. He is the unsolicited best friend of Chinese leaders and the Chinese people. In fact, the Chinese leaders need his help and the help of the Tibetan people if they are truly to garner the respect and admiration of the global community. They aim to achieve personal glory as great leaders in the succession from Mao Zedong and Deng Xiaoping, two of the founding leaders of the People's Republic of China, and from Jiang Zemin, their immediate predecessor. They aim to make China the number one superpower in the world, with internal prosperity and stability, and external military power, economic respect, and cultural admiration. And they wish to lift all their people to a sufficient quality of life and lifestyle that will make them satisfied with the government and the Communist Party, so as to preserve harmony between not-too-rich and not-too-poor, and between the Han Chinese majority and the fifty-six minorities, especially the Tibetans, Uighur and Hui Muslims, Manchus, and Mongolians.

But if they persist in overextending their military-industrial territorial control, in reckless industrialization that causes environmental destruction and pollution, and in excessive polarization between super rich and dirt poor, they will spoil their relations with their neighbors, lose the goodwill of their own masses, lose their personal health and wealth, eventually lose Tibet, and fragment their union for generations.

For almost a thousand years, Chinese empires have thrived with the spiritual blessings of the Tibetans, flowing down to them out of the pristine mountain highlands along with their vital lifelines, the great Yellow and Yangtse rivers. Whenever a shortsighted Chinese or foreign dynasty lost touch with their spiritual sources and neglected or oppressed the highland people, the result has always been tragic. The current Chinese leaders only embarrass themselves in the eyes of the world by treating a friend as an enemy.

WHAT THE FUTURE COULD LOOK LIKE

Tibet could be free and thriving under true autonomy, making more money for China than now, sustainably. The Dalai Lama could give the Chinese government the legitimacy in Tibet they have lacked, while they repair the damage previous Chinese leaders caused and Tibetans voluntarily decide to join as independent participants in a Chinese Federal Union or People's Republic. He can help them see how they can achieve the wealth, power, sustainable society, and harmony with their neighbors and respect from the world that they want, by ceasing to continue on their anachronistic and self-destructive path of nineteenth-century imperialism. Just by their own insight and change of heart they can transform the Dalai Lama from being a liability to becoming a precious asset and, in that way, discover in him the golden key that unlocks the solution to their greatest problems. On the website of the Chinese Embassy in the United States, President Hu Jintao is quoted as saying that success in life "requires resolve, attention to concrete matters, and courage in making decisions." So perhaps he could be the leader to enact the Chinese revolution. If President Hu does not seize this golden opportunity, then it will be one of his successors who wishes to achieve real global eminence for himself and for China.

In regard to the larger world, China's successful turnaround from obsolete military-industrial policies will lead the way for America and Russia to also do the same, imitated as they are by almost all the nations of the world, even poor nations that cannot take care of their people's needs. The huge resources everywhere tied up in militarism then will be freed to invest in the environment and in the poor and destitute throughout the world. Thus, we will move beyond the sea of violence in which we are drowning and enter the long-promised new age of peace, prosperity, and positive evolution through universal education that we all deserve.

Such a new age can fulfill in a nonviolent way the prophecies of all the world religions about a time of great fulfillment, when all conflict and competition among them ends. The world scientists can then turn their energies away from wars—between nations, between empires, with nature, with women, with drugs—and their genius and creativity can be unleashed to solve the life and death problems of global warming, species extinction, population explosion, poverty, famine, drought, and environmental devastation and pollution. The Dalai Lama, empowered by the Chinese insight and creative action, could become their spokesperson for global spirituality and the living icon of China's ideological tolerance. Once China is with him instead of against him, he and his teachings of nonviolence, dialogue, and kindness would be all the more recognized by all the nations as the key to peace for the planet this century. This could repeat on a global scale the way the Tibetan people discovered and deployed his previous incarnations as the key to peace in their land, following the transformation of their own fifteenth-century renaissance, during which a majority in the society came to see the unlimited potential of each human being. From then on, large numbers of individuals dropped all worldly preoccupations and turned their lifetime efforts toward evolutionary education, and the mass monastic social system spread throughout the land.

The Christians are awaiting the second coming of the Christ; the Muslims, the advent of either the Mahdi or the Hidden Imam; the Hindus, Vishnu as Kalki, destroyer of evil; the Jews, their Messiah; the Buddhists, either Maitreya the next buddha or the king of Shambhala; and the Native Americans, their Ghost Dancers or other Great Ones. Every suffering people dreams of its time of restoration and fulfillment. They all want a better life on Earth for themselves and their loved ones and are not content to wait for heaven or the pure land after death. The Dalai Lama is none of these apocalyptic saviors, though he is a kind of day-to-day savior for the Tibetans and Mongolians. He stays with his people, reincarnating life after life, and brings the warm glow of love and joy to their hearts and minds.

As an international figure today, he does not seek in the slightest to take an allegiance from other countries or from the various expected saviors of other religions, but he does inspire nations, leaders, and individuals to think positively. He encourages us, as he struggles—without fear or anger—with the great adversity afflicting himself and his people, not to give in to an unsustainable present course, and not just to wait for some violent disruption to come from outside in the future. He leads us by example to act right now as if all our highest models of existence, or our most beloved saviors, were here with us already. What would they have us do to solve our common, individual, and shared planetary crisis?

Imagine how it would be if environmentalism, tolerance, respect for diversity, generosity, and gentleness were taught every day to every child, in every home and place of worship. Imagine if we had a model of how to resolve conflict—personal or national—through respectful dialogue and peaceful coexistence. Imagine if these teachings were made widely available on television and the Internet, plentiful for all traditions. Imagine if people were thus taught widely and open-mindedly about the commonalities between their faiths and those of others, becoming immunized against religious prejudice and hatred.

Imagine these things happening worldwide and you are seeing the world the Dalai Lama leads us toward. To empower him here, to make his act of truth inspire more widely, the world needs his country and his people to be free. Not necessarily independent from China, but free to enjoy and preserve and develop their beautiful Tibetan culture, within their traditional homeland, and to share it openly with the world.

PART I

Who Is the
Dalai Lama and
Why Is He the Key?

1

WHO IS THE DALAI LAMA?

In the forty-three years that I have known the Great Fourteenth Dalai Lama, he has never failed to impress me with his sincerity, his compassion, and his commitment to his purpose. As one of the few living non-Tibetan people to have a longstanding personal relationship with the Dalai Lama, I'm hoping that my familiarity can bring him closer to you. He is so many things to so many people—spiritual teacher, scholar, scientist, and friend.

The Dalai Lama is a giant of spiritual development—a living exemplar of the best qualities of a Buddhist monk, an inspired practitioner and teacher of the ethical, religious, and philosophical paths of the *bodhisattva*, a Sanskrit term suggesting a cross between a wise saint and a compassionate messiah. He is believed to be a conscious reincarnation of Avalokiteshvara, the bodhisattva of universal compassion. As such, it might seem that his great attainments and vast deeds in this lifetime have spontaneously emerged from his practice in previous lives, as if he had done nothing special to develop himself during this life.

If we think that way, we might feel he is so far beyond our capacity, though we might enjoy his presence, learn from his teaching, and thrive on devotion to him, there is nothing much we can do to emulate him. This would not please him at all. In relying on a Buddhist teacher or "spiritual friend," veneration through devotion and service through actions are important, but it is far more important to actualize his teachings by putting them into practice in our own lives.

Throughout this book, it will be helpful, but not essential, to know a little bit about Buddhism. If China's Buddhists were counted, Buddhism would join Christianity, Islam, and Hinduism as a religion of over a billion adherents. Among these religions, Buddhism is fundamentally a scientific worldview and a variety of therapeutic practices, aiming at healing suffering through understanding and compassion more than through a particular credo or the intercession of a creator deity. It teaches that the human lifetime is extraordinarily precious for the being that obtains it—an achievement that is gained through an arduous evolution over numerous lifetimes. Such a human life offers the best opportunity for that being to develop herself or himself to gain permanent liberation from suffering in the state known in Buddhism as nirvana, enjoy unimaginable bliss, and wield the ability to share such freedom and bliss with others. Buddhism offers an education for happiness and an art of compassion, with as many methods and curricula as there are individuals with different aptitudes.

During the last half century, as Tibetan Buddhism has gained visibility in the wider world, it has become more and more known for being a treasury of the whole variety of Buddhist sciences and arts developed over fifteen hundred years in India rather than strictly a religion in the sense of creed or dogma. Tibetan Buddhist wisdom teachings have thus been found useful by many people for improving the quality of their lives, many of them using this or that element of practice or outlook, while retaining their own original religious heritage.

Many fine books and resources are available on Buddhism and its history in Tibet. The list on page 229 offers readers a place to start.

Shakyamuni Buddha himself was not some sort of primal divinity or a buddha from the beginning. He was human like us, even an animal, in many previous lives. He struggled with passions and flaws, misunderstandings and inabilities, just as we do. Yet he practiced the Dharma—the path to personal liberation and enlightenment—and finally overcame his inadequacies and ultimately became the shining, perfect Buddha who showed us the way to freedom, love, and happiness. Similarly, we must remember that while the Dalai Lama is a monumental spiritual force, he is still human like us and it is within our means to strive to emulate him.

PERSONAL ENCOUNTERS

When I first met the Dalai Lama in 1964, he was a young man of twenty-nine. We met in the audience room at his hotel in Sarnath, India, where he was the guest of honor at the World Fellowship of Buddhists meeting. I remember feeling a guardedness about him, a sense of his being from far away and high above, and not quite relaxed in his surroundings. I also remember his friendliness toward me, especially when he heard me speak in clear Tibetan, which I could already manage to some degree. I was presented to him as a beginning student of Buddhism (around two years into it by then with my first spiritual friend, the Mongolian Geshe, Ngawang Wangyal) who wanted to study under his tutelage and, if possible, to become a Buddhist monk. He said that after the conference was over, I should be brought to see him again in Dharamsala, his Himalayan home in exile, and he would then decide how my studies should proceed. Then he swept out into the autumn sunshine to give his speech to the world's Buddhists assembled at the conference.

I don't remember that first speech very well, as he gave it through an interpreter, and it came out somewhat strained and formal. He had a hard task before him. In those years, he was beginning to introduce Tibetan Buddhism to an international Buddhist audience that regarded Tibetan Buddhism as a provincial corruption of real Buddhism. But there is no doubt that, even then, he commanded great respect and attentiveness, and his combination of being a simple Buddhist monk as well as a sincere and dedicated spokesperson for his suffering people was effective in moving people's hearts, slowly but surely.

During the next year, I remained largely unaware (At twenty-three I was blissfully unaware of a lot of things, even though I was all fired up to get enlightened!) of the good fortune I had by in meeting him regularly, almost every week, to discuss my studies and progress, as well as quite a few other things as it turned out. At that time, the Dalai Lama lived above Mcleod Ganj in a former mountain trekkers' hostel called Swarg Ashram (heavenly abode), on a steep slope with a beautiful view of the Dhauladhar sector of the Himalayas. When we met, our conversations followed an invariable pattern. First, he would listen to my brief recital of what I had been learning from my teachers (he had assigned me to the Abbot of Namgyal Monastery and to his own senior tutor, Kyabje Ling Rinpoche). Then I would address a few questions to him, especially on my favorite topic of that time, the Madhyamika philosophy of voidness and relativity. He would make a few interesting points and observations and ask counter-questions, but then he would refer me to my assigned teachers to take me more deeply into these questions.

Then, he would invariably begin asking me questions about the many things he was wondering about—Darwin and Freud, Einstein and Thomas Jefferson, life in the Americas and in Europe. I would answer as best I could, coining new words in Tibetan for some concepts—the subconscious, the id, relativity, natural selection—and using English terms in other cases. Trying to explain complex subjects to the Dalai Lama's brilliant and eagerly inquiring mind was quite a challenge, and it caused me to rethink many of my own ideas. I am afraid I disappointed him on subjects connected with the hard sciences, since I had been an English major and a would-be poet with strong philosophical and psychological leanings.

But we had a fine time, often annoying his secretaries by spending too much time talking, perhaps taking time away from his other duties. He seemed slightly stressed, lonely, and a little sad, though basically energetic and cheery. I was so intent on Buddhist philosophy and contemplation and knew so little about Tibet and the real sufferings of his people at the hands of the Chinese Communists that I could not really understand his situation. At the time, I had very little idea what a tremendous blessing those meetings were for me.

Eventually I was ordained, and some time after that I returned to the United States to live in the Lamaist Buddhist Monastery of America in New Jersey. As the '60s heated up with war protests and the civil rights movement, I was drawn back into society through my peers; by early 1967 I had resigned my monkhood and returned to lay life. I had the sense that the Dalai Lama was strongly disappointed with me for quite a while after that, since I was the first Westerner he had ordained as a full mendicant (*bhikshu*), and I had firmly expressed my lifetime determination, only later to change my mind.

I returned to my former university, Harvard, and went on to graduate school, focusing on East Asian Studies for my master's and on Sanskrit and Buddhist Studies for my Ph.D. On a dissertation research year in India in 1970, I came again to see the Dalai Lama in Dharamsala, who by then had moved down into more adequate quarters near the newly constructed central cathedral. This time I was married, with children, and far from a monk, but he quickly adapted to my new status as a young Tibetan Buddhist Studies scholar and gave my family his gracious blessing.

The topic I had chosen for my dissertation was a translation and study of Jey Lama Tsong Khapa's *Essence of True Eloquence*, which turned out to be the Dalai Lama's favorite work of critical philosophy. This text was a fifteenth-century treatise exploring the finer points of the theories of Buddhist physics, specifically ultimate voidness and relative relativity. Once he discovered what I was working on, he assigned me to a teacher, as before, and then invited me to a series of discussions with him on this text and the philosophical issues it addresses.

During this second series of conversations in 1971, I noticed an astonishing, exciting change in him since our earlier meetings six years prior. He had come alive philosophically. No longer did he refer questions to other teachers. He had many points to make about Tsong

Khapa's treatise, which is considered his most difficult and is in fact nicknamed "Tsong Khapa's iron bow," which no one else can bend. The Dalai Lama obviously had studied it thoroughly and knew many passages by heart. He was lucid and lyrical in explaining the deep impact and extensive ramifications of the fine points, especially the critical differences between the dialecticist and the dogmaticist approaches to the Madhyamika central way.

Forgetting for a moment that he was the Dalai Lama and so should know it all naturally anyway, it was breathtaking to observe his powerful philosophical development of the previous six years that shone through his clear insight and infectious enthusiasm.

I spent the next eight years in the sword-dance of overachievement required to get tenure as a college professor. I had no chance to get back to Dharamsala, and the Dalai Lama continued to be denied visas to the United States as part of the Kissinger China policy, maintained also by Zbigniew Brzezinski. In 1979 I got tenure and the Dalai Lama got his first visa, thanks to Cyrus Vance, Jimmy Carter, and Thomas Beard. I had a year's sabbatical in India with the whole family. That fall, I was lucky enough to host the Dalai Lama on his first trip to both Amherst College and Harvard University, and then to travel with him back to India to continue my sabbatical in Delhi and Dharamsala.

When the Dalai Lama arrived in New York City on that trip, I couldn't believe the further change he seemed to have undergone in the eight years since 1971. I remember having an early morning dream-vision of him that first day, seeing him as a giant Kalachakra Buddha (a divine buddha-couple embodying the union of wisdom and compassion), standing magnificently high in the sky over New York, his feet planted atop the Waldorf–Astoria® where he was staying, shining gloriously in that deity's luminescent pastel hues, the ecstatic energy attracting a swarm of mostly pin-stripe–suited bees of diplomats, politicians, business people, princes of the church, and other assorted dignitaries.

During that trip and the following year, I couldn't get over the rich power of his charismatic energy. He had always had charisma of office;

now he had ten times more charisma of person. Obviously he had been studying and practicing the Unexcelled Yoga Tantras, the most advanced of all meditational technologies developed over millennia in the Indo-Tibetan spiritual tradition. He had especially deeply immersed himself in the study and practice of the mandala visionary world of the Kalachakra—wheel-of-time or time machine—Buddha, the iconic embodiment of the Buddha's compassionate determination, not to lose people's evolutionary progress in the undertows of history, but to stay with them compassionately to help them throughout all time. The Time Machine Buddha Tantric yoga meditations aim to open the inner energy pathways of the spine and heart and brain, kindling the inner heat that melts negative thought structures and generating the inner bliss of cosmic liberation. It certainly seemed that the Dalai Lama had been successful in these practices, to exactly what extent I would of course not be able to judge, having no such attainments myself.

During that winter in India, we had our third series of conversations. The Dalai Lama was, at that point, forty-four years old and had reached twenty years in exile. The period during the 1970s when Chinese pressure on all governments restricted his world travel had been put to good use: his sustained series of retreats, capping his thirty years of intense study of all levels of Buddha's teaching, brought him to a manifest fruition. Perhaps a Dalai Lama just naturally has all the knowledge, abilities, and compassion. However, I can certainly testify that there was a clear appearance of massive development through tremendous focused intelligence and untiring effort.

In these meetings, we discussed every topic under the sun. My main interest by then was the Tantras, the advanced esoteric meditation techniques, and he had many profound and helpful things to say. He still seemed interested in everything, especially history, politics, sociology, ethics, and what I might call the psychology of compassion.

Since then, he has published many books, conversed with many thinkers and authors, and given innumerable teachings and speeches. The constant progress I observed during those first sixteen years still continues apace, still advances by quantum leaps. Especially since around the time he won the Nobel Peace Prize in 1989, his general talks—on kindness, the common human religion; on nonviolence, even disarmament; on science, focusing on the ecology of the environment; and on comparative religion, focusing on the Buddhist-Christian dialogue in particular—have gotten better and better, more moving, lucid, and powerful in understanding and passion.

A LIVING EMBODIMENT OF THE BUDDHA

It seems that the Dalai Lama's reincarnation continuum makes possible an endless advancement, growth, and enrichment of his skill in liberative arts. Lately when I witness the Buddhist teachings he gives to large assemblies, I have an odd sensation: it feels as if I have entered a time warp and am actually witnessing Shakyamuni Buddha himself in all his glory as a teacher—as the Noble Vimalakirti Sutra puts it, "Dominating all the multitudes, just as Sumeru, the king of mountains, looms high over the oceans, the Lord Buddha shone, radiated, and glittered as he sat upon his magnificent lion-throne."

Over many years, I attended his teachings and found them informative and inspiring, but I always felt that it was the normal Dalai Lama I knew sitting there before me. Buddha was often mentioned as a remote founding figure, far back in ancient history. Sure, this new sense I have of him as the Buddha is just subjective, but it gives me a clue about what the Dalai Lama has come to mean for the world.

The Dalai Lama has grown so close to Shakyamuni Buddha that their manifestations have become indistinguishable; the Dalai Lama has become a living proof of the Mahayana vision of Buddha's inexhaustible compassionate presence. I think people sense that fact, each one according to his level of insight, as constrained by preconceptions, experience, and understanding.

This does not mean that the Dalai Lama is a "God-king" or a "living God," as is sometimes written in the press. For Buddha is not God, who, if He did exist as conceived by Western monotheists, would be absolutely unimaginable, forever trans-human. Buddha on the relative level, though ultimately inconceivable, is a being who was thoroughly human at one time, like you or me, and then through many lives evolved into something more than human and more than any god. He is a wise and compassionate, omnipresent but not omnipotent, universal awareness and powerful energy traditionally called Realized One (*Tathagata*), Blissful One (*Sugata*), Teacher of Humans and Gods (*Devamanushyanaam Shasta*), and many other names. He is everywhere embodied/disembodied as reality, manifested as seeming individuals in sensitive response to needs of beings. Any particular manifestation of Buddha is thus a kind of living doorway to each person's own happiness, a mirror of the reality that the individual must understand to realize wisdom, freedom from suffering, immortality, and supreme happiness.

It is natural that this—the high-flown, challengingly optimistic philosophy (or buddhology) of the Mahayana Buddhist Sutras—might seem merely hypothetical and unrealistic; it becomes concrete only in the live encounter with such a buddha-manifestation. It takes a living personification of the buddha qualities to make our own freedom and enlightenment seem really possible, a live exemplar of the buddha-happiness to make our own mouths water for the taste of our own real happiness. This is the real meaning of the Dalai Lama's presence.

WHAT THE DALAI LAMA REPRESENTS TODAY

It is not merely that the Dalai Lama represents Buddhism. He is much more than a nominal leader of an organization. He does not seek to convert anyone to Buddhism. "Buddhism" is not a world organization competing with other organized world religions, seeking strength in numbers. It is an age-old movement of education and conscious evolution. It seeks to educate people's hearts and minds for freedom and happiness, no matter what their ideology. It is a teaching of the reality of selflessness and global interconnectedness. The Dalai Lama is a simple

Buddhist monk, an adept mind scientist, a thorough scholar, a spiritual teacher, a diplomat, a Nobel Peace Prize Laureate, an apostle of nonviolence, an advocate of intelligence and universal responsibility, and the living exemplar of what he calls "our common human religion of kindness."

We live in an era of extreme contrasts: Technology informs us more than ever and yet makes us feel weaker and more frightened than before. The art of caring for the sick seems more sophisticated than ever, and yet the food chain is becoming poisoned and the environment polluted. Pluralism on all levels seems more essential than ever, yet the cruelty of fanatics rages more violently than ever. Knowledge and technical advances have infinite potential to positively transform our world, yet all around us devastation marches on. In this climate of manifold desperations, both quiet and shrill, the Dalai Lama seems to emerge from another civilization, to descend from another dimension—a living example of calm in emergency, patience in injury, cheerful intelligence in confusion, and dauntless optimism in the face of apparent doom. Inspired by Jesus, Mahatma Gandhi, and Martin Luther King, Jr., he carries on that tradition under the extreme duress of the half-century-long agony of Tibet.

Especially since the emergency call of 9/11, the world seems headed into a tailspin. Instead of a peaceful post-Cold-War century, endless war is declared from several sides. Instead of increased prosperity and joyful, optimistic sharing, we have a gulf between rich and poor that is growing cataclysmic, and the world economy heads for collapse. Instead of a scientifically sound era of healthy living, new man-made plagues rear their terrifying heads. Hopelessness and fear send everyone rushing for an exit, diving into an isolated personal shelter.

In the midst of this devastation, the Dalai Lama remains undaunted, even cheerful. He doesn't give up the responsibility for his own people, a nation of six million very close to succumbing to systematic genocide with no one in official power to protect them. He doesn't revile the harmful leaders as evil. He calls for dialogue and reconciliation, even after more than fifty years of violence and oppression. He insists that intelligence and kindness together can solve any situation. Though he is a simple monk, what the Zen people call a "true man of no rank," without any powerful organization, recognized nation, institutionalized religion, or rich industry or foundation, he still stands out as a natural leader of the plain people, a vital symbol of nonviolence.

What is the Dalai Lama? I have come to see him as a living Prince of Peace, a teacher of intelligence, an inspirer of goodness of heart, a reincarnation of the Buddha of universal compassion. He comes to join us in our world today, offering us hope and help in our stressed-out lives and calling upon us to take up our own wild joy of universal responsibility.

THE DALAI LAMA ACCORDING TO THE BUDDHIST SCIENCES

The Dalai Lama has been called a "Buddhist Pope," a "bodhisattva," a "head of state" in exile, and so on. Each of these is incomplete but has a grain of truth. He describes himself as a "simple Buddhist monk," though he is not unaware of the other dimensions of his being.

To understand him better, while appreciating his own intellectual background and education, we can try to see him the way Tibetans see him in the context of Tibetan culture. In the next sections, we'll examine the views of the major Buddhist sciences: the Buddhist psychological analysis of identity, both subjective and objective; the Buddhist physicists' analysis of physical (including mental) nature or reality; and the Buddhist biologists' analysis of life and death. With this new perspective, we can better understand the Tibetan version of reality and more fully appreciate what the Dalai Lama is and what he means to the Tibetan people.

THE DALAI LAMA ACCORDING TO BUDDHIST PSYCHOLOGY

In regard to personal identity, the Buddha's *Transcendent Wisdom Discourses* say that a person who thinks, "I am a buddha, a bodhisattva, a god, a person," and so on is none of those things but suffers under a delusion. For Buddhist psychology does not understand a person's identity as something rigidly fixed. Like any other image in the mind, the self-image is always relational, changing in different situations. The more one is aware of the self as a living process, the more resilient and adaptable one becomes, the more able to transform qualities from negative to positive. In this light, when the Dalai Lama says he is a simple Buddhist monk, he is reporting that when he turns his attention to himself, he resorts to that basic concept of his role in life, which does not preclude his being capable of other roles in other situations.

The Dalai Lama is vitally aware of his own multiplicity of identities. He is a human being, of course, a male, the descendant of farmers, herdsmen, and strong working women of the province of Amdo in far northeastern Tibet, born right on the border with Mongolia to the north, China to the east, Turkestan to the northwest. He is a Tibetan. His family naturally speaks a thick Eastern dialect, and he is familiar with central Tibetan and even conversant from childhood with the provincial Chinese of the Seeling (Xining) district. Though she had no idea she was about to receive the reincarnation of the Dalai Lama in her womb, his mother had a vivid dream of a special incarnation that came to her from the southwest, the direction of Lhasa, in the form of a bright blue dragon, escorted by two playful green snow lions! That auspicious dream was to prove prophetic for us all, as dragons in Tibet and China symbolize oceans of jewels of prosperity and wisdom, and this Dalai Lama has turned out to be just such an ocean. It also happens that green has always been his favorite color; green symbolizes the spiritual energy called the all-accomplishing wisdom, the creative energy released when the emotional addiction of competitive jealousy is transmuted into harmonious cooperation. The Dalai Lama daily presents the potential of this alchemy to us all.

"Just a simple Buddhist monk!" When the Dalai Lama says this phrase, people usually smile and think that he is striking a pose of studied humility, earnestly contradicting his obvious charisma, radiant good humor, and flashing intelligence. Is he that modest? In an interview, his response revealed just how much he really means it. The writer and actor Spalding Gray asked him if he ever has erotic dreams or is ever tempted by worldly desires. The Dalai Lama responded by acknowledging that such imagery can emerge in the dreamtime but that he guards against losing control to it by remembering that he is a Buddhist monk and retreating to the fortress of his celibate renunciation vow. He added that sometimes he dreams of aggression, of confrontations with knives or guns, but that he reflects on his deepest identity as a simple Buddhist monk to withdraw from his instinctual patterns of hostility. He never thinks, even in his dreams, "I am the Dalai Lama!"

His Buddhist monk identity is that of a person who has taken and maintains vows of personal nonviolence, poverty, celibacy, and spiritual honesty, and who spends most of his waking energy in the pursuit of a perfect enlightenment believed to last for all time, to satisfy the self with unimaginable fullness, and to benefit countless other beings. Simplicity is a cardinal virtue of a homeless mendicant monk. Being free of family obligations, professional concerns, possessions, and all social pretense minimizes the monk's distractions and maximizes his use of his most productive vital energies in education, contemplation, and conscious evolutionary transformation. As a monk, one works on dissolving habitual egotism, including the unconscious rigidities of one's human, sexual, and national identities. As a monk, one lives close to the bone, while also striving to become a universal being.

The Dalai Lama also constantly creates his working identity as a bodhisattva, having dedicated all his lives to the attainment of perfect enlightenment, complete wisdom, and inexhaustible compassion, in order to be able to help all others find freedom from suffering. He calls this "shaping his motivation." Though others in the Buddhist world consider him to be the incarnation of Avalokiteshvara (in Chinese *Guan Yin*), the divine bodhisattva of universal compassion—and he certainly seems to have grown into manifesting that grand personage—he clearly does not hold on to such a self-image.

He does say his religion is the common human religion of kindness, love, compassion, and universal responsibility. He once was asked in an interview, "Who do you consider to be your spiritual peer on this planet?" He considered the question for a moment and then answered with unmistakable sincerity as if he had just rediscovered this fact afresh, "Actually every person in the world is my spiritual peer!" His empathetic identification with others is so strong that he feels he is just like each of us. As the *Transcendent Wisdom Sutra* declares again and again, "He who thinks to himself, 'I am a bodhisattva!' that one is not a bodhisattva. Only one who sees no bodhisattva, who sees no being as intrinsically real, that one is a bodhisattva with true compassion for all beings."

The Dalai Lama labors daily to lead his people and fulfill his responsibility to preserve and rule his nation. This in itself is a huge task. The nation of Tibet has been under genocidal pressure for over half a century, in such mortal danger that Tibetans should be on an Endangered Humans list. He is a statesman, a politician, a diplomat, a personnel manager, and a chief executive officer. He maintains these vital duties in exile as a refugee.

He is a committed scholar and a prolific writer who deeply researches the philosophical, psychological, and religious literature of his sophisticated civilization while also exploring the modern sciences and literatures. The book list from his website counts sixty-nine separate volumes the Dalai Lama has written in English, most of them translated into over thirty languages, including Chinese—and these do not include books written in Tibetan. He studies incessantly with a variety of tutors and teaches extensively, both advanced students in the Tibetan Buddhist monastic community and the entire Tibetan populace, as well as an ever-growing public of spiritual seekers around the world. He speaks to all with clarity and sincerity, a good sense of humor, and unfailing optimism.

He also is an accomplished vajra master, or diamond teacher, of the esoteric ritual and contemplative traditions that his people consider the crown jewels of the Indian Buddhist tradition they inherited and have done so much to preserve, refine, and extend. His precise knowledge of the architecture of the sacred mandala environment, of the details of elaborate ritual arts and procedures, and his graceful gestures, magnificent chanting, and eloquent elucidation of the advanced contemplative practices leave even his veteran disciples still prone to feel amazement.

Finally, he is a peacemaker for the world, a Nobel Peace Prize Laureate, an inspirer of the many world leaders, both political and religious, who have been fortunate enough to encounter him. His example and advice can help—and in many instances have helped—them not to settle for harmful policies propelled by blind institutional momentum but to take responsibility for the poor and the oppressed, to use good sense and good will to solve the problems that beset our world, and not to give in to despair and cynicism while hiding behind power and privilege. He is ready to be a good friend to everyone, even those who have harmed him or others, and patiently offers the alternative of constructive dialogue as balm for violence and prejudice.

THE DALAI LAMA ACCORDING TO BUDDHIST PHYSICS

The Buddhist physicists' analysis of reality is thoroughly relativist and causal. The ancient epitome of the Buddha's teaching stated, "The Realized Lord said that all things arise from causes, what those causes are, and how they terminate—such is the theory of the Great Retreatant!"

Thus according to the discoveries of Buddhist physics, all things exist only in relationship to other things. They arise and disappear based on causal processes. There is no such thing as nothing, as everything is related to other things. The universe, then, is beginningless (since there was always some cause before any effect) and endless (since all effects cause other things), infinite (since any boundary requires something on the other side), and immeasurably open to possibility (because all so-called laws of nature are only locally observed probabilities).

Most importantly, our human minds—and the minds of all living beings—are participants in reality; they are material in the sense of being energies or forces, though extremely subtle in comparison to gross matter and energy. They are so subtle that, as Buddhist physicists see it, beings' minds exist at the quantum level, beneath the level where atoms and even subatomic particles are discerned. Even though extremely subtle, minds are powerfully functional on the quantum level, impossible to pin down by gross material mechanisms. Yet our living minds can tolerate such ultimate uncertainty and can master relative probabilities with resilience and adaptability. Our minds have their own beginningless and endless continuity—they can never come from nothing or go to nothing, as *nothing* is not a source or destination but a term for precisely that which does not exist. And so our imaginations are unlimited in their ability to shape reality, building up from the quantum level, as our imagery is what guides the patterns of subatomic energies and their crystallizations into particles and bodies. So a Dalai Lama is understood to be a person who has developed such tremendous mental stability and penetrating acuity that he can consciously reach down to this quantum level of his mind and body and use his powerful imagination to shape his soul journey through death to a new life in a human womb, as long as he chooses out of compassion to return to the world to accomplish a helpful mission.

In trying to evoke the Buddhist vision of physical/mental reality for modern people, I am ever grateful to the creators of the movie *The Matrix*, since the matrix realm is a perfect analogy for how the real world is for an enlightened person. In the movie, there are two planes of reality, the matrix reality and the world outside. The matrix reality is a robot-controlled computer simulation of a human environment that incorporates the brains of millions of humans whose bodies are maintained in giant test-tube-like machines that keep them stimulated, nourished, and alive—but not truly living.

The people in the simulation think they are really there, walking and talking, bound by gravity, living and dying. A few humans have escaped from this robot world and are leading a resistance movement, intending to liberate all the others. The hero, Neo, is freed by them because they think he is the one, namely a being who can function in the *Matrix* world while knowing it is a simulated illusion. Because Neo realizes that the matrix world isn't reality, he can overcome the robots' control with pow-

ers and actions that seem to be magical, but truly come from his identification with the matrix simulation and his ability to manipulate its
illusory constructs. According to Buddhist physics, this world we are in
is an illusory product of our interwoven subjectivities and, once we
know that viscerally, we feel liberated from bondage to its solid-seeming
laws and can transform this world's negative aspects into positives for
ourselves and others. So the matrix world in the drama is a good analogy for how the Buddhists think enlightened beings can manifest.

THE DALAI LAMA ACCORDING TO BUDDHIST BIOLOGY

In the Buddhist biologists' vision of life and death, life is an evolutionary
process wherein the habits of living beings crystallize into patterns of
form and function according to a cause-and-effect process. In this way,
the quality of one's mind determines the shape of one's embodiment
(whether one is born a human, a fish or a goat, etc.), and one's instinctual and conscious behavioral tendencies. The variety of life forms possible in this evolutionary process is unlimited by space, time and
experience, in both negative and positive directions. Charles Darwin's
genius insight into how all life forms are interrelated through their evolutionary histories is completely in line with the insights of Buddhist
biologists, except for one important distinction. Darwin reduced the
mind or soul to the agency of unconscious, material genes. Darwin
adopted his view in rebellion against the dogmatic theories of the Western church. He did not know of, and probably would not have believed
in, the Buddhist discovery that animals' and humans' individual minds
are the agents of evolutionary actions. According to this Buddhist view,
the effects of these actions become encoded at a super-subtle energy
level in a "mental gene" or "soul gene," which then shapes the experience
and quality of the individual being's gross mind and body as it evolves
through its many lifetimes.

To Buddhist biologists, death is never a state but refers only to a
point (no size) or a boundary line (no width) of transition of one's sub-
tlest mental energy levels. There, one loses connection with particular

gross embodiments and goes into truly matrix-like states—known as the death-point-between, the reality-between, and the potentiality-between—before entering into a new relationship with a gross embodiment as a zygote. This process is commonly referred to in Buddhism as rebirth when instinctually driven and as reincarnation when consciously chosen. From this perspective, the life process itself is analyzed into similar phases called waking-(or life)-between, dreaming-between, and trance-between (similar to deep sleep between). The use of the term "between" is unusual but important here, as it reminds us that this evolutionary process is a continuum of states and experiences, without a fixed, material beginning or end.

This whole ongoing process of life and death of us living beings is called *karma*, meaning "evolutionary action and reaction." It boils down to our creating our own states of being from our own actions and our going on endlessly acting and interacting in this chain of causes and effects. Much of what we experience is determined by the force of past actions serving as underlying causes, and yet our ongoing choices are free and do determine results for us in our future experiences.

Since all this acting and interacting is totally interrelated with other beings, the freer we become, the broader our sense of identification with surrounding beings is, and the more bound we become, the more constricted our sense of relationship is. A buddha is a fully awakened and gloriously blossomed being that embraces all life with its unimaginably expanded awareness and so breaks through the self-other barrier and identifies completely with infinite other life forms and their awarenesses. A hell-being is a fully alienated, self-isolated being, almost totally barricaded against all other life forms. In the effort to ward off all contact with other beings due to fear and hatred of them, the being has imprisoned itself in a defensive iron shell that has become a prison, under the extreme pressures of trying to avoid the entire universe of others.

Luckily for beings tending toward embodiments in such extreme paranoid hell-states, buddha beings fully identify with them as well as with less traumatized beings. So they do not abandon them to their miserable fates but embrace them with loving energy and nurse them out into relationships with others, bit by evolutionary bit. The Dalai Lama is believed to be just such a being, one who attained perfect enlightenment and therefore the ability to manifest whatever different beings need to free themselves and find happiness. Due to that attainment, he returns to the world again and again, in recent centuries focusing on the Tibetans, but certainly manifest in all countries and among all animals in various less well-recognized ways. The Tibetans' and Mongolians' amazing institution of the Dalai Lamas is a formal pattern of specifically inviting the Buddha of Infinite Compassion to reincarnate again and again as a leader and teacher of the nation.

ANOTHER VISION OF REALITY

We have briefly thought through a few of the details of these Buddhist sciences in order to open our minds to the Tibetan vision of reality that stands behind the Dalai Lama, both as an individual being and as a social institution. For only against this psychological, physical, and biological background can we begin to imagine what a Dalai Lama is. The Buddhist sciences are vast fields of collective endeavors of many researchers in large institutions over many centuries, just like the so-called modern or Western sciences but with a much greater sophistication in the psychological area, as that was their priority—but not neglecting physics and biology.

The Dalai Lama is a being in our world who, in previous lives, became so highly aware of his mind and body and the nature of the world that he became able to manifest himself in whatever form is educational and beneficial to whomsoever. He's chosen to reincarnate in a special relationship with the Tibetan people for the last several thousand years in embodiments that are able to help his people. But according to the Buddhist view, there are many such highly developed beings in our world. The Buddhist scientists' sense of the omnipresent activities of enlightened beings is such that they perceive or imagine (depending on their level of awareness) them as manifest everywhere, in all realms among all human nations and nonhuman species and even on other worlds throughout the infinite universe. However, among all the emanations of the infinite compassion of all buddhas, the form of Avalokiteshvara that reincarnates as the Dalai Lama to teach and lead the Tibetan people is the focus of the special institution the Tibetans created to recognize him, find him as a child life after life, educate him, and rely on him to solve their problems and lead them toward peace and a happier existence.

A Dalai Lama is a recognized conscious reincarnation of that celestial bodhisattva, Avalokiteshvara (in Tibetan *sPyan ras gZigs [Chenrayseek]*), considered the iconic figure embodying the universal compassion of all buddhas. In his celestial manifestations, this "god (*Ishvara*) who looked down (*Avalokita*)" compassionately on the plight of beings can be female or male, be mild or fierce, have one face and two arms, one face and four arms, three faces and six arms, ten faces and one thousand arms, and have many other variant forms in between these. The idea is that the Dalai Lama is manifest in whatever way best educates or civilizes whomsoever (in Tibetan *gang la gang 'dul de la de ston pa*).

TIBETAN ORIGIN MYTHS

In order to understand even better how ordinary Tibetans regard the social institution of the Dalai Lama, there are several prominent myths that are important to consider. These myths help us fathom the depth of feeling the Tibetan people have toward him. When properly appreciated and understood, these myths should also help the Chinese leaders realize that it is impossible to eradicate the Dalai Lama from the Tibetan soul. They should embrace the Dalai Lama as an ally, working with him to liberate the Tibetans culturally and politically, and trust him to persuade them that once free, they should join with China voluntarily, as truly autonomous partners.

It is also the case that throughout Buddhist history, Avalokiteshvara has been envisioned in various cultures as the bodhisattva that incarnates as the benevolent rulers of nations. This either happened during or was exploited by numerous dynasties in China, Japan (Shotoku Taishi), and even Sri Lanka long ago. In short, Avalokiteshvara is the Jesus figure in Mahayana Buddhist cultures and, as these myths show, he is believed to have appeared numerous times in many different forms.

AVALOKITESHVARA, SAVIOR OF TIBETANS

In the primal origin myth for the Tibetans, their precious savior, Avalokiteshvara, is born as a monkey, a conscious one who takes the monastic vows of celibacy, poverty, gentleness, and truthfulness and the messianic bodhisattva vow to save all beings from suffering by becoming a buddha as soon as possible. He retires to the Himalayan mountains to meditate in solitude until he achieves the capability to fulfill his vow. Dwelling in a cave high on a mountain above the Yarlung Valley near present-day Tsetang in Tibet, he meets a mountain demoness (*Brag-srin-mo*) who falls madly in love with him. She begs and begs for his love and finally threatens suicide if he does not wed her, so he resolves that his bodhisattva vow takes priority over his monastic vow, and he gives up his monk's vow, abandons celibacy, and marries her. They live together happily on the mountain and engender the Tibetan race, some coming from previous lives as gods, some as titans, some as humans, some as animals, some as hungry ghosts (*pretans*), and some as hell-dwellers.

This myth establishes the Tibetan sense of Avalokiteshvara, in all his emanations and incarnations, as father and messianic savior of the Tibetans. In 1981, during some lectures in Emerson Hall at Harvard, the Dalai Lama joked that he very much wanted to go to Arkansas to join Carl Sagan to testify at an evolution vs. creation trial concerning the Arkansas school books. When asked why he wanted to do that, he smiled broadly and said, "Because we Tibetans think that we are descended from God too, but we think that that God also happened to be a monkey! So maybe I could mediate!" And he burst into gales of laughter, along with the whole audience.

THOUSAND EYES OF THE THOUSAND BUDDHAS

The second myth comes from the Universal Compassion White Lotus (*Mahakarunika-pundarika*) Sutra. The scene is set in the presence of the celestial buddha, Amitabha (Buddha of Infinite Light), Avalokiteshvara being one of the two primary disciples of that buddha, along with Mahasthamaprapta. Avalokiteshvara looks down compassionately on the wayward, deluded, violent, greedy Tibetan people and, feeling sorry for them, decides to take Tibet, with all the peoples of the high Himalayan plateau, as his special protégés. He considers them particularly hard cases and so vows to go there and meditate among them until all their fears are soothed and all their wants satisfied, and they become gentle and enlightened. He becomes so earnest in his intention that he vows before Amitabha, "And if I should ever become discouraged at the difficulty of the task, may my body be torn to shreds and my head split in ten pieces!"

So he incarnates in Tibet, again and again, lifetime after lifetime. It is not too long—after only a few centuries of lifetimes—before he realizes what tough-minded and hard-hearted people the Tibetans are. He begins to despair at ever satisfying them or turning them away from their fighting, toward a more spiritual and evolutionarily progressive lifestyle. He weeps, but his first two tears turn into emanations of the goddess Tara (in Tibetan *Drolma*), the right one Green Tara (*Droljang*) and the left one White Tara (*Drolkar*). Radiantly beautiful, powerful, and determined, they cheer him up and promise they will always help his efforts and together will certainly prevail over all obstructions, so he should not give up.

He does cheer up for a few more centuries but finally loses it altogether. He decides it is really hopeless—the Tibetans will just not listen to reason and stop their stupidity and cruelty, his whole effort has been wasted, and there is nothing more that he can do. At that moment, his original vow takes effect, and his body is shattered into a thousand

shards and his head is split in ten. His great groan of pain is heard all
the way up to the Blissful Buddhaverse. Instantly, Buddha Amitabha
appears on the mountainside amidst the shattered pieces of the bodhisattva and says, "You must always be careful of what you wish for,
because whatever it is, sooner or later it will come to pass!" He then
blesses his disciple with a wave of his hand, and the thousand pieces of
body became a thousand arms, each with an all-seeing eye in the palm
of the hand, and the ten pieces of skull became a stack of ten heads—
three front, left, and right on three levels going up, with a dark-skinned
head of Yama, lord of death, as the top head. Above that single dark
head appears a smiling ruby red head of Buddha Amitabha himself,
indicating his indivisibility from his bodhisattva disciple. From this
myth emerged the common Tibetan prayer verse:

> With the thousand arms of the thousand wheel-turning emperors,
> And the thousand eyes of the thousand buddhas of this good eon,
> You who manifest whatsoever necessary to educate whomsoever—
> I salute you, noble Avalokiteshvara!

TIBETAN HISTORY MYTH
The third myth is really the whole history of Tibet, as told on the level
of what Tibetans call "history in extraordinary perception" (in Tibetan
thun mong ma yin pa'i snang ba'i lo rgyus). For example, in this history, Avalokiteshvara and his two (or however many necessary) Taras dwell
together in bliss on the Potalaka mountain somewhere near the seashore
in south India. From there, with their divine eyes, they overlook the
activities of various cultures and civilizations around the world and
emanate where needed whenever. For example, judging the time to be
right around the beginning of the seventh common era century, a rainbow meteor shot forth from Avalokiteshvara's heart and landed in the
womb of the empress of Tibet, triggering the conception of the
Emperor Songzen Gambo (ca 617–698 CE). At the same time, similar
meteors shot forth from the hearts of White and Green Taras and

landed in the wombs of the empress of China and the queen of Nepal, respectively, causing the conceptions of the two princesses who eventually became two of Songzen's nine consorts, bringing with them from Tang China and Licchavi Nepal important buddha statues and much Buddhist knowledge and inspiration.

After Songzen Gambo, emperors who were believed to be incarnations of other bodhisattvas continued expanding the Tibetan empire as well as adding to the Buddhicisation of Tibetan culture. The Avalokiteshvara incarnations in the next stage were led by the great adept, the Afghan Padmasambhava, who was a yogin and magician, a teacher of kings or "King of Dharma," rather than a political king. The Dalai Lama reincarnation lineage is traced back in these popular stories to a Brahmin boy who met Shakyamuni Buddha near the tree of enlightenment at Bodhgaya and offered him a crystal rosary. Many subsequent incarnations of Avalokiteshvara in India are mentioned in the history of the lineage up until the first Tibetan incarnation, the ordained lay Buddhist teacher Dromtonpa (1004–1064 CE), who was the Bengali master Atisha's foremost disciple and the founder of Reting monastery and the Kadam order.

Century after century—as leader, saint, scholar, yogic adept—Avalokiteshvara appeared in many guises to save the Tibetan people, one by one and as a culture and society. He often accomplished this working in tandem with incarnations of the bodhisattvas Manjushri and Vajarpani, with the omnipresent incarnations and emanations of the noble Tara always in active partnership as well.

SUCCESSION OF REINCARNATIONS

The evolutionary theory of karma existed from Buddhism's beginnings, and the concept of conscious, voluntary reincarnation (as opposed to involuntary, instinct-driven rebirth) developed quite early. The Buddha himself popularized the principle in his Jataka and Avadana stories that illustrate the multilife-continuum perspective. Thus, many small children in Buddhist cultures routinely astounded parents and relatives by announcing that they were in fact merely the rebirth of a specific deceased person known to everybody. It is thus interesting that only in Tibet, as far as we know, did formal reincarnation lineages become institutionalized, as a way of preserving traditions of leadership and authority in religious settings primarily, but also eventually in the political arena. This clearly was connected to the scale of monasticization that occurred in Tibet, unparalleled in any other country on Earth under the banner of any religion. Monastics being celibate, blood lineage eventually became too weak of a consideration in choosing leaders and was replaced by a commonly accepted notion of individual spiritual evolution in continuing reincarnations. Beginning in the thirteenth century, Tibetans turned to reincarnation pedigree as a factor in choosing their leaders, and by the seventeenth century, it had become the dominant consideration.

His Holiness the Victor Karmapa was the first of such formal reincarnations, as far as we know. His first incarnation, Dusum Khyenpa (1110–1193) wrote a letter before he died in which he predicted his reincarnation in specific circumstances, a prediction realized ten years after his death with the birth of the Second Karmapa Lama, Karma Pakshi (1203–1283), who soon asked to be taken back to his monastery at Tsurpu to continue his teachings. The Karmapa reincarnations have continued to develop their institution and perform great service to the people of Tibet and now the whole world. The current Seventeenth Victor Karmapa, Orgyen Trinley Dorje (1982–), has recently escaped from Chinese-occupied Tibet and is living in Dharamsala near the Dalai Lama, showing every promise of becoming another major teacher of the Dharma.

The second important reincarnation began more formally with the birth of Gendun Gyatso in 1475, as he soon declared himself the reincarnation of the famous Gendun Drubpa (1391–1474) and expressed the wish to return to his disciples at the Tashi Lhunpo Monastery, which he had built during the last twenty-five years of his previous life. He was accepted as the true incarnation by his parents, tutors, and attendants, so he was taken in glory back to the monastery. However, some of the abbots of that large monastic university were reluctant to recognize him. So at a certain point in his studies, he had the good fortune of escaping from his duties of office and spending a number of years in intermittent retreat in the sacred area near Olkha and the Ode Gungyel mountain, where Tsong Khapa (1357–1419), his spiritual grandfather, had taken his six-year retreat. Eventually the reincarnation was established beyond question as the main teacher of the Gelukpa order, his primary seat located in the Ganden Palace at Drepung Monastery.

The third formal reincarnation, Sonam Gyatso (1543–1588), was invited to northeastern Tibet to the encampment of Altan Khan, a major Mongolian ruler, on which occasion a major step was taken in converting the Mongols to Buddhism, building on the changes they had undergone when Khubilai ruled in China three hundred years earlier. During the festive atmosphere of this transformative event, the Mongol Khan dubbed Sonam Gyatso the Oceanic Lama (in Mongolian, *Dalai Lama*), and he became known as the "Third" reincarnation in acknowledgment of his conscious connection to Gendun Drubpa and Gendun Gyatso. Sonam Gyatso did great work of teaching and monastery founding among the Mongols and the Amdo people in northeast Tibet but still had no direct political responsibility in Tibet.

It was the Fifth Dalai Lama, Losang Gyatso (1617–1682), who presided over the momentous changes of the seventeenth century that were to produce Tibet's modern form of society. During the mid-sixteenth century, there had been intermittent conflict between the secular rulers of southern Tibet and those of central Tibet, which some historians have attributed to sectarian conflict between the Karmapa Lamas and their followers and the Gelukpa Lamas and their followers. More accurately, the unrest was the result of a conflict between the secular warlord rulers of feudal Tibet and the increasing monastic institutions and their spiritual leaders.

In all Buddhist (and Christian, for that matter) societies throughout history, monasticism and militarism have opposed each other as institutional competitors for land, resources, manpower, and womanpower. Whenever and wherever monasticism dominated, militarism was weakened. Whenever warlords or a single emperor dominated and increased militaristic activities, monastic institutions were purged, their resources confiscated, and their monks turned into warriors. The fifteenth and sixteenth centuries in Tibet saw a vast increase in monasticism, reaching a point by 1600 when aristocratic rulers saw their authority and resources dwindle to a danger point. They considered their opponent the whole new "mass-monastic" social system itself.

The most powerful secular leader of the time was the King of Tsang, but he had to use an important religious leader for legitimacy in the eyes of a people more interested in spiritual pursuits and less interested in feudal wars. He chose the young Victor Karmapa Lama, H. H. Choying Dorje (1604–1674), who was just growing up at the time. The King of Tsang proclaimed himself the lama's disciple, sanctifying his aggressive intention to maintain secular power, and then set about trying to break the power of mass monasticism. The Dalai Lama institution, which had up to that point declined to enter the political arena, devoting itself to the continuous expansion of the monastic universities and their demilitarized lifestyle, reached out for defense from its Mongolian patrons. They came into Tibet and defeated the Tibetan warlord coalition (which included a non-Buddhist, Bonpo ruler of eastern Tibet, so it cannot properly be dubbed a Karmapa coalition). Then, in 1642 the Fifth Dalai Lama took an unprecedented step: He assumed political responsibility for the whole country, demilitarized and bureaucratized the secular warlords, de-feudalized the ownership of land and the networks of relationships between people at all levels, and formalized mass monasticism as the social system of Tibet, what is called the Dharma-state coordination system (*Chös-srid zung-'brel*). Dharma means "teaching," the Buddha teaching of personal liberation and scientific enlightenment, and so Dharma-state coordination intends that the central purpose of the national life is the evolutionary education of all citizens, more like university-state unity than church-state unity.

As Buddhists are not monotheistic, the ruler is not thought to represent an inscrutable, omnipotent, authoritarian God, but rather to be himself a selfless, intercessionary, messianic angel of a bodhisattva. The monastic ruler as a Buddhist monk holds solemn vows of gentleness, poverty, chastity, and honesty, among other essential virtues. Hence he is dedicated to principles of nonviolence, support of individual freedom and education, and selfless service. The Tibetan people preferred a monk king to a warlord king with his armies, coercive demand for labor service, and self-aggrandizing ambitions for his dynastic progeny. This new Tibetan society was unique then and is still now and, therefore, terms like *feudal, theocratic,* even *traditional* or *pre-modern*, are not accurate in describing it.

The Fifth Dalai Lama embarked on the building of the Potala, symbol of the new Ganden Palace government, a remarkable fusion of royal palace, monastic establishment, and Tantric mandala or celestial paradise. He patronized the building of more monasteries for all the orders, not only the Gelukpa order, the leadership of which he designated to the senior abbot of Ganden Monastery so he himself could represent all the people and all religious orders. He gave the former warlord families bureaucratic ranks and salaries for service to the government, but only after revoking their feudal rights over their own lands and peasants and, most important, the right to maintain a private army. He gave land and sustenance, not only to all Buddhist orders, but he also protected the followers of the Bön religion, gave land to the Muslim residents of Lhasa to build their mosques and worship freely, and gave his permission and support to Christian missionary activities. Reaching out from Tibet, he made a pact with the newly triumphant Manchu rulers of China (1644–1911) to keep the peace in Inner Asia and discouraged the Mongols from rebuilding their empire, inspiring them to pursue the demilitarized Buddhistic lifestyle Tibet was further along in adopting.

The Great Fifth died in 1682, but his regent concealed his death for over a decade in order to complete the building of the Potala Palace and the restructuring of the Tibetan Ganden Palace government. This required a long delay in official recognition of the secretly discovered reincarnation, who was kept incognito with his family in a prison-like atmosphere. Due perhaps to the rigidity of the monastic government or the oppressiveness in the manner of his upbringing, the Sixth Dalai Lama turned away from his monastic avocation and more or less refused his state responsibilities. He became a legendary partygoer and lover of women, and his love poems are celebrated by Tibetans with great joy and affection to this day. In spite of his popularity, his unorthodox layman's behavior caused considerable upset among his Mongolian and some monastic Tibetan followers. Their displeasure led to his deposition, deportation, and possibly assassination in 1706, several dangerous civil conflicts over subsequent decades, and greater Manchu imperial intervention in the affairs of Tibet.

In the 1720s calm returned with the advent of the Seventh Dalai Lama, who restored the institution, maintaining his personal focus on spiritual teaching. He empowered his Cabinet and laid the foundation for a National Assembly. The Eighth Dalai Lama carried on this work in the second half of the eighteenth century. During the nineteenth century, from the ninth through the twelfth Dalai Lamas, Tibet remained stable and peaceful, though static in governance, with the later Manchu rulers intent on keeping Tibet isolated from the imperialist powers of Britain and Russia. The main innovations in many fields were developed in eastern Tibetan areas far from the complacent conservatism of the central authorities. The Manchu rulers of China also became less supportive of Tibet once the Mongol threat was reduced, due to Buddhism's pacifying effect, and the era of European imperialism brought the British and the Russians, for whom Buddhism was a complete enigma, into play around Tibet.

The Thirteenth Dalai Lama (1876–1933) was the first Dalai Lama to grow up and assume the full power of his office since the eighth. His life's work was to respond to the pressures on Tibet from the decaying Manchu empire, Tsarist Russia, the British Raj, the Nationalist Chinese, and finally the Russian and Chinese Communists. Tibet was invaded by the British in 1904, and so he fled to Mongolia and Beijing, where he encountered the modern world for the first time. He then had to flee from the Manchu dowager empress, who tried to have him killed in the last throes of her dynasty, and actually went to India to live under the protection of the British Raj for a while.

Returning to Tibet after the fall of the Manchus in 1911, he declared formal independence from the protected relationship Tibet had enjoyed with the Manchu empire. He tried to develop Tibet in more material ways in order to be able to stand up to the industrial militarism of materialistic modernity. He formed a small national defense force and even made attempts to join the League of Nations and to introduce Tibetan civilization to the world. Though he was supported in this by the leaders of the British Raj in India, the British government's geopolitical policy was determined by the Hong Kong faction and the Taipans in the China trade, who used Tibet as a pawn in dealing with the Manchus and then with the Chinese Nationalists. And so London frustrated the Great Thirteenth's every effort to gain recognition from the nations of the world.

From within also, his own conservative monastic leadership frustrated his efforts to create a modernized secular school system, to build up a viable defense force, and to develop even a modest industrial infrastructure. After hearing detailed reports of the fate of Mongolian Buddhists at the hands of Russian Communists in the early '30s, he claimed that he was going to pass away a decade ahead of schedule in order to reincarnate and grow up soon enough to defend Tibet from China's communist threat.

The present Fourteenth Dalai Lama has already earned the title "Great Fourteenth," due to his profound inner development and his magnificent works of teaching, writing, political leadership, and prophetic engagement with global society. He has resolutely proclaimed his intention to resign from the political responsibilities of the Dalai Lama institution, once resumed dialogue with a future, more pragmatic Chinese government has enabled the fate of Tibet to be resolved in a just and reasonable way.

CHRONOLOGY OF THE DALAI LAMAS

First Dalai Lama Gendun Drubpa 1391–1474

Second Dalai Lama Gendun Gyatso 1475–1542

Third Dalai Lama Sonam Gyatso 1543–1588 (first to be named "Dalai")

Fourth Dalai Lama Yonten Gyatso 1589–1617

Fifth Dalai Lama Ngawang Losang Gyatso 1617–1682

Sixth Dalai Lama Tsangyang Gyatso 1683–1706

Seventh Dalai Lama Kelsang Gyatso 1708–1757

Eighth Dalai Lama Jampel Gyatso 1758–1804

Ninth Dalai Lama Lungtog Gyatso 1806–1815

Tenth Dalai Lama Tsultrim Gyatso 1816–1837

Eleventh Dalai Lama Kedrub Gyatso 1838–1856

Twelfth Dalai Lama Trinley Gyatso 1856–1875

Thirteenth Dalai Lama Tubten Gyatso 1876–1933

Fourteenth Dalai Lama Tenzin Gyatso July 6, 1935–

THE DALAI LAMA'S ROLE GOING FORWARD

The Dalai Lama's passion for a democratic Tibet is so great that he has been working with the Tibetan Government in Exile and the worldwide Tibetan exile community to create a constitution for how they order their exile society and to serve as a model for the democratic constitution of the eventually liberated Tibet. I personally have protested his complete resignation from leadership responsibility, which he intends to do in order to have the country run by elected secular presidents and prime ministers in the modern Indian pattern. I have urged him to continue to serve in a symbolic capacity as head of the nation, like the English queen or the Scandinavian royals. And I have argued that the Tibetans will surely insist upon it when they have the free choice.

But he firmly rejected in that conversation my proposal for a constitutional lamarchy (a reincarnate lama monarchy). So it is clear he considers that his duty will change once the occupation and exile has ended and a viable Tibetan democracy has begun to function in a free Tibet.

I still wonder if there is a way to continue the noble experiment begun by the Great Fifth and create a spiritual democracy rather than just conform to the American and Indian pattern of secular democracy, wherein the power of money becomes too great. This spiritual democracy would obviously not elevate any particular religion, order, or sect as the state church, yet should somehow find a way of educating the people to adopt a higher level of ethics, a higher level of spiritual education both in mind and in science, and an exemplary sustainability of lifestyle, balancing material and spiritual goods for the people of the new Tibet. Tibet then could assume its rightful role as a world center of nonviolence studies, methodologies for implementation of social justice, environmentalist methodology, scientific natural healing arts, and spiritual education and development.

Even without a formal political role if the Tibetan people accede to the wishes of the Great Fourteenth and let him resign from political leadership, the Dalai Lama institution consisting of future incarnations could continue as a spiritual incarnation line in his Ganden Palace residence in Drepung Monastic University in Lhasa. Free of political duties, future Dalai Lamas could flourish as a source of spiritual teaching for the larger world. They would follow in our Dalai Lama's footsteps, appeal to followers of all religions, not only Buddhists, and inspire them to curb any dangerous tendencies toward religious intolerance and ideological fanaticism, promoting the beneficial elements of all faiths.

The Dalai Lama is something more and something less than a pope of Tibetan Buddhism. He is more than a pope because he is not merely a vicar of the Buddha; in messianic form as the bodhisattva Avalokiteshvara, he is actually seen as the returning presence of the Buddha himself. He is like Jesus returned, not just for the second time but always returning.

2

What Has the Dalai Lama Accomplished?

To quote his own expression, the Dalai Lama's "Three Main Commitments in Life" are:

1. As a human being, to promote common human values, tolerance, compassion, and so on;
2. As a religious practitioner, to promote world religious harmony, Buddhist self-discipline, and so on;
3. As a Tibetan, to represent his people until oppression by China is solved, then retire from politics even in future incarnations and revert to being a spiritual teacher in Drepung, his traditional monastic university.

Let's examine his first commitment. On the level of a human being, the Dalai Lama promotes what he understands as the prime human values, such as compassion, forgiveness, tolerance, contentment, and self-discipline. All human beings are the same. We all want happiness and do not want suffering. Even people who do not believe in religion recognize the importance of these human values in making their life happier. The Dalai Lama refers to these human values as "secular ethics," not that they are not in harmony with the world religions, but that they don't need the sanction of the world religions to be compelling to everyone, including secularized mainstream modern people. He remains committed to the importance of these human values and shares them with everyone he meets.

As we have glimpsed in the previous chapter, the Buddhist sciences—physics, biology, and psychology—define reality as relational, causal, evolutionary, and a human being as an evolutionarily opportune life form, tending toward self-reflection, gentleness, learning, loving, and happiness. Therefore, the Dalai Lama thinks of a human being as having the evolutionarily predominant nature of kindness, tolerance, compassion, and intelligence.

Regarding his second commitment, on the level of a religious practitioner, the Dalai Lama is committed to the promotion of religious harmony and understanding among the world's major religious traditions. Despite philosophical differences, all major world religions have the same potential to develop good human beings. It is therefore important for all religious traditions to respect one another and to recognize the value of each other's traditions. As far as one truth, one religion is concerned, this may be relevant on an individual level. However, for the community at large, the recognition of several truths and several religions is necessary.

He tends to talk of religion here as a conventional translation of Dharma (in Tibetan *chö*). But he has agreed with me in personal conversation as recently as 2006 that Buddhism is, at the maximum, one-third religion, one-third secular ethical system, and one-third scientific institution. So in order for him to be a good Buddhist practitioner in the Buddhist sense, he must be:

1. A secular ethical leader—a kind of common sense prophet;
2. A religious leader of an infinitheistic religion (meaning the divine as infinite, thus not rigidly this or that form; the Dalai Lama often uses the expression "nontheistic," meaning non-monotheistic in the Abrahamic sense);
3. A first-rate scientific practitioner and philosopher, especially concerned with the discovery of the nature of reality and the fostering of the human ability to evolve through education, to develop, change, and grow.

In "being a good Buddhist" therefore, he:

1. Thinks of secular humanism as another world religion; he brings it into dialogue with spirituality in his book *Ethics for the New Millennium*;
2. Lives an exemplary life of a Buddhist mendicant, traveling the accessible world as Shakyamuni did 2,500 years ago, inspiring people to pursue their higher potentials; engages with all world religions, urging them to focus on their own contributions to human betterment, inviting them to join him in avoiding inter-religious competition and aggressive pursuit of cross-religious converts (exemplified in his many writings on Buddhist teachings, his *Good Heart* venture into inter-religious interpretation of Christianity, his dialogues with rabbis, swamis, ministers, popes, archbishops, imams, muftis, and sheikhs);
3. Studies sciences—Tibetan Buddhist and modern material-ist—and puts them into practice and research in his own mind and teaches them in his various communities of colleagues, Tibetan and non-Tibetan (as exemplified in the Mind and Life series of books, *The Universe in a Single Atom*, and so on).

In terms of his third commitment, the Dalai Lama is Tibetan, and Tibetans place their trust in him. He has a responsibility to act as the

Tibetans' free spokesperson in their struggle for justice. His third commitment will cease to exist once a mutually beneficial solution is reached between the Tibetans and the Chinese. However, he has said he will carry on with the first two commitments till his last breath.

His sense of himself as a Tibetan comes, in this incarnation, from an extraordinary life, detailed in two autobiographies so far, and many works by others. Born in a well-off peasant farmer-trader family, he was recognized as the Dalai Lama very young, was brought up as a monk with a special education, was trained to be a head of state, and was entrusted with the political leadership of his people.

So when he refers to himself as a Tibetan, he refers to his:

1. Family identity;
2. Tribal identity, not very strongly defined in his region;
3. National identity, identifying with the Tibetan nation, which he represents to the Tibetans and to the world, as from many lifetimes of service, according to the Tibetans' (and his own, I'm sure) belief;
4. Perhaps cultural identity, esteeming the nation of Tibet as quintessentially Buddhist, as it enshrines Buddhist principles of transcendental individualism, gentleness and justice, educational humanism, social altruism, and egalitarian freedom; thus his Tibetan-ness and his Buddhist-ness overlap a lot.

Accomplishments and Impacts

In parallel with those three levels of commitment, but adding more detail from an observer's point of view, I divide the Dalai Lama's accomplishments into at least seven levels and kinds of impact, which will be described in this chapter.

As a Buddhist Monk

As a simple Buddhist monk, his Buddhist teachings through his writings in many languages and his lectures around the world have inspired a vastly improved understanding of Buddhism among non-Tibetans, both Buddhist and non-Buddhist. He has been unfailingly careful in his sincere refusal to urge followers of other religions or of secular humanism to convert to Buddhism. He practices what he preaches about how the world religions in the twenty-first century should be careful not to compete with one another for converts so as not to stir up inter-religious conflicts in the pluralistic global society.

If you understand Buddhism not merely as a world religion, religion as primarily a system of belief, and the Dalai Lama as being a great philosopher in the tradition he claims as his own, that of the Seventeen Great Professors (Pandits) of Nalanda University (the great Buddhist Monastic University of classical India), then he emerges not as a religious preacher but as a world teacher. The Dalai Lama can be classified as someone like Albert Einstein, Arnold Toynbee, Bertrand Russell, or Stephen Hawking, who advances human knowledge from a philosophical and scientific point of view. If Buddhism is one-third ethics, one-third psychology and religion as therapy, and one-third scientific wisdom, then the Dalai Lama brings new aspects of those three values to the world.

In ethics, he advances a general call to his "common human religion of kindness," which, he reasons, grounds a secular, humanistic, and environmental ethic. He argues that compassion is not grounded in religious faith or commandments, though it can be reinforced by all of them, but

ACHIEVEMENTS
FROM DALAILAMA.COM

October 22, 2007 **Presidential Distinguished Professor**
Emory University, Atlanta

October 17, 2007 **US Congressional Gold Medal** *US Congress, Washington, DC*

October 8, 2007 **Ahimsa Award** *Institute of Jainology, London*

September 20, 2007 **Doctor Honoris Causa** *University of Müenster, Germany*

June 8, 2007 **Doctor Honoris Causa** *Southern Cross University, Melbourne, Australia*

May 12, 2007 **BILD Award** *BILD newspaper, Germany*

it is grounded in human beings' biology. This is the ancient Buddhist biological theory of karma, which means "evolutionary action," and in advocating this worldview on the ethical and life science level, the Dalai Lama is adding a new perspective to the prospect of human survival, a new reason for a reasonable hope.

In psychology/therapeutic religion, the Dalai Lama does take responsibility for his spiritual dedication and his role as a religious leader. But his main concern is the training of the mind, that is, the psychological knowledge contained in Buddhism, and all other religious traditions, about how to lessen the destructive ideas and emotions in the individual mind and how to fortify the creative and evolutionarily beneficial motives and emotions. The science of meditational practice and the analysis of insight cultivation are the primary preoccupations here. This emphasis on training the mind and advancing in the qualities by all religions' founders helps the Dalai Lama avoid simply claiming that his belief is better than others' beliefs. He can instead follow the ancient adage found among Ashoka's third century BCE pillar edicts: "Never criticize others' religions. Better to advance yourself in the qualities commended in your own tradition."

In scientific wisdom, he has been engaged for more than two decades in dialogue with eminent modern scientists from most fields: physics, biology, neuroscience, psychology, cosmology/astronomy, and various hybrids.

May 9, 2007 **Doctor Honoris Causa** *Smith College, Northampton, USA*

December 10, 2006 **White Lotus Order**
Republic of Kalmykia, Russian Federation

October 14, 2006 **Doctor Honoris Causa** *University of Rome 3, Rome, Italy*

September 19, 2006 **Doctor Honoris Causa**
University at Buffalo, New York, USA

September 9, 2006 **Honorary Citizenship** *Canada*

May 4, 2006 **Doctor Honoris Causa** *University of Santiago, Santiago, Chile*

February 16, 2006 **Ben-Gurion Negev Award**
Ben Gurion University, Be'er Sheva, Israel

He sponsors projects to translate modern scientific treatises into Tibetan and have them taught to the new generations of Tibetan monk scholars in exile, intellectually well-trained students numbering in the tens of thousands. He has also expounded some of the various Buddhist scientific theories of mind and body, which more and more emerge as connected with modern biology, physics, neuroscience, and psychology. His contribution has been so significant, indeed, it warrants a special section below.

AS A BUDDHIST TEACHER

The Dalai Lama's intensive teaching schedule on both philosophy and contemplative methodology has informed and empowered the studies and practice of Tibetan Buddhist monks and lay people of all orders as well as the Bön religious sect, causing a palpable renaissance in the quality and intensity of Tibetan spirituality.

He has directly accomplished a small miracle in exile and indirectly another even larger miracle from a distance in occupied Tibet. The direct miracle is witnessed in the community of the roughly 150,000 Tibetans currently in exile around the world, by the fact that there are approximately 25,000 to 35,000 monks and nuns. They are clustered mainly in large monasteries built and thriving in south India, in Karnataka and Mysore states, and are scattered elsewhere in India and Nepal in smaller monasteries. This has been maintained for almost fifty years within an

November 6, 2005 **Inspiration & Compassion Award**
American Himalayan Foundation, San Francisco, USA

September 25, 2005 **Doctor Honoris Causa** *Rutgers University, New Jersey, USA*

August 12, 2005 **Manhae Peace Prize**
Manhae Foundation, South Korea

July 27, 2005 **Hessian Peace Prize**
Parliament of Hesse, Wiesbaden, Germany

October 7, 2004 **Doctor Honoris Causa**
Universidad Iberoamericana, Mexico City, Mexico

exile population where the young have had plenty of opportunity to gain a secular education, enter lay life, do business, make money, bring up a family, and so forth, within the modern social pattern wherein monasticism is not considered a viable vocation.

The indirect miracle is that, under the Dalai Lama's inspiration, since the end of the cultural revolution in the '70s, there has been a huge increase in monastic vocations in Tibet, combining the usual Tibetan choice of monastic lifestyle as the most meaningful way of living a consciously evolutionary life with a form of civil disobedience against the antireligious communist regime. The Tibetans have also engaged in a large amount of monastery rebuilding as well as pursuing studies under the few surviving senior teachers rehabilitated from various Chinese prisons. This occurred to everyone's surprise after twenty-five years of violent class struggle, thought reform, and the criminalization of religious belief and practice.

The Chinese government was so surprised during the early 1980s that it made little effort to stop the movement, even though it was against the law. Later, after the tumultuous times of 1987 (mass protests violently put down in Tibet) and 1989 (the all-China suppression after the Tiananmen Square events), officials did crack down on these monastic developments and reasserted control over the reconstructed monasteries. They started management committees, instituted communist thought control studies, and expelled monks and nuns who did not toe the party line. They made a

October 5, 2004 **The Gold Medal**
National University of Mexico (UNAM), Mexico City, Mexico

September 27, 2004 **Doctor Honoris Causa**
University of Costa Rica, San José, Costa Rica

September 24, 2004 **Doctor Honoris Causa**
University of Puerto Rico, San Juan, Puerto Rico

September 23, 2004 **Doctor Honoris Causa**
University of Miami, USA

September 18, 2004 **Doctor Honoris Causa**
Nova Southeastern University, Miami, USA

big shift in policy in 1994, frightened by the deconstruction of the Soviet Union, and proclaimed that Tibetan Buddhism, since it involved devotion to the Dalai Lama, was seditious and caused Tibetans to disidentify with the Chinese "Motherland." They accelerated this anti-Tibetan-Buddhism campaign with the Panchen Lama affair in 1995[1] and have been intensifying even more in the new century with their anti–Dalai Lama campaigns. Yet the monastic spirit still flourishes in Tibet.

This is a miracle because the world is almost universally devoted to militarism as the main institution protecting society; Ancient India, Tibet, and Mongolia are the only societies where militarism was largely abandoned, and their unique social form called mass monasticism is the only remedy against rampant militarism human societies have ever developed.[2] Young men and women in formative years, who are not satisfied hanging around the house, either go into armies and set out to conquer something to make their fortunes, as directed by aggressive and greedy leaders, or they have the option of joining schools of self-conquest to seek salvation or enlightenment and to find the higher purpose of human life. Buddhism and non-Protestant Christianity have been the two movements that have used this institution widely, with Jainism, Hinduism, and Taoism joining in Asia.

This miracle is only understandable in the Tibetan case if we gain a sense of the personality or character constellation (to use a concept

May 28, 2004 **Humphreys Memorial Award for Services to Buddhism**
Buddhist Society of UK, UK

April 27, 2004 **International Acharya Sushil Kumar Peace Award**
University of Toronto, Canada

April 27, 2004 **Doctor Honoris Causa** *University of Toronto, Canada*

April 20, 2004 **Doctor Honoris Causa**
Simon Fraser University, Vancouver, Canada

April 19, 2004 **Doctor Honoris Causa**
University of British Columbia, Vancouver, Canada

developed in the sociology of knowledge) that results from acculturation in the Tibetan Buddhist society. Tibetan society is one of only two (barely) surviving mass-monastic societies, in which monastics comprise up to and more than 20 percent of the population. Even medieval Europe or orthodox Russia never reached such a proportion of Christian monastics, nor did any other Buddhist society. For a society to sustain such a huge proportion of celibate monastics, a basic economic sufficiency is required so the other 80 percent can do without the agriculturally productive labor of 20 percent of the work force. Second, a lack of militarism is mandatory, since that 20 percent of manpower in other societies constitutes the military. Third, enough people must have an ambition toward self-purification and self-transformation to enter or stay in (if entered involuntarily as youths) a monastic vocation, as well as enough intellectual ability to undergo the rigorous studies that are required of most Tibetan Buddhist monastics. And fourth, there must be a constant example and source of inspiration, a popular sense that "there be buddhas among us!" The Dalai Lama has provided the inspiration and has exemplified:

a. The generosity needed to support economically unproductive monastics;
b. The gentleness needed to not choose violence no matter how bad the oppression;

April 16, 2004 **2nd Citizens Peace Building Award**
University of California, Irvine, USA

October 9, 2003 **Award for Promotion of Human Rights**
Foundation Jaime Brunet, Madrid, Spain

September 19, 2003 **Human Rights Award**
International League for Human Rights, New York, USA

September 5, 2003 **Doctor Honoris Causa**
University of San Francisco, USA

June 3, 2003 **Manfred Björkquist Medal**
Sigtuna Foundation, Stockholm, Sweden

c. The evolutionary ambition needed for development of self through wisdom and of others through compassion;

d. The wisdom needed to pursue that ambition through systematic self-transformative studies.

Holding such a large refugee community together and enabling its members to preserve their culture throughout three generations in exile are great accomplishments. The Tibetan refugee communities have won UN awards (over protests of Chinese members) as model refugee communities and have prospered wherever they have settled, sometimes inciting the envy of eventually poorer indigenous neighbors in Nepal, Bhutan, and India. Their lamas and reincarnate spiritual teachers have earned the affection of whole populations of countries in which they have opened thousands of Dharma and meditation centers.

The main accusation against the Dalai Lama that surfaces from time to time around the world is that of being ineffective. People have said, "What has the Dalai Lama ever accomplished, for all his running around the world meeting celebrities?" In fact, answering that question is one of the main drives of this book. What they are really saying is, "Violence is the way of the world. The Dalai Lama's dogged nonviolence has gotten Tibet nowhere. He didn't back the guerrilla war in the '60s. The Chinese just laugh and scorn his appeals for dialogue. His

December 5, 2002 **Basavashree Award**
Basavakendra, Sri Murugha Math, Chitradurga, India

November 7, 2002 **Doctor Honoris Causa**
Mongolian University of Science & Technology, Mongolia

November 7, 2002 **Doctor Honoris Causa**
National University of Mongolia, Mongolia

October 14, 2002 **Human Rights Prize** *University of Graz, Austria*

July 6, 2002 **Man of the Year** *Croatian Academic Society, Croatia*

May 21, 2002 **Peace Award 2000** *UN Association of Australia, Australia*

December 5, 2001 **Doctor Honoris Causa** *University of Tromsø, Norway*

own people are demoralized and feel abandoned. He is a pathetic figure, utterly ineffective." In regard to the Dalai Lama's efforts to liberate
his people, Elie Wiesel once said in public, "Your Holiness, prayer is
not enough!"

The Dalai Lama does not answer this challenge directly but instead
politely accepts that he may be unrealistic. However, he could answer
that Afghanistan did succeed in repelling the Russian invaders by violence, but then, once addicted to violence, they have been fighting among
themselves incessantly ever since, staggering around in an endless cycle of
revenge in a destroyed environment. The Israelis have defended themselves with violence, as the Palestinians have tried to defend themselves.
Yet after fifty years, both are locked in an endless cycle of hatred, fear,
and violence. In comparison with these violent liberation struggles, the
Dalai Lama has succeeded in minimizing the violence his people have
been exposed to, though now they are threatened with the slow, less
visible violence of genocide by population transfer, or assimilation by
colonization. When Tibetans do recover their autonomy, they will have
done so nonviolently, and so their newfound freedom will not be accompanied by violent internal struggles as in the Afghani case.

This fits with the wisdom of ancient Buddhist teachings on self-
defense. The rule is always to minimize violence. If you are invaded and
have the manpower to defend yourself and overcome the invader, you

November 26, 2001 **Doctor Honoris Causa**
University of Lusíada Porto, Portugal

June 10, 2001 **Ecce Homo Order** *Kancelaria Kapituly Orderu, Poland*

October 16, 2000 **Doctor Honoris Causa**
Comenius University, Bratislava, Slovakia

December 12, 1999 **Diwaliben Mohanlal Mehta Award for
International Peace & Harmony** *Diwaliben Mohanlal Mehta Charitable
Trust, India*

November 24, 1999 **Lifetime Achievement Award**
Hadassah Women's Zionist, Israel

should do it; then do not pursue the invader back into their own territory but impose a treaty. If you do not have the power to defend yourself successfully, and so by fighting you will anger the invading military more and cause it to be more destructive once you are defeated, you should not fight defensively but surrender peacefully, hoping to minimize the violence inflicted on your people.

As a Religious Practitioner

The Dalai Lama has been tireless in his championing of interreligious dialogue and promotion of mutual understanding and tolerance among world religions in these times of religious extremisms and violence. He has facilitated many interfaith talks and activities and authored *The Good Heart*, a book offering his Buddhist interpretations and appreciations of the Christian Gospels to Christian monks.

In this enterprise, the Dalai Lama has assumed world leadership and continues to do so. I'll never forget the day in 1979 when he sat at a reception at the Harvard Divinity School and gave an informal talk on Buddhist-Christian dialogue. He said that it was time for us all to give up thinking that our beliefs are superior to those of others. He confessed that he used to think that the belief in an omnipotent Creator God was childish and irrational. Then his meeting with Thomas Merton led him to understand that it could be a beautiful and powerful

October 12, 1999 **Bodhi Award** *American Buddhist Congress, USA*

April 16, 1999 **Doctor of Theology** *Florida International University, USA*

April 9, 1999 **Doctor Honoris Causa** *University of Buenos Aires, Argentina*

April 7, 1999 **Doctor Honoris Causa** *University of Brasília, Brazil*

November 11, 1998 **Doctor Honoris Causa** *Seton Hill College, Greensburg, USA*

May 15, 1998 **Doctor of Laws** *University of Wisconsin, Madison, USA*

May 11, 1998 **Doctor of Divinity** *Emory University, Atlanta, USA*

May 8, 1998 **Doctor of Humane Letters** *Brandeis University, Boston, USA*

May 8, 1998 **Juliet Hollister Award** *Juliet Hollister Foundation, New York, USA* worldview and could lead people to discover a great sense of holiness and thereby also help hold communities together in a good way. So he gave up thinking that Buddhism is superior because of its rational rejection of the plausibility of a Creator in the Hindu or Abrahamic sense. Then he said he hoped for the same effort from others—and I remember the caught-in-the-cookie-jar look on the faces of some of my theological colleagues.

He further said that some of those Christians, when they heard that a person such as the Dalai Lama himself was an atheist, might even faint from the stress of it! At the time, I hadn't thought enough about it to argue with him about calling himself an atheist, and I noted that he enjoyed the shock value of using the term for himself.

This is the level of intensity with which the Dalai Lama pursues the development of inter-religious tolerance. In his public teachings—both at home in Dharamsala and around the world—he always spends time and effort in the beginning to urge those who are present who might not be Buddhists *not* to take the coming teachings as any sort of imperative to become Buddhists. He, the Dalai Lama, is not interested in making converts and increasing the number of Buddhists denominationally in the world. In fact, it is a serious step to change one's religion. It can create tension and conflict within one's family and birth society. It has a deep psychological impact on the personality. It's often better to simply

November 25, 1997 **Paulos Mar Gregorious Award**
Paulos Mar Gregorious Committee, India

September 11, 1997 **Doctor of International Diplomatic Science**
University of Trieste, Trieste, Italy

June 1, 1997 **Doctor Honoris Causa** *Regis University, Denver, USA*

May 31, 1997 **Doctor Honoris Causa** *University of Colorado, Boulder, USA*

March 23, 1997 **Doctor of Social Sciences**
National Sun Yat-sen University, Kaohsiung, Taiwan

March 23, 1997 **Doctor of Honoris Causa**
Chu San University, Kaohsiung, Taiwan

learn from other religions, any of them, and understand the commonalities between the teachings and then try to implement the positive practices learned within the framework of one's own tradition. That is the proper way to study the teachings, he says.

When I used to hear him on this subject, I thought he was just covering his steps for public consumption in pluralistic societies, and of course, he hoped for people to wake up to the glorious teaching of the Buddha, its helpful reasonings, sciences, meditations, and ethics. I used to think that out of my own religious sense of the superiority of the Buddhist teachings that had been so useful to me in my life. But finally, I realized I was wrong. The Dalai Lama got to me with his reasoning, and I realized that the way we teach religion in the academy, in a formally and factually nonpartisan, nonproselytizing way, is the way we should present the Buddhist teachings to the general public, even in religious settings, because we are all always in the pluralistic globalizing society no matter where we are. We must not presume our own superiority of belief over those of others, even though we can engage in critical analysis of our own and others' beliefs in the proper settings of inquiry, based on a fundamental sense of equality in the basics.

The Dalai Lama freely admits that he finds Buddhism superior *for him* but then has succeeded in restraining himself from thinking it is superior for any other. That is for each person to decide for herself or himself. It is

July 26, 1996 **The President's Medal for Excellence**
Indiana University, Bloomington, USA

April 5, 1995 **Doctor of Buddhist Philosophy** *Rissho University, Tokyo, Japan*

January 2, 1995 **Doctor of Letters** *Nagpur University, India*

June 4, 1994 **Franklin D. Roosevelt Freedom Medal**
Franklin & Eleanor Roosevelt Institute, New York, USA

April 27, 1994 **World Security Annual Peace Award**
New York Lawyer's Alliance, USA

April 26, 1994 **Doctor of Humane Arts & Letters**
Columbia University, New York, USA

so important, he feels, since the ancient history of religions is full of violent conflicts with each other: crusades, *jihads*, and inter-sectarian warfare even among Buddhists in Tibet, Japan, Sri Lanka, and elsewhere. Then there was the famous Marxist-Leninist-Maoist religious persecution, when the Communist ideology proved itself just as intolerant, violent, cruel, and destructive as any of the religious denominations and groups. The Dalai Lama personally experienced the secular fanaticism of the communists in Tibet. He recounts in his autobiography how, as a young man, he shuddered when Mao leaned over to him at a dinner and said, "You know of course that religion (Sanskrit, *dharma*, Tibetan, *chö*, Chinese, *fa*) is poison!" His Holiness then thought, prophetically, "Ah, so you really are the destroyer of the Dharma!"

Thus, the Dalai Lama has always considered secularism, with all its communist and capitalist forms, to be a kind of world religion, since he has observed that supposedly nonreligious ideology can also become fanatical and therefore powerfully intrusive in molding peoples' lives.

The Dalai Lama has spoken to three popes about his view that religions should cease trying to convert each other's followers. He has spoken to all kinds of rabbis, Muslim leaders in India, Sufis, Hindu swamis, and Protestants of all kinds, as well as whatever Taoists and Confucianists he has met in his far-flung travels. He has also addressed leaders of

April 25, 1994 **Doctor of Humane Letters**
Berea College, Berea, New York, USA

March 20, 1994 **Fellow of University** *Hebrew University, Jerusalem, Israel*

March 14, 1993 **International Valiant for Freedom Award**
The Freedom Coalition, Melbourne, Australia

September 17, 1992 **Honorary Professor** *Novosibirsk State University,*
Buriat, Russia

September 11, 1992 **Honorary Professor**
Kalmyk State University, Kalmykia, Russia

June 6, 1992 **Doctor Honoris Causa** *University of Rio de Janeiro, Brazil* various indigenous religions, who are always relieved to hear that he for-mally renounces missionary activities, since they have suffered much from many such well-intentioned but intrusive believers. He called for a moratorium on conversion efforts around the world long before the emergence of the worldwide fundamentalist, politically engaged religious movements in the late 1990s.

He has been working on and gradually introducing a democratic constitution in the exile community as a way to live in exile and a model for self-rule whenever it is recovered in Tibet. It is a secularist constitu-tion based on separation of church and state, in which all religions are equal under the law. He has consistently supported those in exile and at home who practice Bön, the Tibetan religion closest to Buddhism. His former incarnations gave lands to Christian missionaries and Muslim communities in Tibet, the former never quite hanging on there having so few converts, the latter living happily in Lhasa and other centers of trade but not much bothering with attempting conversions.

At the same time as the Dalai Lama is working in this religiously pluralistic way, Tibetan reincarnate lamas and scholars have spread around the free world and have established around five thousand medi-tation centers, monasteries, and temples. These centers sometimes func-tion as churches in their communities but most often offer a kind of mental hygiene through meditation, therapy, and a sense of connection

May 5, 1992 **Doctor of Laws** *University of Melbourne, Australia*

February 16, 1992 **Doctor of Sacred Philosophy**
Lafayette University, Aurora, USA

October 10, 1991 **Wheel of Life Award**
Temple of Understanding, New York, USA

October 10, 1991 **United Earth Prize** *Klaus Nobel United Earth, USA*

August 23, 1991 **Peace and Unity Award**
National Peace Conference, Delhi, India

April 17, 1991 **Advancing Human Liberty Award**
Freedom House, New York, USA

to the bliss of reality, the ultimate reality of the universe at the deepest level, which Buddhists call "bliss-freedom-indivisible." In the background, people begin to feel an affinity to the beleaguered people of Tibet, under the stress of progressive genocide. The number of people thus seemingly "missionarized" by all these Tibetan teachers is hard to quantify, however, because the centers all encourage people to retain what they can of their birth religions. Therefore, when pollsters ask these people, "Are you a Buddhist?" they often say "no" or "sort of" or "maybe" instead of affirming a distinct faith. An important book by the Dalai Lama that gives a clear sense of how committed he is to inter-religious harmony is *The Good Heart*, the edited transcript of lectures he gave in a Christian monastery on the New Testament of the Christian Bible.

Recently, His Holiness attended, at the invitation of the Imam of Northern California, a conference emphasizing Muslim-Buddhist dialogue. He proclaimed during that meeting that it seemed he might have to become a "defender of Islam," since the media and people in general are picking out Islam as specially guilty of being a religion of hate or a religion of violence. Though he acknowledges that all religions have their share of imperfections as manifested by aberrations of institutions and practices of followers, it is unfair to single out Islam. His Holiness forcefully declared, "There is no such thing as a religion of hate!" His reason is that human beings have a common, unstated, biologically

March 25, 1991 **Shiromani Award 1991** *Shiromani Institute, Delhi, India*

April 6, 1991 **Distinguished Peace Leadership Award**
Nuclear Age Peace Foundation, USA

December 8, 1990 **Doctor Honoris Causa** *Karnataka University, India*

January 14, 1990 **Doctor of Divinity**
Central Institute for Higher Tibetan Studies, Sarnath, India

December 10, 1989 **The Nobel Peace Prize**
Norwegian Nobel Committee, Norway

December 4, 1989 **Prix de la Memoire**
Foundation Danielle Mitterrand, Paris, France

mandated religion of kindness, which is the glue that holds societies together. There might be temporary bands of violent fanatics bent on a crusade or another sort of religious war, but they are misusing the teachings of the founders. Such hate-based movements could not be the long-lasting, universalist movements we call world religions today, as they would be incapable of holding viable communities of people together for long.

The Grand Mufti of Egypt, the Venerable Ali Goma'a of Al-Azhar University, sent a message welcoming His Holiness's beginning of a sincere dialogue between Buddhism and Islam, saying that he wanted "real dialogue, not mere diplomacy." The Dalai Lama was invited by the Imam of Senegal to hold another session of dialogue in that West African country, extending the trip into Ghana and Cameroon. He accepted enthusiastically, but the People's Republic of China government was able to use its influence to block his visa from the local governments, so the trip has not yet happened.

The Dalai Lama has caused an enormous amount of progress in developing dialogue, mutual understanding, and real tolerance between the various world religions. He could have an even greater impact if the People's Republic of China government would support his activity in this direction, making religious pluralism, moderation, and tolerance a priority objective for China's influence in the world, sending him to

September 23, 1989 **Recognition of Perseverance of Times of Adversity**
World Management Council, USA

September 15, 1989 **Doctor of Humanities, Honoris Causa**
Columbia University, USA

June 21, 1989 **Raoul Wallenberg Congressional Human Rights Award**
Human Rights Foundation, USA

June 16, 1988 **Leopold Lucas Award** *University of Tüebingen, West Germany*

September 28, 1987 **Albert Schweitzer Humanitarian Award**
Human Behavior Foundation, USA

January 16, 1984 **Honorary Doctor Degree** *University of Paris, France*

African countries, holding substantial inter-religious conferences in Shanghai and Beijing, inviting him to address the UN on this topic, and making this a priority for UNESCO type agencies at the UN.

One of the Dalai Lama's innovations in inter-religious dialogue has been to issue a call to secularists to join the dialogue, since their world-view is itself a sort of religion, in the sense of belief system. His aim is to encourage all human bearers of worldviews, ideologies, and religions to emphasize a mutually harmonious bottom line of ethical restraint, responsibility, and altruistic kindness, which is essential to enhancing the life of all beings of all species and the planet itself.

AS A PHILOSOPHER AND SCIENTIST

Since our first conversations about science in 1964, the Dalai Lama has shown great interest in all the major modern sciences. In Europe in the 1970s, he held conversations with physicist David Bohm and others. In 1984, at Amherst College, we organized a five-day Inner Sciences Conference, during which he dialogued with psychologists, medical doctors, biologists, and cognitive scientists. Soon thereafter, a series of dialogues with other scientists was convened, and the Mind and Life Institute was formed in order to continue them in the United States, Europe, and India. Visits were arranged to important scientific laboratories at places such as M.I.T. in Cambridge and CERN in Switzerland. And more

MEETINGS WITH WORLD DIGNITARIES
FROM DALAILAMA.COM

December 14, 2007 **Giovanna Melandri**, *Italian Minister of Youth & Sports Activity*
December 13, 2007 **Franco Marini**, *President of the Italian Senate*
December 13, 2007 **Fausto Bertinotti**, *President of the Italian Chamber of Deputies*
December 13, 2007 **Gianni Vernetti**, *Undersecretary to the Italian Foreign Affairs*
December 12, 2007 **Ricardo Illy**, *President of the Friuli Venezia Giulia Region*
December 7, 2007 **Roberto Formigoni**, *President of the Lombardy Region*
October 30, 2007 **Stéphane Dion**, *Leader of the Canadian Liberal Party*
October 30, 2007 **Gilles Duceppe**, *Leader of the Canadian Bloc Québécois Party*

recently, programs of research on the effects of meditation on the brain and mind have been sponsored at various universities. The impact of the Dalai Lama's dialogues with scientists has been remarkable. It's spawned a dozen books published by the Mind and Life Institute[3] as well as high profile public discussions at MIT, Stanford, Emory, and Harvard in the United States, not to mention universities in Europe, India, and Australia. The Dalai Lama was invited to address the 25,000-member Neuroscience Association in Washington, DC, and he wrote a highly regarded book of his reflections on sciences, Buddhist as well as Western, called *The Universe in a Single Atom*.

Buddhism is all about science. As Shantideva says, "Everything the Buddha ever taught comes down ultimately to a question of wisdom—it was all for the sake of wisdom." That is so simply because it is the attainment of wisdom that enables a being to attain liberation from suffering. Faith, love, and kindness are in fact the products of true wisdom; they are released and empowered by it. The wisdom that understands the visceral interrelatedness of self and other opens the heart to the feeling of natural compassion for the sufferings of those others. Faith, love, kindness are excellent, but none by itself can make liberation possible. Only wisdom can liberate us from suffering. Only when we know that the deepest nature of life is, itself, freedom, only then do we feel free, and feeling free, feel inexhaustible bliss. If science is the systematic

October 30, 2007	**Jack Layton**, *Leader of the Canadian New Democratic Party*
October 29. 2007	**Michaëlle Jean**, *Governor General of Canada*
October 29, 2007	**Stephen Harper**, *Prime Minister of Canada*
October 29, 2007	**Maxime Bernier**, *Canadian Minister of Foreign Affairs*
October 29, 2007	**Stockwell Day**, *Canadian Minister of Public Safety*
October 29, 2007	**Jason Kenney**, *Secretary of State for Multiculturalism and Canadian Identity*
October 29, 2007	**Peter Milliken**, *Canadian Speaker of House of Commons*
October 19, 2007	**John Negroponte**, *US Dep. Secretary of State*
October 17, 2007	**Nancy Pelosi**, *Speaker, US House of Representatives*
October 17, 2007	**Harry Reid**, *US Senate Majority Leader*

pursuit of the accurate knowledge of reality, then science is Buddhism, Buddhism is science.

The analogy with modern science goes even further. The Buddhist theory of emptiness or voidness is not a theory about the essential nothingness of the universe. It is the original theory discovered millennia ago that proposes the *relativity* of the universe. Things are not empty of their own existence. They are empty of any nonrelational essence or isolated core reality, therefore possessing only the reality of their interrelatedness with other relational things. All things being relational, whenever anything is sought as an absolute by the kind of analytic inquiry that seeks the ultimate nature of that thing, that thing dissolves under the analysis and disappears from view. It cannot be found as an absolute. This is obvious, in a way, because if it is found at all, the finder has related to it by finding it and so has voided its absoluteness. Therefore, the voidness theory means that all theories about all things are from a particular perspective, relational, valid, or invalid only in a certain context. All theory is hypothetical, awaiting further refinement by experimental or experiential discovery of further aspects of the realities in question.

This is like Karl Popper's definition of working science as the construction of hypotheses based on existing evidence, which means hypotheses await falsification by yet further evidence. Voidness means

October 17, 2007 **Mitch McConnell**, *US Senate Minority Leader*
October 17, 2007 **Steny Hoyer**, *US House Majority Leader*
October 17, 2007 **John Boehner**, *US House Minority Leader*
October 17, 2007 **Harry Reid**, *US Senate Majority Leader*
October 16, 2007 **George W. Bush**, *U.S President*
September 23, 2007 **Angela Merkel**, *Chancellor of Germany*
September 22, 2007 **Roland Koch**, *Minister President of Hessen*
September 20, 2007 **Dr. Jürgen Rüttgers**, *Minister President of North Rhine-Westphalia*
September 20, 2007 **Alfred Gusenberger**, *Chancellor of Austria*
September 18, 2007 **Dr. Jörg Haider**, *Governor of Carinthia*

reality is elusive to our concepts, including mathematical concepts, although once we are more relaxed about their absoluteness, our concepts can be creative and useful in living with relational realities.

Therefore, the Dalai Lama has become one of the world's greatest scientists, an Einstein of our day. In dialogue with Nobelists of all fields, the Dalai Lama brings to life the sophisticated inner science, or mind science, derived from thousands of years of Buddhist research and experiment. The technologies for human betterment based on the Buddhist inner science have been field-tested for millennia in the most diverse human populations and have been proven in their value by helping hundreds of millions of people in places such as India, Sri Lanka, China, Central Asia, Thailand, Korea, Japan, Vietnam, Burma, Laos, and Mongolia enjoy a better quality of life, not to mention the ultimate liberation claimed for so many of these practitioners and experimenters.

The Tibetan Buddhist tradition is bringing forward this science and technology, which it received originally from ancient India and refined for 1,300 years in its mountain wildernesses and previously had shared mainly with the Mongolians and some Manchurians who were Tibet's geographic neighbors. Buddhists are introducing it to the modern world, slowly creating for the globe as a whole what I call the Second Renaissance, by analogy with the first, exclusively European, Renaissance. The first Renaissance came from Europe's rediscovery of the Greek

September 17, 2007 **Dr. Erwin Pröll**, *Governor of Lower Austria*
September 14, 2007 **Mário Soares**, *Former President of Portugal*
September 14, 2007 **Jorge Sampaio**, *Former President of Portugal*
September 13, 2007 **Jaime Gama**, *President of Portuguese Parliament*
September 10, 2007 **Ernest Benach i Pascual**, *President of Catalonia Parliament*
September 10, 2007 **Josep-Lluís Carod-Rovira**, *Vice President of Catalonia Government*
June 19, 2007 **Winston Peters**, *Foreign Minister of New Zealand*
June 15, 2007 **John Howard**, *Prime Minister of Australia*
June 14, 2007 **Helen Clark**, *Prime Minister of New Zealand*
June 12, 2007 **Kevin Rudd**, *Leader of Opposition in Australia*

humanism and naturalism, which lifted Europeans out of the Dark Ages of church-dominated thought suppression. But its progress is now, five hundred years later, blocked by the dogma of materialism and a lack of systematic attention to the exploration, understanding, and cultivation of the mind. So now it is the job of the Tibetans to help us rediscover the ancient science of the mind, the interior science and its derivative technologies perfected by the Buddhists, but also quite well known by Hindus and Taoists, as it permeated the Asian cultures for millennia. With the help of that science, complementing our sophisticated outer, or physical, sciences we have before us the prospect of a Second Renaissance, a flourishing of human enlightenment, insight, and creativity. And this time the renaissance will be global, not just Western. The Dalai Lama continues to be a major force in making this introduction—another huge accomplishment.

From the earliest times I began meeting with the Dalai Lama, he was fascinated by science and technology. He queried me on all sorts of topics involving physics, astronomy, chemistry, and biology. I was not a very good informant on these, as I had focused on literature and the humanities in my education, but we struggled through some of the main points of various disciplines. He was delighted by how wrong some of the Indo-Tibetan Buddhist outer sciences could be about the solar system, genes, the stability of atoms, and many other things. In his autobiogra-

May 4, 2007 **Walter Mondale**, *Former US Vice President*
May 3, 2007 **Jim Doyle**, *Governor of Wisconsin*
April 27, 2007 **Nancy Pelosi**, *Speaker, US House of Representatives*
October 13, 2006 **Massimo D'Allema**, *Italian Foreign Minister*
October 13, 2006 **Pope Benedict XVI**, *The Pope, Vatican City*
October 12, 2006 **Franco Marini**, *President of the Italian Senate*
October 12, 2006 **Fausto Bertinotti**, *Speaker of the Italian Parliament*
October 10, 2006 **Sasha Vondra**, *Czech Foreign Minister*
October 9, 2006 **Václav Havel**, *Former President of Czech Republic*
September 26, 2006 **Arnold Schwarzenegger**, *Governor of California*
September 22, 2006 **Bill Clinton**, *Former US President*

phies, he recounts how, in his early years, he loved watches, clocks, and other kinds of mechanisms. Heinrich Harrer famously recounted the pleasure the young Dalai Lama took in learning the operation and maintenance of a movie projector. This has been considered by the media, as they have become more and more interested in this remarkable man, as something quaint and fantastic, that a religious pope, or nonviolent mystical ascetic, would take an interest in hard and soft sciences. But if we understand Buddhism, as you now do having read the earlier preamble, as an educational process of becoming more and more realistic about the nature of life, then inquiry into the nature of physical and mental reality can be seen a normal part of the quest of enlightenment.

In this regard, we can claim the distinctive greatness of this Dalai Lama as an inner scientist, a scientific philosopher, a world-class scientific discoverer in the ranks of Albert Einstein, Werner Heisenberg, Niels Bohr, and other genius thinkers.

AS THE POLITICAL REPRESENTATIVE OF THE TIBETAN PEOPLE

The Dalai Lama continues to be persevering, skillful, and patient in speaking up for the Tibetan people to the world and to China in particular, following his Middle Way Approach. Though the dialogues of the last few years are presently stalled due to Chinese insincerity, he never gives up the

September 17, 2006 **Queen Noor**, *Former Queen of Jordan*
September 16, 2006 **Oscar Arias Sánchez**, *President of Costa Rica*
September 9, 2006 **Monte Solberg**, *Canadian Minister of Citizenship and Immigration*
September 9, 2006 **Jason Kenney**, *Secretary to the Canadian Prime Minister*
September 8, 2006 **Gordon Campbell**, *Premier of British Columbia Canada*
June 22, 2006 **Prince Ghazi Bin Mohammed**, *Personal Envoy & Senior Advisor to the King of Jordan*
June 21, 2006 **King Abdullah II & Queen Rania** *of Jordan*
June 20, 2006 **Ahmad Helail**, *Imam to the Royal Hashemite Court and Supreme Judge, Jordan*

cause of true autonomy for Tibet (meaning internal independence within the Chinese Union), knowing full well that many people think it is one of the great lost causes, an idea we are here reversing.

In 1959, Chairman Mao heard via Deng Xiaoping, the official in charge of taking over Tibet, that Chinese troops had crushed all Tibetan resistance against their occupation of Lhasa, but the Dalai Lama had escaped the Chinese troops that encircled his residence and had fled out of Tibet to India. Mao is reported to have said, "Ah, then we have won the battle for Lhasa, but lost the war for Tibet!" As demented as Mao eventually became, this is a statement showing prescience. It is much more far-seeing than Joseph Stalin's "How many divisions does the Pope have?" In spite of his materialistic philosophy, Mao knew that personal power and spiritual determination were key in leadership. Mao was acknowledging that the Dalai Lama, at only twenty-four years old, would be able to represent Tibet personally, so the Chinese presence there would never be legitimate in the eyes of either international law or the international community.

Clearly, when they had met in Beijing in 1954, though the young incarnation was only nineteen, Mao had encountered the power of his presence, charisma, eminence, vitality, and purity—an indefinable, almost divine, quality. Mao knew that the Tibetan nation was actually an independent country and its people not Chinese in any sense of the

June 1, 2006 **Armand De Decker**, *Belgian Minister of Development*
June 1, 2006 **Herman De Croo**, *President of the Belgian House*
June 1, 2006 **Anne Marie Lizen**, *President of the Belgian Senate*
June 1, 2006 **Guy Verhofstadt**, *Prime Minister of Belgium*
May 31, 2006 **Josep Borrell**, *President of the European Parliament*
May 31, 2006 **Günter Verheugen**, *Vice President of the European Commission*
May 30, 2006 **Wolfgang Schüssel**, *Chancellor of Austria & President of the European Council*
May 30, 2006 **José Manuel Barroso**, *President European Commission*
May 14, 2006 **Karin Gastinger**, *Austrian Minister of Justice*
May 14, 2006 **Maria Rauch-Kallat**, *Austrian Minister for Health*

term. He knew that governments seeking wealth from China might pretend to accept China's annexation of Tibet, either being ignorant of the true facts or thinking it unimportant to protest. But studied in terms of international law of nations and the sanctity of 1947 borders on which the UN was founded, China's case would be found wanting. And with the Dalai Lama free to speak his powerful truth to the people of many countries, Tibet would not disappear from the heart of the world.

There is much evidence of the Dalai Lama's almost superhuman presence. For example, before the Dalai Lama came to the Indian border in Assam (now Arunachal Pradesh), just east of Bhutan, the Indian government was loath to accept any of the Tibetan refugees fleeing the violence of the People's Liberation Army. The Indian President Nehru and his foreign minister, the Keralese Communist Krishna Menon, wanted above all to get along with China and didn't want to provoke Mao over Tibet. In the greatest mistake of his career, Nehru was willing to let the Chinese take Tibet, though the Indian government had a legation in Lhasa inherited from the British.

Both India and Britain knew full well that the Tibetans were a separate people and country, and that the Chinese invasion was a case of international aggression and territorial expansion. But when the Dalai Lama himself came to the border, Nehru opened the country to all the Tibetan refugees, and the international press came in large numbers to

May 14, 2006 **Hubert Gorbach**, *Vice Chancellor of Austria*
May 14, 2006 **Dr. Jörg Haider**, *Governor of Carinthia*
May 11, 2006 **Mario Iguarán**, *Attorney General of Colombia*
May 7, 2006 **Elaine Karp de Toledo**, *First Lady of Peru*
May 6, 2006 **Sergio Espejo**, *Chilean Minister of Transpor*
May 5, 2006 **Felipe Harboe Bascuñán**, *Deputy Minister of the Interior, Chile*
May 5, 2006 **Cardinal Errázuriz Ossa**, *Archbishop of Chile*
May 5, 2006 **Paulina Urrutia**, *Chilean Minister of Culture*
May 5, 2006 **Martín Zilic**, *Chilean Minister of Education*
May 4, 2006 **Antonio Leal Labrín**, *President of the Chilean House of Chambers*
May 3, 2006 **Jaime Naranjo Ortiz**, *Vice President of the Chilean Senate*

that remote spot to greet the legendary "God-King." How on earth did this happen? A young and unknown ruler flees an obscure and little-known country during a time of much more high-profile international events, and the world suddenly takes notice; he is featured on the covers of magazines across the globe, including *Life* magazine in America, *Stern* in Germany, and *Paris Match*. Why was this of such interest to the whole world? It can only be what we might call the magic of the Dalai Lama's special presence.

There is a story about the Third Dalai Lama, Sonam Gyatso, who accepted in 1573 the imperious invitation of the Mongolian Great Emperor of that time, Altan Khan, to his court in Inner Mongolia. This Khan was curious about the Lama, who was not at that time the ruler of Tibet, but an important religious teacher. The legend is that as the Dalai Lama was riding across the steppe with his relatively small entourage toward the vast encampment of the Great Khan—who was not a Buddhist but a warrior and a shamanistic practitioner, a sacrificer of prisoners of war—the Tibetans were feeling a bit intimidated. Just then a fierce, blood red deity, what the Tibetans call a Dharma Protector, or Begtse Jamdrel, showed up alongside the Dalai Lama's party with a vast army of hundreds of thousands mounted demon warriors, so that the Dalai Lama arrived in the Mongolian tent city with a larger army than the Great Khan! The Khan was so impressed, overwhelmed by this demonstration of spiritual

May 1, 2006 **Adolfo Pérez Esquivel**, *1980 Nobel Peace Prize Winner*
April 26, 2006 **Gilberto Gil**, *Brazilian Minister of Culture*
April 26, 2006 **José Luiz de França Penna**, *Brazilian Green Party President*
February 19, 2006 **Rabbi Shlomo Amar**, *Sephardi Chief Rabbi of Israel*
February 19, 2006 **Rabbi Yona Metzger**, *Ashkenazi Chief Rabbi of Israel*
November 18, 2005 **Dr. M. G. Buthelezi**, *President of Inkatha Freedom Party, South Africa*
November 16, 2005 **Harry Reid**, *US Senate Minority Leader*
November 16, 2005 **Nancy Pelosi**, *US House Minority Leader*
November 16, 2005 **Dennis Hastert**, *US Speaker of the House of Representatives*
November 9, 2005 **Condoleezza Rice**, *US Secretary of State*

might, that he at once ordered the destruction of the ancestral idols propitiated in the prisoner sacrifices and set himself humbly to become the disciple of the Lama. In fact, in his admiration for Sonam Gyatso, for his combination of power and gentleness, integrity, courage, and intelligence, Altan Khan is the one who gave him the name Dalai, which in Mongolian means "vast," "oceanic" (*gyatso* in Tibetan means "ocean"), which must express how the Khan perceived the simple Buddhist monk, Sonam Gyatso, from the Drepung Monastery University.

Whatever the interpretation of this legendary account, the impression conveyed by a Dalai Lama is similarly oceanic, vast, and energizing. I have seen it again and again when our present Dalai Lama has given audience to contemporary dignitaries of various nations, political, business, and artistic celebrities, as well as simple people. The effect of his presence is galvanizing; people often burst into tears, forget what they were planning to say, commonly change their preconceived attitudes completely. The noted economist J. K. Galbraith once hosted a meeting between the Dalai Lama and Professor John Fairbank, the famous Harvard China scholar, who had just returned from a tour in China. Fairbank was practically dragged into the room, not wanting to be there but of course unwilling to offend his host, the cheerfully towering Galbraith. He approached the Dalai Lama, who was forty-four at the time, as if he were approaching a possibly dangerous wild animal, no doubt filled with all sorts of horrid

November 9, 2005 **George W. Bush**, *US President*
November 6, 2005 **Jimmy Carter**, *Former US President*
October 27, 2005 **Renuka Chowdhury**, *Tourism Minister of India*
September 11, 2005 **Dirk Kempthorne**, *Governor of Idaho*
September 9, 2005 **Frank H. Murkowski**, *Governor of Alaska, USA*
August 16, 2005 **Natwar Singh**, *Foreign Minister of India, USA*
August 4, 2005 **Pascal Couchepin**, *Interior Minister of Switzerland*
August 1, 2005 **Giuliano Amato**, *Former Prime Minister of Italy*
June 18, 2005 **Wolfgang Thierse**, *President of the German Parliament*
June 17, 2005 **Dr. Angela Merkel**, *Leader of the CDU/CSU Party*
June 15, 2005 **Kjell Magne Bondevik**, *Prime Minister of Norway*

propaganda tales from his Chinese hosts in Beijing. But as the two men shook hands, the distinguished elder professor and the young Lama, Fairbank's whole posture melted; he visibly relaxed and then became enchanted when he realized that the Dalai Lama could converse either in Chinese or English. Fairbank smiled, became animated, and remained holding the Dalai Lama's hand for some time. You would have thought they had been old friends in reunion. The transformation was unforgettable.

I tell such anecdotes because they reveal how the Dalai Lama is a force of nature, how people find him extraordinary, and how effective he is at representing the special qualities and precious value of the Tibetan people. People who meet the Dalai Lama intuitively feel that this amazing person is a product of a unique culture—one that should not be wiped out, one worth preserving. The Tibetan people under occupation and in exile, then, could not have a more effective representative in their quest for freedom.

As my wife, Nena, once brilliantly put it, Mahatma Gandhi was able ultimately to oust the British from India nonviolently because his people outnumbered the British hugely, and so their nonviolent resistance to the British rule was ultimately effective. The Dalai Lama is in the opposite situation. His numerically few people are swamped in an ocean of Chinese, so even if his nonviolent policy led to entire Tibetan population rising in nonviolent resistance, it would not make Tibet ungovernable by the Chinese overlords. But the world's people outnumber the Chinese

June 14, 2005 **Jorgen Kosmo**, *President of the Norwegian Parliament*
May 19, 2005 **Prince Ghazi Bin Mohammed**, *Advisor to the King of Jordan*
May 19, 2005 **Bill Clinton**, *Former US President*
May 18, 2005 **King Abdullah II & Queen Rania** *of Jordan*
May 18, 2005 **Bassem Awadallah**, *Finance Minister of Jordan*
November 7, 2004 **Dr. M. G. Buthelezi**, *President of the Inkatha Freedom Party, South Africa*
November 5, 2004 **Nelson Mandela**, *Former President of South Africa*
October 5, 2004 **Santiago Creel**, *Secretary of Interior of Mexico*
October 1, 2004 **María del Carmen Aceña**, *Education Minister, Guatemala*
October 1, 2004 **Jorge Briz Abularach**, *Guatemalan Foreign Minister*

people five to one. So only if the Dalai Lama can move the hearts of the world's people—including the Chinese people—to really care about Tibet, really disapprove of the Chinese cultural genocide of the Tibetan people, really express their refusal for that to happen, only then will the nonviolent, moral liberation movement of the Tibetans stand a chance of succeeding. And even then, the analogy with the Gandhian movement is not complete. For the Chinese cannot be forced out of Tibet by any sort of material power, either arms and threats or nonviolent resistance. They must be moved from the heart, from within their own minds, to decide for themselves that it is better for them to leave Tibet alone, whether federated with them or not. They must decide that Tibet is Tibet, that it deserves to exist as itself, and that a Tibet standing free and open as a friend of the world is more valuable to China than a Tibet without Tibetans. Such a Tibet would be a land of ghosts where uncomfortable Chinese people, feeling themselves languishing without much oxygen in barren exile, would welcome you to their own stolen prize of empty land, their own theater of genocide, their own scene of crimes against humanity, their own vast Auschwitz under which the six million (amazingly the same number) Tibetans would have been interred. Such a land would be far worse than worthless to the Chinese.

Both United States presidents Bill Clinton and George W. Bush, for all their other problems and failings, have sensed that the leadership of

October 1, 2004 **Eduardo Stein Barrillas**, *Vice President of Guatemala*

October 1, 2004 **Óscar José Rafael Berger Perdomo**, *President of Guatemala*

September 29, 2004 **Francisco Laínez**, *Foreign Minister of El Salvador*

September 29, 2004 **Ana Vilma de Escobar**, *Vice President of El Salvador*

September 29, 2004 **Antonio Saca González**, *President of El Salvador*

September 27, 2004 **Mario Redondo Poveda**, *Speaker of the Costa Rican Parliament*

September 27, 2004 **Gerardo González Esquivel**, *President of the Costa Rican Congress*

September 27, 2004 **Roberto Tovar Faja**, *Foreign Minister of Costa Rica*

September 27, 2004 **Lineth Saborío**, *Vice President of Costa Rica*

China would be moved from the heart in this positive way should they have the fortune to meet the Dalai Lama while they are still in power. That's why Clinton told former President Jiang in Shanghai that he should really meet the Dalai Lama; he would really like him. And why Bush II said in the fall of 2007, during the awarding of the Congressional Gold Medal of Honor to the Dalai Lama, that Hu Jintao and Wen Jiabao should meet and talk to the Dalai Lama to find out what a good guy he is.

The Dalai Lama's presence thus has the positive impact of helping world leaders to look up from their immediate worries and fears and to feel encouraged to look at the big picture for the long term, to see from a fresh perspective. The Dalai Lama himself has always supported the various summit meetings held around the world, since he feels that world leaders, especially those with conflicting agendas, need to get to know each other personally, as human beings.

AS THE LEADER OF THE TIBETANS

The Dalai Lama continues to inspire restraint and nonviolence among the Tibetan youth in exile and all the Tibetans in Tibet, in spite of their mounting frustration at the lack of progress made in achieving economic self-sufficiency, religious freedom, and human and other rights due to the Chinese government's oppressive and destructive policies.

September 27, 2004 **Abel Pacheco**, *President of Costa Rica*
September 26, 2004 **Guido Sáenz**, *Minister for Culture of Costa Rica*
September 23, 2004 **Sila Calderón**, *Governor of Puerto Rico*
September 17, 2004 **Jeb Bush**, *Governor of Florida, USA*
July 3, 2004 **Dr. Manmohan Singh**, *Prime Minister of India*
July 3, 2004 **Sonia Gandhi**, *Chairperson of Ruling UPA, India*
May 28, 2004 **Michael Howard**, *Leader of UK Opposition*
May 28, 2004 **Prince Charles**, *Prince of Wales, UK*
May 27, 2004 **Jack Straw**, *Foreign Secretary of UK*
May 27, 2004 **Dr. Rowan Williams**, *Archbishop of Canterbury, UK*
May 6, 2004 **Dalton McGuinty**, *Premier of Ontario, Canada*

Some Tibetans nowadays, freely in exile and underground in Tibet, complain about the Dalai Lama's leadership because of his insistence on nonviolence and his offering to accept autonomy within China rather than the full independence that Tibet deserves under international law. But so far, they still follow him and restrain their urge to do violence.

Actually, the whole debate of autonomy versus independence is mainly the result of a general confusion. The Dalai Lama never questions that every Tibetan wants and has a right to have independence; he always says that all persons and all countries flourish with it, and all value it supremely. However, once independent, they and their neighbors have to relate to one another. They have to trade, exchange, tolerate, and connect to each other. There is no such thing as absolute independence. Everything is interdependent.

So to ask for *true autonomy* within China is simply to be realistic. The Dalai Lama is essentially saying to the Chinese, "Well, you want to own Tibet, but that is not possible. Tibet is naturally free and Tibetans are Tibetans, not Chinese. Since you are, however, determined to play a large part in Tibet's future, and we do need your help to modernize and to repair the immense damage your predecessors have wrought in our land, we will voluntarily join with you in federation, in a "One-Country, Two-Systems" arrangement such as you have with Hong Kong and should soon have with Taiwan. As we are a minority people in union

May 6, 2004 **James Bartleman**, *Lt. Governor of Ontario, Canada*
April 23, 2004 **Paul Martin**, *Prime Minister of Canada, Canada*
April 22, 2004 **Stephen Harper**, *Leader of the Conservative Party, Canada*
April 18, 2004 **Gordon Campbell**, *Premier of British Columbia, Canada*
November 28, 2003 **Mikhail Gorbachev**, *Former President of USSR.*
November 27, 2003 **Marcello Pera**, *President of the Italian Senate*
November 27, 2003 **Pope John Paul II**, *The Pope*
November 26, 2003 **Massimo D'Aleama**, *Former Italian Prime Minister*
November 26, 2003 **Pier Ferdinando Casini**, *President of the Chamber of Rome*
November 26, 2003 **Margherita Boniver**, *Deputy Foreign Minister of Italy*
October 15, 2003 **Jean-Louis Debré**, *President of the French National Assembly*

with you, your own constitution dictates that you cannot swamp us in Chinese ("Han")[4] colonization. So once you remove your colonists and internal occupation armies, you can keep your troops on the borders to protect us, and then let us have our own internal basic law, just as Hong Kong does. Then we will vote, and I will campaign to persuade my countrymen to vote for joining you in a legitimate, voluntary union. And just so you don't worry too much, I cast my vote for union right now, ahead of time!"

The point is, the Dalai Lama does not need to call for independence, since Tibet actually *has* independence, historic, moral, and legal. It always has been independent and always will be a free highland under the vast sky, ringed with high snow peaks, where only people with special genes can be comfortable with the lack of oxygen at almost three miles of altitude.[5] Their independence is not only in the minds of all living Tibetans, including the Dalai Lama, but also in the mind of anyone who has seen through the propaganda and the diplomatic lies of present governments and done even cursory research into the history and the issues under international law. Just because the Chinese have troops and colonists there, and just because the UN and other nations' executive branches are prevented by fear and greed from bringing international law to bear on the question, that does not mean that the Chinese occupation has legitimacy, that their preposterously false historical

October 14, 2003 **Christian Poncelet**, *President of the French Senate*
October 12, 2003 **Alejandro Toledo**, *President of Peru*
September 11, 2003 **Nancy Pelosi**, *Minority Leader of the US House*
September 10, 2003 **George W. Bush**, *US President*
September 9, 2003 **Colin Powell**, *US Secretary of State*
September 9, 2003 **Tom Daschle**, *US Senate Minority Leader*
September 9, 2003 **Bill Frist**, *US Senate Majority Leader*
June 6, 2003 **Anders Fogh Rasmussen**, *Prime Minister of Denmark*
June 4, 2003 **Per Stig Møller**, *Foreign Minister of Denmark*
June 3, 2003 **Björn von Sydow**, *Speaker of the Swedish Parliament*
May 30, 2003 **Wolfgang Thierse**, *President of the German Parliament*

claims can ever convince anyone. In fact, a number of the world's important parliaments—the United States Congress, the German Bundestag, the French and Italian Parliaments, the Costa Rican Parliament, the European Parliament—all have passed resolutions similar to that of the United States Congress, which pronounced unequivocally that Tibet is an independent country under foreign occupation.

So no wonder the Chinese keep shouting that the Dalai Lama really wants independence, even though he keeps repeating "autonomy, autonomy, autonomy within China." The Chinese are giving the Dalai Lama more credit than do the Tibetan patriots who are thinking he has betrayed their right of independence. Actually, the Dalai Lama does not need to "want" independence—*he knows that his country has it*. It is just not being respected by the Chinese nor by the other world powers who cater to them. Since the Dalai Lama is confident in Tibet's essential independence, he can choose to cede it to China conditionally, if that is the only way he can get the unsustainable and smothering hordes of colonists out of his country, off his peoples' land, and move China to adopt the role of a helpful, federated neighbor, supporter, and colleague.

Everyone should have independence, including the Chinese. Karl Marx once said, "The nation that enslaves another nation, thereby forges its own chains." After all, nirvana is ultimate independence from suffering, the supreme goal of all Buddhists. China also needs independence

May 30, 2003 **Claudia Roth**, *German Commissioner for Human Rights*
May 30, 2003 **Joschka Fischer**, *Foreign Minister of Germany*
May 27, 2003 **George Fernandes**, *Defense Minister of India*
November 7, 2002 **Nambar Enkhbayar**, *Prime Minister of Mongolia*
October 13, 2002 **Benita Ferrero-Waldner**, *Foreign Minister of Austria*
October 8, 2002 **Bhairon Singh Shekhawat**, *Vice President of India*
October 8, 2002 **Dr. A. P. J. Abdul Kalam**, *President of India*
July 8, 2002 **Ivica Račan**, *Prime Minister of Croatia*
July 6, 2002 **Dr. Dimitrij Rupel**, *Foreign Minister of Slovenia*
July 5, 2002 **Milan Kucan**, *President of Slovenia*
July 4, 2002 **Borut Pahor**, *President of Slovenian National Assembly*

yet has lost it due to its colonial imperialism, since as a colonialist you must depend on possessions as much as they must depend on you. Since you must violently oppress the people you are colonizing, you end up violently oppressing your own people. And it bears repeating that Tibet is independent; it is simply smothered at the moment by a foreign military power's overwhelming presence. So the Dalai Lama has decided to invest Tibet's undying independence in the Chinese union, to become one of the United States of China. He sees that it is best for his people in the present circumstances, since China is the big power neighbor most convenient to join. Of course, he himself cannot simply close the matter just by casting his one vote. His whole people first have to be acknowledged as having the free situation in which to vote without fear or coercion in an internationally observed vote.

To allow this to happen, the Chinese leaders must trust in the Tibetans' love of him and trust in him, and their good common sense. There is no doubt that the Tibetan people would follow his suggestion and vote to become voluntarily part of China, as long as China follows its own laws and truly respects Great Tibet's[6] (not just the Tibet Autonomous Region's) autonomy and internal self-rule.

This is why the Dalai Lama has offered to visit China in person, on pilgrimage, to meet with the Chinese leadership privately so they could know him and realize they could trust him not to betray his agreements

July 4, 2002 **Dr. Janez Drnovšek**, *Prime Minister of Slovenia*
July 2, 2002 **Václav Havel**, *President of Czech Republic*
May 28, 2002 **Phil Goff**, *Foreign Minister of New Zealand*
May 28, 2002 **Jim Anderton**, *Prime Minister of New Zealand*
November 30 2001 **Giovanni Alemanno**, *Italian Minister of Agriculture*
November 28 2001 **Jorge Sampaio**, *President of Portugal*
October 24, 2001 **Simeon II**, *Prime Minister of Bulgaria*
October 24, 2001 **Nicole Fontaine**, *President of the European Parliament*
July 3, 2001 **Atal Behari Vajpayee**, *Prime Minister of India*
June 24, 2001 **Valdas Adamkus**, *President of Lithuania*
June 23, 2001 **Andris Berzins**, *Prime Minister of Latvia*

with them. In an internally democratic Tibet, those who oppose the Dalai Lama's call to join the Chinese union could campaign against him and call upon their compatriots to ignore his advice and vote in the eyes of the world for full independence from China. This is the risk the Chinese leadership must think they would have to take, which is why they back away and simply shout, "He wants independence! Independence!" Because they haven't met him and don't realize the depth of the Tibetans' devotion to him, and they can't imagine that a people whom they have so egregiously suppressed, dispossessed, tormented, and killed would still vote to join in union with them.

I remember once when I was traveling a long distance in Tibet, and my tent was always pitched near the tent of the Tibetan drivers of the trucks and jeeps. I regularly overheard a running debate every night around the campfire, stimulated by the many large trucks that passed our caravan all through the days carrying borax to market from the dried up lakes in western Tibet. One side in the debate argued that, after regaining its independence, Tibet should never sell any borax to the Chinese, to punish them for all the harm they have caused every Tibetan family over several generations. The other side argued that such vindictiveness was silly since the Chinese could more easily transport the borax and were used to getting it and marketing it, and so should be considered as valid bidders for the borax along with any Westerners or the Japanese, so

June 21, 2001	**Vaira Vike-Frigbera**, *President of Latvia*	
June 19, 2001	**Maart Laar**, *Prime Minister of Estonia*	
May 23, 2001	**George W. Bush**, *US President*	
May 22, 2001	**Richard Armitage**, *US Deputy Secretary of State*	
May 22, 2001	**Colin Powell**, *US Secretary of State*	
May 13, 2001	**John Kitzhaber**, *Governor of Oregon USA*	
May 10, 2001	**Michael Leavitt**, *Governor of Utah, USA*	
May 9, 2001	**Jesse Ventura**, *Governor of Minnesota, USA*	
May 6, 2001	**Ruth Dreifuss**, *Interior Minister of Switzerland*	
April 7, 2001	**Hsiu-lien Annette Lu**, *Vice President of Taiwan*	
April 7, 2001	**Chang Chun-hsiung**, *Prime Minister of Taiwan*	

that Tibet could get a good price for it! Though a lot of emotions were stirred and the talks went on and on, the debate was eventually won resoundingly by the pragmatists who would let bygones be bygones and would engage in business with the Chinese along with anyone else in their much dreamed-of future freedom!

In 1985 in Bodh Gaya, the city in India famous for being the place where the Buddha attained enlightenment, I witnessed the Dalai Lama speaking to more than a hundred thousand Tibetans from Tibet, during a break from the Kalachakra initiation and teaching he was giving to them and a hundred thousand more Tibetans from exile communities and from ethnically Tibetan Indian Himalayan areas, such as Ladakh, Sikkim, and Arunachal. He spoke to them of his deep compassion for them and the sufferings they had gone through, losing family members, lands, and property, and being tortured in prisons and labor camps. He himself wept as he recited the litany of their ordeals.

And then he launched into the Dharma, specifically the great Indian philosopher Shantideva's superb teaching on the conquest of anger and hatred; on how the enemy is our greatest teacher, giving us the supreme teaching on tolerance by harming us and so giving us the chance to practice it under duress and pain; on how the greatest challenge is not to hate that enemy no matter how horrible the injuries they have dealt us. And then he connected that with the Tibetan struggle for

April 5, 2001 **Chen Shui-bian**, *President of Taiwan*
April 2, 2001 **Wang Jin-pyng**, *Speaker of the Parliament, Taiwan*
January 29, 2001 **Atal Behari Vajpayee**, *Prime Minister of India*
October 21, 2000 **Mary McAleese**, *President of Ireland*
October 16, 2000 **Václav Havel**, *President of Czech Republic*
October 13, 2000 **Janos Martonyi**, *Foreign Minister of Hungary*
October 11, 2000 **Viktor Orbán**, *Prime Minister of Hungary*
July 3, 2000 **Madeleine Albright**, *US Secretary of State*
June 21, 2000 **Richard Holbrooke**, *US Ambassador to U.N*
June 20, 2000 **Bill Clinton**, *US President*
May 23, 2000 **Jens Stoltenberg**, *Prime Minister of Norway*

freedom, their fight to regain their land and self-respect. He insisted that this struggle with their own hatred and wish for revenge against their enemy—this conquest of their inner demon of violence and anger—was the true liberation struggle. This would also have the practical effect of bringing the world to their side. This heroic self-conquest would make them victorious, not only in the long run by the fact that eventually they would have their freedom again, but also in the short run, that no matter how much suffering their oppressors inflicted upon them, they would not add to it by tormenting themselves with rage, anger, and hatred that would destroy their minds, their health, the deep spirituality of their bodhisattva vow, and their spirit of enlightenment.

He offered them such a powerful teaching that it had most of them in tears. They saw that he was not just sitting back and giving them some routine teachings, and that, though he himself had not been physically in Tibet with them undergoing the thirty years of agony they had suffered, he was with them with his powerful compassionate awareness, that he had felt the blows and the torments. They also understood the teaching, knowing full well that anger against anyone, inner hatred, even justified, is a sure destroyer of one's own internal happiness and peace of mind. I was deeply moved that these people—mostly simple farmers and nomads who were not highly educated in spiritual practices—so well understood this most exalted teaching, a message needed by all of

May 22, 2000	**H.M. King Harald of Norway**, *King of Norway*
May 22, 2000	**Thorbjørn Jagland**, *Foreign Minister of Norway*
May 21, 2000	**Poul Nyrup Rasmussen**, *Prime Minister of Denmark*
May 17, 2000	**Göran Persson**, *Prime Minister of Sweden*
May 16, 2000	**Birgitta Dahl**, *Speaker of Parliament, Sweden*
May 16, 2000	**Anna Lindh**, *Foreign Minister of Sweden*
May 11, 2000	**Jerzy Buzek**, *Prime Minister of Poland*
May 10, 2000	**Maciej Ptażynski**, *Speaker of Parliament, Poland*
November 24, 1999	**Yossi Sarid**, *Minister of Education, Israel*
November 24, 1999	**Abraham Burg**, *Speaker of the Knesset, Israel*
October 28, 1999	**Pope John Paul II**, *The Pope*

humanity so caught up in violence and rage. These people still could aspire to practice it and could conceive of a kind of heroic resistance to oppression that involved overcoming one's own inner oppressors, such as anger and hatred.

This is the great leadership the Dalai Lama has given his people. His accomplishment cannot be overestimated; he has inspired a tough-minded, courageous, intelligent, and fierce people to resist genocidal oppression by developing their internal fortitude and maintaining non-violence as their campaign. He has dissuaded them from turning to violence and terrorism as almost any other people in the world would have and as many others have done in similar circumstances. In fact, their achievement was not perfect: Tibetan warriors did fight for over a decade as guerrillas (with a low level of support from CIA until betrayed by Henry Kissinger and President Richard Nixon), against the Dalai Lama's instructions, but admittedly with his admiration for their bravery. Occasionally there are riots here and there, and individual Chinese are sometimes beaten or killed during agitations that sporadically occur. But overall, in spite of massive oppression, Tibetans have maintained the nonviolence the Dalai Lama has asked of them. The greatness of this achievement cannot be overstated.

Nowadays the world is spinning out of control in a "war on terror," which is endless in principle because violence simply breeds more counter-

October 26, 1999 **Massimo D'Alema**, *Prime Minister of Italy*
October 18, 1999 **Wim Kok**, *Prime Minister of The Netherlands*
October 18, 1999 **J. J. Van Aartsen**, *Foreign Minister of The Netherlands*
June 17, 1999 **Otto Schily**, *Interior Minister of Germany*
June 16, 1999 **Joschka Fischer**, *Foreign Minister of Germany*
May 12, 1999 **Prince Charles of England**, *Prince of Wales, UK*
May 12, 1999 **Robert Cook**, *Foreign Secretary of England*
May 11, 1999 **Dr. George Carey**, *Archbishop of Canterbury, UK*
May 10, 1999 **Tony Blair**, *Prime Minister of UK*
May 4, 1999 **Jean-Luc Dehaene**, *Prime Minister of Belgium*
April 13, 1999 **Eduardo Frei**, *President of Chilee*

violence. Then to our amazement, we encounter a people who eschew terrorism and violence from the beginning, before they have gotten anything external out of it. While they are still under the gun of oppression, they make peacefulness and gentleness their method as well as their goal, and we sit back blinking uncomprehendingly and say, "What have they accomplished?" As if the violence we deplore, we are vowed to fight against, can only be met with more violence, even though we see it does not work and only produces more violence. And yet we despise the real method, which does work, which is for all involved to free themselves from inner as well as outer violence, and thus ultimately disarm their enemies.

As a Trans-Religious Prophet to the World

The Dalai Lama has carried out his exemplary role as Nobel Peace Prize Laureate with great effectiveness, especially by maintaining his teaching and practice of nonviolence in the midst of extreme challenges. To elucidate this, I'll quote in full his remarkable Nobel Peace Prize acceptance speech, which he gave at the University Aula, in Oslo, Norway, on December 10, 1989, with commentary grounded on his own noble and powerful words.

Your Majesty, members of the Nobel Committee, Brothers and Sisters. I am very happy to be here with you today to receive the Nobel Prize for Peace. I feel

April 7, 1999 **Fernando Henrique Cardoso**, *President of Brazil*
December 8, 1998 **Mary Robinson**, *UN High Commissioner for Human Rights*
December 8, 1998 **Kofi Annan**, *Secretary General of the United Nations*
December 8, 1998 **Lionel Jospin**, *Prime Minister of France*
December 8, 1998 **Jacques Chirac**, *President of Franc*
November 10, 1998 **Madeleine Albright**, *US Secretary of State*
November 10, 1998 **Al Gore**, *US Vice President*
November 10, 1998 **Bill Clinton**, *US President*
June 17, 1998 **Laurent Fabius**, *President of the French National Assembly*
June 9, 1998 **Wolfgang Schüssel**, *Foreign Minister of Austria*
May 11, 1998 **Jimmy Carter**, *Former US President*

honored, humbled, and deeply moved that you should give this important prize to a simple monk from Tibet. I am no one special.

His humbleness is remarkable. I had worked on nominating him for three years in a row, along with many other people. When I called to congratulate him after the prize announcement, I spoke to his secretary who told me about his "no big deal" approach to the news. To me and the people who had been working to nominate him it was a very big deal and, we hoped, a tipping point in the world's coming to know the true story of Tibet, the true nature of this incredible man, and the power of nonviolence. But, true to form, the Dalai Lama did not let the honor go to his head and insisted that he is "no one special." This "simple monk" humility is truly meant by him, as he remains aware of the ordinariness of being human, and he cleaves to his duty to guard body, speech, and mind within the moral and emotional fortress of the robe of the Buddhist mendicant. At the same time, he also recognizes that he has the responsibility to bear the burden of a specially eminent person, all the more so because, from then on, he would be a laureate of the most distinguished peace prize on our planet.

But I believe the prize is a recognition of the true value of altruism, love, compassion, and nonviolence which I try to practice, in accordance with the teachings of the Buddha and the great sages of India and Tibet.

May 7, 1998 **Christine Todd Whitman,** *Governor of New Jersey, USA*
May 5, 1998 **Mary Robinson,** *UN High Commissioner for Human Rights*
May 4, 1998 **Bill Richardson,** *US Ambassador to UN*
April 6, 1998 **Mikhail Gorbachev,** *Former President of USSR*
April 2, 1998 **Krishan Kanth,** *Vice President of India*
April 2, 1998 **K. R. Narayanan,** *President of India*
September 5, 1997 **Václav Havel,** *President of Czech Republic*
June 16, 1997 **I. K. Gujral,** *Prime Minister of India*
April 23, 1997 **Madeleine Albright,** *US Secretary of State*
April 23, 1997 **Al Gore,** *US Vice President*
April 23, 1997 **Bill Clinton,** *US President*

He accepts the prize as given to compassion and altruism itself, so fitting for one believed to be the reincarnation of the universal compassion of all enlightened beings throughout the multiverse. He steps up to his responsibility as the upholder of the teaching, practice, and performance of kindness, altruism, love, and compassion—to him the essential human qualities that make life on this earth viable.

I accept the prize with profound gratitude on behalf of the oppressed everywhere and for all those who struggle for freedom and work for world peace. I accept it as a tribute to the man who founded the modern tradition of nonviolent action for change, Mahatma Gandhi, whose life taught and inspired me.

His generosity shines through, as Mahatma Gandhi never did receive the Nobel Peace Prize, much as he deserved it, presumably because he was assassinated before it could be conferred. The Dalai Lama had been short-listed for the Nobel Peace Prize for several years, each time being blocked at the last minute, I have heard, by the Norwegian Foreign Ministry's fear of provoking the Chinese, who they hoped under Deng Xiaoping were slowly trying to improve their human rights behavior and normalize their relations with other nations. In 1989, with Deng having shown at Tiananmen Square and throughout China the ruthless brutality of his dictatorship, it made no sense to deny the Dalai Lama the award

March 27, 1997 **Lee Teng-hui**, *President of Taiwan*
October 23, 1996 **Jacques Santer**, *President of the European Union*
October 23, 1996 **Dr. Klaus Hänsch**, *President of the European Parliament*
October 23, 1996 **Halmo van Mierlo**, *Foreign Minister of The Netherlands*
September 14, 1996 **Alexander Downer**, *Foreign Minister of Australia*
September 14, 1996 **John Howard**, *Prime Minister of Australia*
September 11, 1996 **Don McKinnon**, *Foreign Minister of New Zealand*
September 11, 1996 **Jim Bolger**, *Prime Minister of New Zealand*
August 23, 1996 **F. W. de Klerk**, *Former President of South Africa*
August 21, 1996 **Nelson Mandela**, *President of South Africaa*
August 20, 1996 **Bishop Desmond Tutu**, *Nobel Laureate, South Africa*

he obviously deserved just to avoid provoking a government already over the top in naked atrocity.

> *And, of course, I accept it on behalf of the six million Tibetan people, my brave countrymen and women inside Tibet, who have suffered and continue to suffer so much. They confront a calculated and systematic strategy aimed at the destruction of their national and cultural identities. The prize reaffirms our conviction that with truth, courage, and determination as our weapons, Tibet will be liberated.*

Here we see the ancient Indian tradition known as "the act of truth." It is said in India that an act of truth can make the Ganges flow backward. Indeed, there are many stories of a person in extreme circumstances who takes a stand on her or his own integrity, and nature and societies respond against all odds. By bluntly stating his knowledge of the systematic cultural genocide policy of the Chinese government, the Dalai Lama challenged Goliath and exposed his brutal nature to the world. By expressing the plight of the Tibetans in such a public and globally visible forum, he broke the taboo imposed by the Chinese, who pretend there are no such people as suffering Tibetans. According to the standard propaganda line, Tibetans are just a variety of Chinese. The Chinese taboo was also enforced for a

July 17, 1996 **Douglas Hurd**, *Foreign Secretary of England*
May 28, 1996 **Bjørn Tore Godal**, *Foreign Minister of Norway*
May 23, 1996 **Lena Hjelm-Wallén**, *Foreign Minister of Sweden*
May 20, 1996 **Pope John Paul II**, *The Pope*
May 15, 1996 **Niels Helveg Petersen**, *Foreign Minister of Denmark*
July 5, 1994 **Ernesto Leal**, *Foreign Minister of Nicaragua*
July 5, 1994 **Violeta Chamorro**, *President of Nicaragua*
June 17, 1994 **Pope John Paul II**, *The Pope*
June 7, 1994 **Willy Claes**, *Foreign Minister of Belgium*
June 6, 1994 **Alois Mock**, *Foreign Minister of Austria*
June 4, 1994 **Princess Juliana of The Netherlands**

long time by the Indian government as a condition of their hosting the Tibetans in exile, and tends also to be imposed by many countries as a condition of granting the Dalai Lama a visa to visit for "religious purposes only."

The Dalai Lama's act of truth is set forth in the context of the web of international relations, which is too often a web of lies—the kind of lies put forward in praise of the magnificent wardrobes of naked emperors. Individuals and governments know all too well that Tibet does not belong to China. They know that Mao invaded, occupied, and annexed a foreign country against the essential rule of respect for sovereignty of the New World Order that gave birth to the United Nations Organization. Yet they cater to China's preposterous propaganda for the sake of military alliance and advantage, as well as the hope of business profit. So in that world of woven lies—a world in which Tibet is a lost cause or never existed and does not exist—the Dalai Lama performs his act of truth and states his grand strategy: reliance on truth, courage, and determination to win his people's liberation from oppression. "Tibet will be liberated." He does not budge one iota from this determination. If upon liberation, Tibet chooses to federate with its great neighbor China, Tibet has the right to make that free choice. Indeed, for the moment the Dalai Lama has made that choice for himself, hoping that his people will follow him whenever given the freedom to choose.

June 14, 1993 **Dr. Thomas Klestil,** *President of Austria*

May 17, 1993 **Lech Walesa,** *President of Poland*

May 12, 1993 **Douglas Hurd,** *Foreign Secretary of England*

May 10, 1993 **George Leonard Carey,** *Archbishop of Canterbury, UK*

April 27, 1993 **Al Gore,** *US Vice President*

April 27, 1993 **Bill Clinton,** *US President*

September 12, 1992 **Dr. Shankar D. Sharma,** *President of India*

June 20, 1992 **Patricio Aylwin,** *President of Chile*

June 11, 1992 **Carlos Menem,** *President of Argentina*

May 13, 1992 **Don McKinnon,** *Foreign Minister of New Zealand*

May 13, 1992 **Jim Bolger,** *Prime Minister of New Zealand*

No matter what part of the world we come from, we are all basically the same human beings. We all seek happiness and try to avoid suffering. We have the same basic human needs and concerns.

He states his first principle as a philosopher, scientist, and enlightened teacher—the basic sameness of not only humans but all living beings. This teaching comes from Buddha and resonates down the millennia through the insights of millions of enlightened sages; this great tradition of compassionate altruism and universal responsibility comes through the great Indians Nagarjuna (second century) and Shantideva (eighth century), both great masters of Nalanda University in Central India, and Atisha (eleventh century). This lineage continued with the Tibetans Tsong Khapa (fifteenth century), Patrul Rinpoche (nineteenth century), and again the Indian Ladakhi, Khunu Lama Tenzin Gyaltsen (twentieth century), with hundreds of great sages in between and parallel to these luminaries. The vision is that of the basic heart of beings, a heart that longs for happiness and fears suffering. And among human beings, these drives are expressed in common ways. By empathizing with these drives in others, the messianic bodhisattva adopts the aims of others as his or her own, realizes the futility of seeking his or her own happiness in struggle with countless others, turns away from that struggle to an insightful harmony, and so finds a greater happiness through striving

May 8, 1992 **Paul Keating**, *Prime Minister of Australia*
May 6, 1992 **Gareth Evans**, *Foreign Minister of Australia*
May 4, 1992 **Son Sen**, *Prime Minister of Kampuchea, Cambodia*
March 3, 1992 **P. V. Narasimha Rao**, *Prime Minister of India*
December 8, 1991 **Gro Harlem Brundtland**, *Prime Minister of Norway*
December 7, 1991 **Lech Walesa**, *President of Poland*
December 7, 1991 **Bishop Desmond Tutu**, *Nobel Laureate, South Africa*
December 5, 1991 **Uffe Ellemann-Jensen**, *Foreign Minister of Denmark*
December 4, 1991 **Margaretha af Ugglas**, *Foreign Minister of Sweden*
December 3, 1991 **King Carl XVI Gustaf and Queen Silvia**, *Sweden*
December 2, 1991 **John Major**, *Prime Minister of England*

for the happiness of all. The Dalai Lama mentions this as a truism, but the firmness of his conviction is based on his insight, his rediscovery of the ancient enlightenment insight into the biological reality of life.

All of us human beings want freedom and the right to determine our own destiny as individuals and as peoples. That is human nature.

He expands from that universal insight about human nature into the modern dream of democracy and its expansion in the international arena through the principle of self-determination. Again it seems simple enough, and some might think he was merely pandering to some modern Western people. This is not so. His statement comes from the words of Buddha and is backed up by his practice with his own government. First, for nine years in Tibet he tried to implement reforms in his inherited government to take it in the direction of democracy. But he was hampered by the communist campaigns to break the spirituality of Tibetans and destroy their unique culture while exploiting their resources and depriving them of their long-accumulated treasures of gold, silver, precious stones, and priceless religious artifacts. He continued the quest for democracy in subsequent years, reaching safety in exile in 1959, publishing the first democratic constitution in 1962, and continually refining it and improving its practice for thirty years.

October 5, 1991 **Zhelyu Zhelev**, *President of Bulgaria*
October 4, 1991 **Indrek Toome Kadriorg**, *Foreign Affairs Commission of Estonia*
October 4, 1991 **Olo Nugis**, *The Supreme Council of Estonia, Tallinn, Estonia*
September 30, 1991 **K. Palkalniskis**, *Deputy Prime Minister of Lithuania*
September 30, 1991 **Gediminas Vagnorius**, *Prime Minister of Lithuania*
September 29, 1991 **Vytautas Landsbergis**, *President of Lithuania*
August 19, 1991 **Rene Feler**, *Foreign Minister, Switzerland*
August 16, 1991 **Prince Hans-Adam II**, *Liechtenstein*
July 9, 1991 **P. V. Narasimha Rao**, *Prime Minister of India*
April 16, 1991 **Jeane Kirkpatrik**, *Former US Permanent Representative to the UN*
April 16, 1991 **Jiri Dienstbier**, *Foreign Minister of Czechoslovakia*

*The great changes that are taking place everywhere in the world, from Eastern
Europe to Africa, are a clear indication of this.*

His Holiness had just come to Oslo from Berlin, where he visited
the wall that was beginning to come down. He was excited about the
outbreak of freedom occurring through the nonviolent opening up of
the Soviet Union and the gentle and joyous velvet revolution in Eastern
Europe. He was also in touch with Nelson Mandela, urging him on in
the conversion of the African National Congress to nonviolence; he was
enthusiastic about the first steps of progress happening as cracks were
appearing in the edifice of apartheid.

When we feel depressed about China, Darfur, Burma, Tibet and
think of them as lost causes, we are forgetting how completely unreason-
able it would have been to predict, say, that in 1987 the Soviet Union
would release Eastern Europe, the Baltics, and even the immensely valuable heartland province of Ukraine and the oil depository of Kazakhistan without a shot being fired. And yet these miracles did occur, right
before our eyes. Oppressive countries with huge armies, enormous populations, and powerful interests found themselves unable or—more
importantly—unwilling to maintain their oppressive behaviors, not only
because of their immorality but because of the miserable state they
found themselves stuck in. The jailer has to live in or next to the prison

April 16, 1991 **Dan Quayle**, *US Vice President*
April 16, 1991 **Violeta Chamorro**, *President of Nicaragua*
April 16, 1991 **George Bush**, *US President*
March 27, 1991 **Dr. Carl Sagan**, *Scientist, USA*
March 22, 1991 **Mary Robinson**, *President of the Irish Republic*
March 21, 1991 **Neil Kinnock**, *Leader of Opposition in the Parliament, UK*
March 20, 1991 **Bernard Weatherhill**, *Speaker of House of Commons, UK*
March 20, 1991 **Lord James Mackay**, *Lord Chancellor, UK*
March 18, 1991 **Prince Charles, Prince of Wales**, *UK*
March 18, 1991 **Prince Richard**, *Duke of Gloucester G.C.V.O., UK*
January 29, 1991 **Chandra Shekhar**, *Prime Minister of India*

where he keeps the prisoner. The perpetrator may feel twisted bursts of sadistic satisfaction or sensations of power and self-importance, but when it is a continuous grinding routine, the misery is shared by both parties. Human nature is too sensitive, too empathetic; we are mammals and bear our young inside our own bodies. Brutality requires special training and tremendous effort, and it is ultimately destructive to the brutalizer as well.

In China the popular movement for democracy was crushed by brutal force in June this year. But I do not believe the demonstrations were in vain, because the spirit of freedom was rekindled among the Chinese people and China cannot escape the impact of this spirit of freedom sweeping many parts of the world. The brave students and their supporters showed the Chinese leadership and the world the human face of that great nation.

The Dalai Lama was pleased with the students and workers in Tiananmen and their efforts at maintaining nonviolence. For example, they prevented extremists among them from defacing Mao's portrait, they called for dialogue with the politburo, they appealed to the People's Army troops not to attack the people, and they brought the dictatorship to a standstill for quite a while. Deng had suffered badly in Mao's cultural revolution (his son was made paraplegic from being thrown out a

December 1990 **Shankarachariya of Kanchi Kamakoti**, *India*
October 4, 1990 **Richard von Weizsäcker**, *President of Germany*
September 10, 1990 **Hans van den Broek**, *Minister of Foreign Affairs, The Netherlands*
September 5, 1990 **Gabriel Canellas**, *President of the Autonomous Government of the Balneares, Spain*
June 4, 1990 **Gabriel Urralburu Tainta**, *President of the Autonomous Government of Navarre, Spain*
June 1, 1990 **Pope John Paul II**, *The Pope*
April 24, 1990 **Mark Eyskens**, *Minister of External Affairs, Belgium*
February 3, 1990 **Václav Havel**, *President of Czechoslovakia*

second story window by Red Guards), and some expected that he would therefore never commit violence against these protesting students who were simply calling for dialogue, for honesty, for democracy, for communism living up to its own ideals. Of course, in this case they underestimated the corrupting influence of absolute power, and the Deng who eventually had many of them killed and imprisoned was a different Deng than the one who had suffered under Mao. At the time the Dalai Lama said that he was very sad that Deng, who had done so much to liberate China from the devastating influence of Mao's more demented policies, would have his reputation tarnished by this final act of atrocity against the best and the brightest of Chinese youth. But the Dalai Lama doesn't dwell on this. Rather, he welcomes the first signs of opening up of Chinese society and celebrates the human face of the great nation of China.

Last week a number of Tibetans were once again sentenced to prison terms of up to nineteen years at a mass show trial, possibly intended to frighten the population before today's event. Their only "crime" was the expression of the widespread desire of Tibetans for the restoration of their beloved country's independence.

With this passage, the Dalai Lama showed immense courage. Tibet's "hard-line" communist managers treat the Tibetan people as

BOOKS IN ENGLISH
FROM DALAILAMA.COM

Yoga Tantra: Paths to Magical Feats, with Dzong-ka-ba and Jeffery Hopkins, Snow Lion Publication, Ithaca, 2005.

The Universe in a Single Atom: The Convergence of Science and Spirituality, Morgan Road Books, New York, 2005.

The Wisdom of Forgiveness, with Victor Chan, Riverhead Books, New York, 2004.

Many Ways to Nirvana, Penguin Books, India, 2004.

365 Dalai Lama: Daily Advice from the Heart, Element, London, 2003.

Warm Heart Open Mind, The Dalai Lama Trust NZ, 2003.

hostages against the Dalai Lama's open speech about their situation. Up into the 1980s, they let him know that if he said certain things in certain venues, Tibetans under their power would suffer torture, summary executions, long prison terms, destruction of monasteries, and so forth. In this case, the Chinese leaders were so furious about his getting the Nobel Peace Prize that the Nobel Committee members said they had the worst reaction of any government angered by the awarding of the prize to someone they opposed since Germany's reaction to imprisoned journalist Carl von Ossietzky's award in 1936. The Chinese ambassador to Norway was invited to the ceremonies, of course, but instead he threatened a break in diplomatic relations if the king and prime minister attended the ceremony. When the Norwegians did attend, the ambassador left the country, spewing threats and veiled curses—but he returned shortly thereafter when three busloads of Taiwanese turned up wishing to upgrade relations with Norway!

The suffering of our people during the past forty years of occupation is well documented. Ours has been a long struggle. We know our cause is just. Because violence can only breed more violence and suffering, our struggle must remain nonviolent and free of hatred. We are trying to end the suffering of our people, not to inflict suffering upon others.

The Compassionate Life, Wisdom Publications, Boston, 2003.
Illuminating the Path to Enlightenment, Thubten Dhargye Ling, Long Beach, 2002.
How to Practice: The Way to a Meaningful Life, Simon & Schuster, New York, 2002.
Essence of the Heart Sutra, Wisdom Publications, Boston, 2002.
Advice on Dying, Random House, London, 2002.
Stages of Meditation, trans. G. L. Jordhen, et al., Snow Lion, Ithaca, 2001.
An Open Heart, Little Brown and Company, New York, 2001.
Transforming the Mind, Thorsons Publications, London, 2000.
A Simple Path, Thorson Publications, London, 2000.
The Dalai Lama's Book of Transformation, Thorson Publications, London, 2000.
Training the Mind, Wisdom Publications, Boston, 1999.

This philosophy is why the Nobel Committee awarded him the prize. Many conflicts around the world could certainly be solved if the option of a resort to violence were taken off the table. Under conditions of dialogue seeking truth and justice, with no fear of others' anger erupting violently, there is no situation that cannot be resolved through compromise. Getting something out of the negotiation, even if less than you want, is better than being killed. And even if you get everything by killing others, you can count on losing it again soon enough in the form of revenge.

Here the Dalai Lama begins his Nobel Peace Laureate great work, as an articulate spokesperson, an exemplary practitioner of nonviolent conflict resolution in a life-and-death situation. This is where he represents the key to the solution for every conflict situation on this earth—approximately 118 major armed conflicts between 1990 and 2004, according to archives kept by the Carter Center in Atlanta. And only if these conflicts are stopped and everyone, even the big powers, understands that they cannot use violence and need not fear violence will the world be able to muster the resources needed to turn around the deadly process of global warming and save life on earth.

It is with this in mind that I proposed negotiations between Tibet and China on numerous occasions. In 1987, I made specific proposals in a Five-Point Plan for the restoration of peace and human rights in Tibet. This included the conversion

The Little Book of Buddhism, Penguin Books, New Delhi, 1999.
The Heart of the Buddha's Path, Thorsons Publications, London, 1999.
Consciousness at the Crossroads: Conversations with the Dalai Lama on Brain Science and Buddhism, Snow Lion Publications, Ithaca, 1999.
Ancient Wisdom, Modern World: Ethics for a New Millennium, Little Brown and Company, London, 1999.
The Political Philosophy of His Holiness the Dalai Lama: Selected Speeches and Writings, Tibetan Parliamentary and Policy Research Center, New Delhi, 1998.
The Path to Tranquility: Daily Meditations, Penguin Books, New Delhi, 1998.
The Four Noble Truths, Thorsons Publications, London, 1998.
The Art of Happiness, with Howard C. Cutler, Riverhead Books, New York, 1998.

of the entire Tibetan plateau into a Zone of Ahimsa, a sanctuary of peace and nonviolence where human beings and nature can live in peace and harmony.

In September of 1987, the Dalai Lama appeared at the US Congress for a session of the Congressional Human Rights Caucus chaired by Representative Tom Lantos (D–California). He was there to take the courageous step of internationalizing the Tibet-China conflict, responding to a Chinese Five Point Plan, which only had to do with the personal disposition of the Dalai Lama and did not resolve any of the problems of the Tibetan people. The Dalai Lama appealed to the People's Republic of China government, requesting other governments' support, to implement the following:

1. *Transformation of the whole of Tibet into a zone of peace;*
2. *Abandonment of China's population transfer policy, which threatens the very existence of the Tibetans as a people;*
3. *Respect for the Tibetan people's fundamental human rights and democratic freedoms;*
4. *Restoration and protection of Tibet's natural environment and the abandonment of China's use of Tibet for the production of nuclear weapons and dumping of nuclear waste;*
5. *Commencement of earnest negotiations on the future status of Tibet and of relations between the Tibetan and Chinese peoples.*[7]

Sleeping, Dreaming and Dying, narrated by Francisco Varela, Wisdom Publications, Boston, 1997.

Love, Kindness and Universal Responsibility, Paljor Publications, New Delhi, 1997.

The Joy of Living and Dying in Peace, Harper Collins, New Delhi, 1997.

The Heart of Compassion, Foundation for Universal Responsibility, Delhi, India, 1997.

Healing Anger: The Power of Patience from a Buddhist Perspective, Snow Lion, Ithaca, 1997.

The Gelug/Kagyu Tradition of Mahamudra, with Alexander Berzin, Snow Lion, Ithaca, 1997.

The Good Heart: A Buddhist Perspective on the Teachings of Jesus, Wisdom Publications, Boston, 1996.

Last year, I elaborated on that plan in Strasbourg, at the European Parliament. I believe the ideas I expressed on those occasions are both realistic and reasonable, although they have been criticized by some of my people as being too conciliatory. Unfortunately, China's leaders have not responded positively to the suggestions we have made, which included important concessions. If this continues, we will be compelled to reconsider our position.

The key points the Dalai Lama elaborated in Strasbourg, on June 15, 1988, were as follows:

The whole of Tibet known as Cholka-Sum (U-Tsang, Kham, and Amdo) should become a self-governing democratic political entity founded on law by agreement of the people for the common good and the protection of themselves and their environment, in association with the People's Republic of China. The Government of the People's Republic of China could remain responsible for Tibet's foreign policy. The Government of Tibet should, however, develop and maintain relations, through its own foreign affairs bureau, in the field of commerce, education, culture, religion, tourism, science, sports, and other nonpolitical activities. Tibet should join international organizations concerned with such activities.

The Government of Tibet should be founded on a constitution or basic law. The basic law should provide for a democratic system of government entrusted with the task of ensuring economic equality, social justice, and protec-

Beyond Dogma, Souvenir Press Ltd., London, 1996.

The World of Tibetan Buddhism, Wisdom Publications, Boston, 1995.

The Way to Freedom, Harper Collins, New Delhi, 1995.

Violence & Compassion/Power of Buddhism, with Jean Claude Carriere, Doubleday, New York, 1995.

The Spirit of Tibet, Universal Heritage: Selected Speeches and Writings by H.H. the Dalai Lama, Tibetan Parliamentary and Policy Research Center, New Delhi, 1995.

The Power of Compassion, Harper Collins, India, 1995.

The Path to Enlightenment, Snow Lion Publications, Ithaca, 1995.

His Holiness the Dalai Lama: Speeches Statements Articles Interviews from 1987 to June 1995, Department of Information and International Relations, Dharamsala, 1995.

tion of the environment. This means that the Government of Tibet will have the rights to decide on all affairs relating to Tibet and the Tibetans.

As individual freedom is the real source and potential of any society's development, the Government of Tibet would seek to ensure this freedom by full adherence to the Universal Declaration of Human Rights, including the rights to speech, assembly, and religion. Because religion constitutes the source of Tibet's national identity and spiritual values lie at the very heart of Tibet's rich culture, it would be the special duty of the Government of Tibet to safeguard and develop its practice.

The Government should be comprised of a popularly elected Chief Executive, a bi-cameral legislative branch, and an independent judicial system. Its seat should be in Lhasa.

The social and economic system of Tibet should be determined in accordance with the wishes of the Tibetan people, bearing in mind especially the need to raise the standard of living of the entire population.

The Government of Tibet would pass strict laws to protect wildlife and plant life. The exploitation of natural resources would be carefully regulated. The manufacture, testing, stockpiling of nuclear weapons and other armaments must be prohibited, as well as use of nuclear power and other technologies which produce hazardous waste. It would be the Government of Tibet's goal to transform Tibet into our planet's largest natural preserve.

A regional peace conference should be called to ensure that Tibet becomes a genuine sanctuary of peace through demilitarization. Until such a peace

Essential Teachings, Souvenir Press, London, 1995.

Dimensions of Spirituality, Snow Lion Publication, Ithaca, 1995.

Dialogues on Universal Responsibility & Education, Library of Tibetan Works and Archives, Dharamsala, 1995.

Commentary on the Thirty Seven Practices of a Bodhisattva, Library of Tibetan Works and Archives, Dharamsala, 1995.

Awakening the Mind, Lightening the Heart, Harper Collins, 1995.

A Flash of Lightning in the Dark of Night, Shambala Publications, Boston, 1994.

Words of Truth, Wisdom Publications, Boston, 1993.

Freedom in Exile, Harper Collins, New York, 1991.

Path to Bliss, Snow Lion Publications, Ithaca, 1991.

conference can be convened, and demilitarization and neutralization achieved,
China could have the right to maintain a restricted number of military instal-
lations in Tibet. These must be solely for defense purposes.

    In order to create an atmosphere of trust conducive to fruitful negotia-
tions, the Chinese Government should cease its human rights violations in
Tibet and abandon its policy of transferring Chinese to Tibet.

This proposal planted the seed of the Dalai Lama's willingness to
accept for Tibet real autonomy within a union with People's Republic of
China, instead of Tibet's justly deserved outright independence. This is the
maximum concession from the point of view of many Tibetans, and so it
became highly controversial. It was a very courageous and extremely conciliatory step. Many see it as a sign of weakness. But it should be understood rather to be a sign of perfect inner strength, based on a clear
self-confidence about the *actual* independence of Tibet. Here the Dalai
Lama means the whole of Tibet, not the leftover of a nineteenth-century
colonial definition of Outer Tibet as opposed to Inner Tibet, pretended
even then to have been part of China, even though before 1950 few, if any
Chinese had ever settled to live anywhere on the highland. These parts of
real Tibet are comprised of the eleven Tibet Autonomous Prefectures of
other Chinese provinces, administrative units set up in the 1950s, after the
invasion and conquest had succeeded.[8] (See figure 3.)

MindScience: An East-West Dialogue, with Herbert Benson, Robert Thurman,
    Howard E. Gardner, Daniel Goleman, Wisdom Publications, USA, 1991.
Policy of Kindness, Snow Lion Publications, Ithaca, 1990.
The Nobel Peace Prize and the Dalai Lama, Snow Lion Publications, Ithaca, 1990.
My Tibet, with Galen Rowell, University of California Press, 1990.
The Meaning of Life, Snow Lion Publications, Ithaca, 1990.
The Global Community & the Need for Universal Responsibility, Wisdom, Boston,
    1990.
Ocean Of Wisdom, Clear Light Publications, New Mexico, 1989.
The Union of Bliss & Emptiness, Snow Lion Publications, Ithaca, 1988.
Transcendent Wisdom, Snow Lion Publications, Ithaca, 1988.

Any relationship between Tibet and China will have to be based on the principles of equality, respect, trust, and mutual benefit. It will also have to be based on the principle which the wise rulers of Tibet and of China laid down in a treaty as early as 823 AD, carved on the pillar which still stands today in front of the Jokhang, Tibet's holiest shrine, in Lhasa, that "Tibetans will live happily in the great land of Tibet, and the Chinese will live happily in the great land of China."

From this reality of history[9] comes the great strength of the Dalai Lama's position, which the diplomatic community seems incapable of seeing, being so caught up in its web of fabrications of temporary convenience. It must be understood that the Chinese had the only major civilization not to be based on a symbiosis between upland pastoralists and lowland agriculturalists, the only people not to have milk products in their diet, and the only people to build a Great Wall to separate themselves from the upland herders. The Tibetans have genetically adapted to the lack of oxygen at two miles altitude and above by producing a high quantity of nitric oxide in their bloodstream, which carries the oxygen through their system with great efficiency. Without this unique adaptation, no one can live there long-term in comfort and health.[10] (See endnote 5.) If millions of Chinese could live there, of course, they would have been there thousands of years ago.

The Dalai Lama at Harvard, Snow Lion Publications, Ithaca, 1988.

The Bodhgaya Interviews, Snow Lion Publications, Ithaca, New York, 1988.

Opening the Eye of New Awareness, Wisdom Publication, London, 1985.

Kalachakra Tantra Rite of Initiation, with Jeffrey Hopkins, Wisdom, Boston, 1985.

Kindness, Clarity, and Insight, Snow Lion Publication, Ithaca, 1984.

Four Essential Buddhist Commentaries, Library of Tibetan Works and Archives, Dharamsala, 1982.

Collected Statements, Interviews & Articles, Department of Information & International Relations, Dharamsala, 1982.

Advice from Buddha Shakyamuni, Library of Tibetan Works and Archives, Dharamsala, 1982.

As a Buddhist monk, my concern extends to all members of the human family and, indeed, to all sentient beings who suffer. I believe all suffering is caused by ignorance. People inflict pain on others in the selfish pursuit of their happiness or satisfaction. Yet true happiness comes from a sense of brotherhood and sisterhood. We need to cultivate a universal responsibility for one another and the planet we share. Although I have found my own Buddhist religion helpful in generating love and compassion, even for those we consider our enemies, I am convinced that everyone can develop a good heart and a sense of universal responsibility with or without religion.

This is the Dalai Lama's statement of the principles he represents and exemplifies as a Nobel Peace Prize laureate. Indeed it is to carry this banner in our violence-ridden world that the Committee awarded him the prize. His key concept of universal responsibility is mentioned here, which we will go into at further length in chapter 3. His pluralism is implied in recognizing all religions to be capable of producing this sense of universal responsibility, and even his acceptance of the positive world-view of humanistic secularism, whether capitalist or socialist.

With the ever-growing impact of science on our lives, religion and spirituality have a greater role to play in reminding us of our humanity. There is no contradiction between the two. Each gives us valuable insights into the other. Both

Universal Responsibility and the Good Heart, Library of Tibetan Works and Archives, Dharamsala, 1977.

The Buddhism of Tibet and the Key to the Middle Way, Wisdom Publishing, London, 1975.

The Opening of the Wisdom-Eye, The Theosophical Publishing House, Illinois, 1966.

My Land and My People, Potala Publications, New York, 1962.

science and the teachings of the Buddha tell us of the fundamental unity of all things. This understanding is crucial if we are to take positive and decisive action on the pressing global concern with the environment.

He takes the lead in reconciling science and religion in a better partnership, especially in the context of restoring the environment. Besides his natural curiosity about modern science and his admiration of the technological achievements of the scientists, he would like to contribute from the sophisticated inner or spiritual science of Buddhism some perspectives to balance the materialistic reductionism that currently hampers Western scientific progress, especially in the areas of psychology and the subtler levels of the physical sciences. The key point here is that the Buddhist religion does not consider blind faith a good thing, but considers reason a necessary complement to a healthy faith. Buddhism is not caught in the reason versus faith dichotomy found in most present day versions of the Abrahamic and Hindu religions. Hence, a partnership between religions and sciences becomes possible.

I believe all religions pursue the same goal; that of cultivating human goodness and bringing happiness to all human beings. Though the means might appear different, the ends are the same.

Here is his keen insight into the potential—actually, critical necessity—of mobilizing the mainstream religions into campaigning or crusading for nonviolence, critical reform, and attitude change. He demonstrates his respect for the spiritual insight of all traditions as bearing on world problems, especially environmental preservation.

As we enter the final decade of this century, I am optimistic that the ancient values that have sustained mankind are today reaffirming themselves to prepare us for a kinder, happier twenty-first century.

During the 1990s the Dalai Lama frequently gave his four reasons for optimism about the twenty-first century:

1. People at large in all countries are less hopeful that war can ever solve any problem satisfactorily.
2. People do not trust in big massive systems, such as communism and capitalism, so much any more but think individual effort is more important.
3. People are more interested in spiritual perspectives on life's meaning and values choices than in the dictates of materialistic science alone.
4. People no longer take the environment for granted or just throw things away into it carelessly, but make a real effort to preserve it.

He still considers these four trends to be operative. However, as a US citizen, I am embarrassed by our leadership in the last decades, in that these encouraging trends have been resolutely opposed, to disastrous effect. In particular:

1. We have been dragged into a disastrous war under false pretenses with false motives, and we are just beginning to pay the price for it.
2. Instead of our understanding the Russians' grand gesture of withdrawal from military-industrial imperialism in Europe and Central Asia and reciprocating by opening up our system, we were misled into thinking that capitalism was the victor in the cold war. Furthermore, we squeezed Russia and instead rewarded China for imitating our military-industrial hyperdevelopment; we followed "the free market" into a dangerous concentration of wealth in the upper classes, and now an economic collapse is coming at us.
3. We are confusing spiritual insights with fundamentalisms and so have become suspicious of many world religions.
4. We have refused to join the Kyoto accords and have added to the thermal pollution that threatens the entire earth, spurring China to join us in the same destructive polluting practices.

Our leaders have thereby delayed by a decade our embracing the Dalai Lama's vision for the twenty-first century and our energetic turning to the positive trends we really need. Fortunately, the negative consequences of our current trajectory are providing instant feedback, which may yet wake us up by underlining the danger of our persistent folly.

I pray for all of us, oppressor and friend, that together we succeed in building a better world through human understanding and love, and that in doing so we may reduce the pain and suffering of all sentient beings. Thank you.

It is indeed fortunate that such a person as the Dalai Lama is praying for us. We can only respond by making heroic efforts to really build that better world by developing our understanding and our love, and to never stop trying to reduce the suffering of all beings.

Endnotes

1. The Tenth Panchen Lama died suddenly in 1989, and in the process of finding his reincarnation, the Dalai Lama was consulted by the Panchen Lama reincarnation committee of his monastery, Tashi Lhunpo Monastery as is traditional, since the Dalai Lama always oversees the discovery of the Panchen Lama. At the last minute, when the final determination was made by the Dalai Lama, choosing Gendun Chokyi Nyima as the correct candidate, the Chinese government under Jiang Zemin declared that the Communist Party would make the decision. They then rejected the Dalai Lama's choice, even though all Tibetans accepted it, arrested Gendun Chokyi Nyima and his family, and took him away to an undisclosed location where he has been ever since. Jiang then chose another boy, against the wishes of the Tibetans, and the government has been using loyalty pledges to its boy, whom the Tibetans call the False One, as a litmus test of who is loyal to the Dalai Lama and who to Beijing.

2. See my *Inner Revolution* for a greater elaboration of this insight.

3. For more information on this, see www.mindandlife.org.

4. Since the Republic of China was founded in 1912 with the overthrow of the foreigner-imposed Manchu Empire, the Chinese leaders decided to stop treating the Manchurians, Mongolians, Uighur Turks, and Tibetans as foreigners in order to incorporate their lands into China. They began to speak of Manchu Chinese, Mongol Chinese, Uighur Chinese, and Tibetan Chinese and felt a bit strange to then refer to themselves as Chinese Chinese. So they took the name of one of their great classical

dynasties, the Han Dynasty, and called themselves Han Chinese. When the Communists founded the People's Republic of China in 1949, they continued this practice, and, in fact, the five stars on the People's Republic's flag stand for the Han Chinese (the big yellow star) and the four "ethnic" peoples (the four little stars). But the fact is that none of those four groups of people consider themselves Chinese—nor do Chinese people, when meeting any of them in the street, consider them to be fellow Chinese. Thus, both Nationalist and Communist Republics were trying to maintain the Manchu Empire's reach over the four colonized peoples, just as the Soviet Union was trying to maintain the reach of the Tsarist Empire.

5. and 10. The research literature on adaptation to high altitude comparing Tibetans and Chinese is summarized by William Bushell, Ph.D., MIT post-doc; Research Fellow, Tibet House US. "A critical review of the primary several hundred published studies in the medical literature reveals the following regarding genetic/hereditary differences between Tibetans and immigrant Chinese (Han) in high altitude Tibet. Most studies, including those done recently at Chinese research institutions, support the hypotheses that (1) Tibetans possess a range of physiological, biochemical, and molecular adaptations to high altitude that are based on genes and heredity, and that (2) ethnic ("Han") Chinese possess an overall physiology that is, comparatively, genetically unsuited for life there, both in the short and long terms. There are two main related categories of data, pertaining to (1) the quality of daily functioning and (2) disease risk.

"In terms of the first, Tibetans possess a full spectrum of adaptations, most notably in terms of respiratory, cardiovascular, and nervous system adaptations to high altitude, which makes their efficiency, tolerance, quality of life, and all manner of day-to-day functions superior to Chinese at the same altitude.... The physiological adaptations do include nitric oxide; the functions include exercise and/or work performance and sleep, which is extremely important for functioning and quality of life.

"In terms of the second, there is the issue of altitude related disease.... In adults, there is risk, both acutely and in the long term, for serious respiratory, cardiovascular, and nervous system disease and disorder. Most common is acute and chronic mountain sickness (AMS & CMS), which can be extremely debilitating and even lethal; long term chronic versions of the syndrome lead to severe pathology in the heart. As for birth and early life stages, the results, particularly for non-Tibetans, can be equally severe: intrauterine growth restriction (IUGR) and related disorders are associated with higher risks of pregnancy-related morbidity and mortality for the mother, as well as restricted fetal growth, reduced birth rate, increased premature birth, increased infant mortality (both pre- and post-natal), and for infant cardiovascular and respiratory health as well."

For further research on high altitude in relation to Chinese colonization of Tibet, see selected research references in the Resources section.

6. "Great Tibet," as I will explain in detail in Part II, and demonstrate with maps, is what Tibet has always been when the eleven Tibet Autonomous Prefectures (TAP), years ago split off from Tibet and placed in other Chinese provinces, are rejoined to the Tibet Autonomous Region (TAR). As the Chinese's own names indicate, these are areas on the high plateau where only Tibetans can live comfortably, due to lack of oxygen, and together they have always been the homeland of Tibet. Taking the Tibetan word for Tibet, *Böd*, I will refer to the *new* autonomous region I envision as the Böd Autonomous Region (BAR), to distinguish it from the TAR, which is only half of it. I will continue to use the term "Great Tibet" when referring to the area historically designated as Tibet prior to China's twentieth century invasion, again to distinguish it from the smaller area of the current TAR meant when the term "Tibet" is used by the Chinese or in the popular media. Geographically, Great Tibet and the BAR are one and the same.

7. Text quoted from www.dalailama.com.

8. The Tibet Autonomous Prefectures (TAP), Tibet Autonomous Counties (TAC), and other formerly Tibetan regions, as mapped in figure 3, were all created as People's Republic of China administrative units in the 1950s, after the Chinese military occupation.

> *Qinghai Province*: 1. Golmud TAP, created 1955; 2. Yushu TAP, created 1955; 3. Tsonub Mongolian Prefecture and TAP, created 1955; 4. Golog TAP, created 1955; 5. Tsolho TAP, created 1955; 6. Tsojang TAP, created 1955; (Pari TAC) created 1950; (Xining City District); (Haidong Prefecture). *Gansu Province*: 7. Malho TAP, created 1957; 8. Kanlho TAP, created 1957; 9. Ngapa TAP, created 1957. *Sichuan Province*: 10. Kartse TAP, created 1957. *Yunnan Province*: 11. Dechen TAP, created 1957; (Mili TAC).

9. For an enlightening presentation of the entire history of Tibet, both from a Western historian's and the Dalai Lama's perspectives, see Thomas Laird's important book, *The Story of Tibet: Conversations with the Dalai Lama*. New York: Grove Press, 2007.

3

THE DALAI LAMA'S CALL
FOR AN ETHICAL AND
SPIRITUAL REVOLUTION

The Dalai Lama has clear and specific ideas about the ethical and spiritual revolution needed not only for a solution to the Tibet-China problem but also for the world at large. In this chapter, we'll take a close look at his philosophy as exemplified in his remarkable book *Ethics for a New Millennium* and his speech given to the European Union (EU) in 2001.

The Dalai Lama's philosophy emerges clearly in *Ethics for a New Millennium*, where he speaks more distinctly than ever as a world leader with a compelling vision for a viable future. I highly recommend reading the book in full—it is truly necessary for our world community. His wisdom is urgently needed as we look back at a long, hard twentieth century, and forward in hope that the twenty-first, after these initial tough years, will be better. Calling for a spiritual and ethical revolution, he is even a bit ahead of his time, a fact exquisitely ironic for those who assume he speaks from an underdeveloped civilization outside of the progressive modern stream.

His thesis in *Ethics for a New Millennium* is that kindness, love, and altruism are the keys to happiness. Compassion (in Tibetan, *nying-je*) is not just sentimentality but rather a powerful method of living the good life and attaining real happiness. Here is the Dalai Lama in his own words: "*nying-je* [means] a combination of empathy and reason. Empathy we can think of as a very honest person; reason as someone who is very practical ... the combination is highly effective."

On the topic of happiness he says this: "Human beings have the capacity to experience happiness at a deeper level, which, when achieved, has the capacity to overwhelm contrary experiences.... According to my experience, I have found that the principle characteristic of genuine happiness is peace: inner peace ... I cannot claim personally to have succeeded very far in this ... I attribute my sense of peace to the effort to develop concern for others."

On the social level, the human biological and spiritual facts he mentions dictate an ethic of compassion and universal responsibility; the pressure of the postmodern planetary crisis requires a spiritual and ethical revolution. His other main idea is that, if humanity adopts more spiritual outlooks and more ethical actions, the world can be livable in the coming centuries; we can avoid the various doomsday scenarios that are possible. He ends with a powerful appeal to the individual to implement the spiritual and ethical revolution in her or his life.

His Holiness articulates in *Ethics* some of his usual themes:

I. That the common human religion is love and kindness, based on the actual biology of human nature; "alongside our natural ability to empathize with others, we have also a need for others' kindness which runs like a thread throughout our whole life";

2. That spirituality is broader than any specific form of religion and is essential for individual happiness and for keeping the world livable;

3. That ethics are also more universal than specific religious pre-scriptions. For example, he states that "religious belief is no guarantee of moral integrity. Looking at the history of our species, we see that among the major troublemakers—those who visited violence, brutality, and destruction on their fellow human beings—there have been many who professed religious faith, often loudly. Religion can help us to establish basic eth-ical principles. Yet we can still talk about ethics and morality without having recourse to religion;"

4. That nonviolence is essential to solving the manmade disas-ters of conflict and wars;

5. That so-called idealism is not as unrealistic as certain modern cyn-ical secular theories of psyche and society have made it out to be.

His book expresses some important new ideas as well. I have been listening to the Dalai Lama's talks for almost forty years now, and every time he brings something fresh and new into connection with his per-sistent themes. His *Ethics* book fits into the same pattern, demonstrating a new power of conviction and acuity of penetration. His thought never remains static and formulaic but develops bit by bit over time, as he keeps on learning more about life and history and thinks ever more deeply about his own broad experience.

Among the most important new dimensions unveiled in this book are, first, a devastating critique of material progress and soulless mechanical technology. He states, "Although I never imagined that material wealth alone could ever overcome suffering, still, looking towards the developed world from Tibet, a country then as now very poor in this respect, I must admit that I thought it must go further towards doing so than is the case. I expected that, with physical suffering much reduced, as it is for the majority living in the industrially developed countries, happiness would be much easier to achieve ... [However,] the extraordinary advancements of science and technology have achieved little more than linear, numerical improvement ... progress has meant hardly more than greater numbers of opulent houses in more cities, with more cars driving between them. Certainly there has been a reduction in some types of suffering including certain illnesses. But there has been no overall reduction."

A second new dimension his book offers is a passionate call for a spiritual and ethical revolution. Though he is the leader of a people that have suffered as much as any in this terrible past century of genocide and mass destruction, he never deviates from his general theme of world ethics to plead the special case of Tibet, an endangered nation.

Third, he argues adamantly for universal disarmament, sketching a series of systematic steps toward the total prevention of wars and war industries, likening war to a bonfire on which people are heaped like logs, and poignantly recalling his own visits to Auschwitz and Hiroshima.

Fourth, he engages in a courageous critique of excessively luxurious living and over-concentration of wealth and makes a clear appeal for altruism and universal responsibility in policy, based on his well-argued insight that altruism is the essential key to individual happiness and social harmony. He is practical and optimistic about globalization, but not the imbalanced globalization that makes the rich richer and the poor poorer.

And finally, he forcefully calls for religions to focus on personal practice over institutional aggrandizement and tolerant pluralism over bigoted exclusivism. He argues that the practice of spirituality and ethics is more important than doctrinal purity and ritual formalism. He shows a willingness to dispense with religion altogether if it only adds to the burdens people struggle with. He acknowledges the benefit of religion sincerely applied and argues that one can overcome the seemingly insoluble tension between exclusive focus on one's own religion in personal faith and sincerely tolerant pluralism in social practice. "I love my own religion as best for me! And I honor your devotion to your own religion as best for you!"

The Dalai Lama speaks with great sincerity and intelligence like a reasonable and practical, if sometimes challenging, friend rather than a lofty eminence or a dogmatic authority. He does not set himself above his readers but frequently refers to his own shortcomings, admitting how hard he himself has to work to try to live up to the ideals he espouses. Having known the Dalai Lama for so long, and having traveled with him occasionally, I was particularly touched by this passage: "I feel strongly that luxurious living is inappropriate, so much so that I must admit that whenever I stay in a comfortable hotel and see others eating and drinking expensively whilst outside there are people visible who do not even have anywhere to spend the night, I feel greatly disturbed. It reminds me that I am no different from either the rich or the poor. We are the same in wanting happiness and not wanting to suffer. And yet the person who is saying these things is one of those enjoying the comforts of the hotel. Indeed, I must go further. It is also true that I possess several valuable wristwatches. And whilst I feel that if I were to sell them I could perhaps build some huts for the poor, so far I have not.... So I must admit a contradiction between my principles and my practice in certain areas. At the same time, I do not think that everyone can or should be like Mahatma Gandhi and live the life of a poor peasant. Such dedication is wonderful and greatly to be admired. But the watchword is 'as much as possible'—without going to extremes."

One senses no false humility here, as he is more forceful than ever about the practicality, even necessity, of proposals that some might call overly idealistic, and he sharply critiques the so-called realists of realpolitik (ruthless, calculating, amoral geopolitical strategies) as obsolete in their thinking and destructive in their actions.

It is also significant that the Dalai Lama never once mentions the sad plight of his own Tibetan people in this book. Nor does he decry the appalling treatment Tibetans continue to receive from the Chinese government, with the official community of nations in denial about the genocidal danger Tibetans face. I know for a fact that he agonizes moment to moment over the suffering of his people. Yet, thinking over what revolutionary changes the world needs to make as the new millennium was dawning, he did not put forward his own great preoccupation and heavy responsibility. I think this is an excellent exemplification of his central claim that genuine altruism—thinking of others before one-self—is the key to inner peace and happiness.

How does that work in very personal terms? When you feel very sad about some tragedy that has befallen, your compassion can help you step back and notice that it seems to you at that moment as if it is the worst thing that has ever happened to anyone ever. Once you remember that even worse has happened to others, compassion expands toward them. So many things remind you of others' tragedies—remembering the mishaps of people you know, hearing the news of disasters, or recalling history. As the vastness of human suffering fills your awareness, your own tragedy becomes smaller and smaller by comparison, and, at the very least, you feel some relief that the many other worse things have not yet happened to you. Your perspective has widened and your own tragedy becomes more bearable, and indeed you identify more strongly with the sufferings of others. This is the way compassion moves you toward great tolerance of your own hardships and even happiness, and thus greater intolerance of others' sufferings.

And this is the secret of the Dalai Lama's famous cheerfulness and grace under pressure.

THE VASTNESS OF THE DALAI LAMA'S "OCEAN"

The Dalai Lama's international role, in his many books, his honors received all over the world, and his meetings with dignitaries and celebrities begins to give a sense of his impact around the globe.

These accomplishments reveal him as the Dalai, the grand ocean of intelligence, kindness, and responsibility. Since beings are only inter-relational, their personages constituted not only by their own self-identity notions and constructions but also by their connections with others, the Dalai Lama has become a "network being," connected to many of the world's ruling and former presidents, ministers, intellectuals, executives, financiers, media celebrities, artists, actors, and private individuals of wealth and influence, as well as millions of ordinary people through his lectures, books, films, and media appearances. The running list in the previous chapter catalogues mainly the political and religious leaders whom he regularly meets throughout the free world. The numerous private individuals are not listed. And the leadership and influential circles of Communist China—and Russia to a lesser degree, as there were some connections established during the Gorbachev/Yeltsin era—were the only ones planet-wide to have been deprived of almost all connection with this ocean, although in 1954 the young Dalai Lama did meet all the early People's Republic of China leadership, including Mao Zedong, Zhou Enlai, Deng Xiaoping, and Liu Xiaoqi.

The Dalai Lama should certainly be included in any international register of the ten most influential living people in the world, much more so than many heads of state. In addition to each of the many honors he has received, he has personally met, impressed, and touched the heart of kings and queens, prime ministers, mayors, chancellors, university presidents, provosts, state governors, congresspeople, and senators. During these award ceremonies, he has reached out heart to heart with the community—32,000 at Rutgers University, 20,000 at Harvard, 26,000 at Emory, plus large crowds in Europe and Australia. The books he has written on many subjects have been read by millions of people in more than thirty languages, a number of them becoming bestsellers in many countries. It can be evidently seen how the Dalai Lama, through his deep connections to the minds and hearts of many beings around the world, has a truly oceanic influence.

Speaking Truth to Power: The Reluctant Prophet

An excellent example of his prophetic role is his speech to the European Parliament in Strasbourg on October 14, 2001, delivered shortly after 9/11 and twelve years after receiving the Nobel Peace Prize. In it we see him in action being a Dalai Lama for the larger world, in a time of great stress and danger. I will cite it here and draw out the meaning his words have for our current state of affairs.

> *Madame Speaker, Honorable Members of the Parliament, ladies, and gen-tlemen. It is a great honor for me to address the European Parliament. I believe the European Union is an inspiring example for a cooperative and peaceful coexistence among different nations and peoples, and deeply inspiring for people like myself who strongly believe in the need for better understanding, closer cooperation, and greater respect among the various nations of the world.*

The Dalai Lama here hints at his longing for an Asian Union, with an Asian Parliament, wherein China, India, and Japan would naturally be dominant members, like Germany, France, and England, but with room still for smaller nations, Tibet emerging most fittingly as the Switzerland of the group. This would prevent the kind of tension throughout Asia that has caused two major wars, the Korean and the Vietnamese, and numerous smaller conflicts throughout the twentieth century. A century ago, one would have thought that Germany and France would always be at war, not to mention Spain and England, who had multi-century global competitions, yet today they work coopera-tively in a virtually borderless community with a common market and a common currency. The Asian nations fear China and India—the two giants left over from past conquest empires, the Manchu and the British, respectively—continuing the trajectories of military-industrial imperialism and colonialism. And of these two giants, China is central in its position in Asia. The people of Korea, Mongolia, Turkestan, Tibet, India, Nepal, Bhutan, Burma, Laos, Vietnam, the Philippines, and Taiwan can feel the intense pressures of the need for "living space" for China's 1.3 billion people, the appetite for resources of its growing military-industrial economy, and the relentless determination of its atti-tude that it is culturally superior. So the question is, does China, as

Germany did in Europe several times, try to dominate all these surrounding people by forms of military-industrial tribal conquest? Or does China follow the example of today's Germany and nonviolently participate as an equal state in a mutually beneficial community of nations? China could lead the formation of an Asian Union, an Asian common market, and even a United States of Asia.

Tibet is the key point where now conquest and colonial domination prevail, evident to all nations though unacknowledged by the giant. And so, Tibet is the key point where China can show its superiority by avoiding the past century's futile and destructive attempts at world conquest by various Western nations and a Westernized Japan and go straight to a nonviolent economic, cultural, and pluralistic union. The Dalai Lama can help China make that historic turnaround.

I thank you for this kind invitation. I consider it as an encouraging gesture of genuine sympathy and concern for the tragic fate of the Tibetan people. I speak to you today as a simple Buddhist monk, educated and trained in our ancient traditional way. I am not an expert in political science. However, my lifelong study and practice of Buddhism and my responsibility and involvement in the nonviolent freedom struggle of the Tibetan people have given me some experiences and thoughts that I would like to share with you.

It is evident that the human community has reached a critical juncture in its history. Today's world requires us to accept the oneness of humanity. In the past, communities could afford to think of one another as fundamentally separate. But today, as we learn from the recent tragic events in the United States, whatever happens in one region eventually affects many other areas. The world is becoming increasingly interdependent. Within the context of this new interdependence, self-interest clearly lies in considering the interest of others. Without the cultivation and promotion of a sense of universal responsibility, our very future is in danger.

This is his prophetic clarion call, set against the background of the global event of 9/11, and directly challenging the reactions of the United States, Britain, and other nations on the one side and the alienated segment of the Muslim world on the other. (It must be noted that the spiritual leadership of the Muslims, Sunni through the Mufti of Al-Azhar University in Egypt, and Shia through the Mullahs of Iran, condemned the terrorists who attacked the World Trade Center in New York, supported the US intervention in Afghanistan, and did not condemn America until the invasion of Iraq two years later.) The Dalai Lama presents the more viable response to such a disaster: everyone acknowledging responsibility and accepting the oneness of humanity. Enlightened self-interest calls upon us to develop altruism. The Dalai Lama's key solution is that principle. He personally exemplifies it and holds his nation on the excruciating path of exemplifying it as a group, for the most part.

> *I strongly believe that we must consciously develop a greater sense of universal responsibility. We must learn to work not just for our own individual self, family, or nation but for the benefit of all mankind. Universal responsibility is the best foundation both for our personal happiness and for world peace, the equitable use of our natural resources, and, through a concern for future generations, the proper care for the environment.*

The universal responsibility to pursue the happiness of all as the core of life, nonviolence in the face of conflict, generosity in sharing wealth, and prudent self-restraint in preserving the natural environment—these are his unvarying recommendations of the values humanity must elevate above all others in order to achieve everyone's goal of a viable global lifestyle in this century.

> *Many of the world's problems and conflicts arise because we have lost sight of the basic humanity that binds us all together as a human family. We tend to forget that despite the diversity of race, religion, culture, language, ideology, and so forth, people are equal in their basic desire for peace and happiness: we all want happiness and do not want suffering. We strive to fulfill these desires as best we can. However, as much as we praise diversity in theory, unfortunately*

often we fail to respect it in practice. In fact, our inability to embrace diversity becomes a major source of conflict among peoples.

The basis of true tolerance is the ability to identify with others by recognizing in yourself the common qualities you share with others, transcending all the categories that the shortsighted ego can take up as the basis for lethal prejudices.

A particularly sad fact of human history is that conflicts have arisen in the name of religion. Even today, individuals are killed, their communities destroyed, and societies destabilized as a result of misuse of religion and encouragement of religious bigotry and hatred. According to my personal experience, the best way to overcome obstructions to inter-religious harmony and to bring about understanding is through dialogue with members of other faith traditions. This I see occurring in a number of different ways. In my own case, for example, my meetings with the late Thomas Merton, a Trappist monk, in the late '60s, were deeply inspiring. They helped me develop a profound admiration for the teachings of Christianity. I also feel that meetings amongst different religious leaders and joining together to pray from a common platform are extremely powerful, as was the case in 1986 during the gathering at Assisi in Italy. The recent United Nations Millennium World Peace Summit of Religious and Spiritual Leaders held last year was also a laudable step.

However, there is a need for more of these initiatives on a regular basis. On my part, to show my respect for other religious traditions I went on pilgrimage to Jerusalem, a site holy to three of the world's great religions. I have paid visits to various Hindu, Islamic, Christian, Jain, and Sikh shrines both in India and abroad. During the past three decades I have met with many religious leaders of different traditions and have discussed harmony and inter-religious understanding. When exchanges like these occur, followers of one tradition will find that, just as in the case of their own, the teachings of other faiths are a source of both spiritual inspiration as well as ethical guidance to their followers. It will also become clear that irrespective of doctrinal and other differences, all the major world religions help to transform individuals to become good human beings. All emphasize love, compassion, patience, tolerance, forgiveness, humility, self-discipline, and so on. We must therefore embrace the concept of plurality in the field of religion too.

As a religious leader himself, he here chronicles his own insights and efforts to do his part to overcome the extremely dangerous potential of religious self-definitions. Extremist interpretations of sacred writ often support lethal alienation among people, ethnicities, nations, and even whole religious denominations. Religious self-identity can trump tribal, national, racial, cultural, and gender identities, and yet, in the absence of a broad acceptance of what the Dalai Lama calls "the common human religion of kindness," there is no self-identity that can trump religious self-identity. Secularism tried to do this, culturally in the free or capitalist world and politically in the communist world. But then secularism itself became a kind of religious self-identity with a tendency to extremism in its own right, while failing to provide a high percentage of people with a sense of universal human identity that could restrain religious exclusivism. But the Dalai Lama does not attempt any such universal religion in any formal sense, except to express his perception that all religions value kindness, ethical commitment, and universal responsibility. He urges existing world religions to emphasize these common transcending qualities and practices.

In the context of our newly emerging global community, all forms of violence, including war, are totally inappropriate means of settling disputes. Violence and war have always been part of human history, and in ancient times there were winners and losers. However, there would be no winners at all if another global conflict were to occur today. We must, therefore, have the courage and vision to call for a world without nuclear weapons and national armies in the long run. Especially in the light of the terrible attacks in the United States, the international community must make a sincere attempt to use the horrible and shocking experience to develop a sense of global responsibility, where a culture of dialogue and nonviolence is used in resolving differences.

This is the crux of the Dalai Lama's key solution, his act of truth. Non-violence is the only solution to the war on terrorism. Many of those who believed that terrorism required a violent response have admitted the strategy's futility by proclaiming that the so-called "war on terror" cannot be won and is therefore endless. The Dalai Lama's vision is clear. We must first conquer terror within ourselves. We must not give in to it and become fearful and desperate. We will lose our effective judgment if we become terrified and merely lash out and incite more terror in others who will lash back. This was the message of Buddha, Mahavira of the Jains, Confucius, Mencius, the ancient Hebrews, Jesus, Krishna, and Muhammad. Once people's fear and terror subsides, both from the courage of not letting terror control one's reactions and from practicing—and observing others practice—nonviolence, then there is time and calm for dialogue about the causes of conflict and the methods to overcome it peacefully.

> *Dialogue is the only sensible and intelligent way of resolving differences and clashes of interests, whether between individuals or nations. The promotion of a culture of dialogue and nonviolence for the future of mankind is a compelling task of the international community. It is not enough for governments to endorse the principle of nonviolence without any appropriate action to support and promote it. If nonviolence is to prevail, nonviolent movements must be made effective and successful. Some consider the twentieth century a century of war and bloodshed. I believe the challenge before us is to make the new century one of dialogue and nonviolence.*

This is truly remarkable to hear proclaimed in such a forum during a time when the drums of war are being loudly beaten in some of the leading industrial countries, especially America.

> *Furthermore, in dealing with conflicts, too often we lack proper judgment and courage. We fail to pay adequate attention to situations of potential conflict when they are at an early stage of development. Once all the circumstances have progressed to a state where emotions of the people or communities involved in*

disputes have become fully charged, it is extremely difficult, if not impossible, to prevent a dangerous situation from exploding. We see this tragic situation repeated time and again. So we must learn to detect early signs of conflict and have the courage to address the problem before it reaches its boiling point.

This should be the charter principle causing all national governments and the UN to endow large-scale, mainstream peace institutions, universities, think tanks, and schools that are committed to gradually building up the sciences, technologies, arts, institutions, and industries of peace to match and balance the widespread complex of institutions devoted to war.

I remain convinced that most human conflicts can be solved through genuine dialogue conducted with a spirit of openness and reconciliation. I have therefore consistently sought a resolution of the issue of Tibet through nonviolence and dialogue. Right from the beginning of the invasion of Tibet, I tried to work with the Chinese authorities to arrive at a mutually acceptable, peaceful coexistence. Even when the so-called Seventeen Point Agreement for the Peaceful Liberation of Tibet was forced upon us, I tried to work with the Chinese authorities. After all, by that agreement, the Chinese government recognized the distinctiveness and the autonomy of Tibet and pledged not to impose their system on Tibet against our wishes. However, in breach of this agreement, the Chinese authorities forced upon Tibetans their rigid and alien ideology and showed scant respect for the unique culture, religion, and way of life of the Tibetan people. In desperation the Tibetan people rose up against the Chinese. In the end in 1959, I had to escape from Tibet so that I could continue to serve the people of Tibet.

Here he turns away from his prophetic call to a new rule among nations, encouraged by the very example of the EU, as he said, in that their organization is based on a turning away from World Wars I and II, and the creation of a forum wherein a larger-than-the-nation sense of identity grounds a culture of dialogue. He turns to his primary responsibility as the leader of all Tibetans, the tragic situation of Tibet.

During the past more than four decades since my escape, Tibet has been under the complete control of the Government of the People's Republic of China. The immense destruction and human suffering inflicted on the people of Tibet are today well known, and I do not wish to dwell on these sad and painful events. The late Panchen Lama's 70,000-character petition to the Chinese government serves as a telling historical document on China's draconian policies and actions in Tibet. Tibet today continues to be an occupied country, oppressed by force and scarred by suffering. Despite some development and economic progress, Tibet continues to face fundamental problems of survival. Serious violations of human rights are widespread throughout Tibet and are often the result of policies of racial and cultural discrimination. Yet they are only the symptoms and consequences of a deeper problem. The Chinese authorities view Tibet's distinct culture and religion as the source of threat of separation. Hence as a result of deliberate policies, an entire people with its unique culture and identity are facing the threat of extinction.

He depersonalizes the genocidal policies and practices of the People's Republic of China, understanding their cause in the Chinese perception that the very Tibetan-ness of Tibetans makes them unable to identify themselves as Chinese, and so, logically, in order to keep long-term ownership of Tibet, the Chinese judge that they have to eliminate the Tibetans, either by eliminating the Tibetan-ness of the Tibetans or by eliminating the Tibetans altogether, whichever comes first.

When this is pointed out to Chinese thinkers, they tend to excuse this inherently genocidal policy by citing its normality and inevitability. They compare a sort of Chinese manifest destiny to the example of the North and South American genocide of most of the Native Americans, which has been going on during the five-hundred-year-long Columbian period. As a North American, I have been asked by Chinese dissident colleagues if I am ready to give back the land to the Iroquois, Lakota, Hopi, Kwakiutl, and so forth. They are shocked and incredulous when I say yes. But when we go on to discuss the details—where are these tribes' descendants, what do they want, how difficult would it be to begin true reparations—they realize that nothing is impossible and it is never too late to strive for some elements of justice to ameliorate a tragic situation. At this point it is also helpful to remind them that Tibet is different from the American heartland; I used to make a joke about this, "Ah! Mao's Louisiana Purchase—How sad! The land is three miles too high! Instead of waving fields of grain, he found only waving tails of yaks!"

I have led the Tibetan freedom struggle on a path of nonviolence and have consistently sought a mutually agreeable solution of the Tibetan issue through negotiations in a spirit of reconciliation and compromise with China. With this spirit in 1988, here in Strasbourg at this Parliament, I presented a formal proposal for negotiations, which we hoped would serve as a basis for resolving the issue of Tibet. I had chosen consciously the European Parliament as a venue to present my thoughts for a framework for negotiations in order to underline the point that a genuine union can only come about voluntarily when there are satisfactory benefits to all the parties concerned. The European Union is a clear and inspiring example of this. On the other hand, even one country or community can break into two or more entities when there is a lack of trust and benefit, and when force is used as the principal means of rule.

Here he refers to his speech in Strasbourg (quoted earlier) thirteen years before he became a Nobel Laureate. He again avows his friendly spirit toward China and its leadership, wishing them to have the benefit of a just and compassionate solution to the problem caused by their inability to digest Tibet without destroying it. And his very mention of the EU as an example of what he sees the Chinese can achieve by relenting in Tibet shows his profound understanding of the present moment in history and the dangers and opportunities attendant upon the choices made now. Brute force no longer works, he is saying, and nonviolent dialogue and reconciliation must replace the rule of domination and desperation.

My proposal, which later became known as the "Middle Way Approach" or the "Strasbourg Proposal," envisages that Tibet enjoy genuine autonomy within the framework of the People's Republic of China. However, not the autonomy on paper imposed on us fifty years ago in the Seventeen-Point Agreement, but a true self-governing, genuinely autonomous Tibet, with Tibetans fully responsible for their own domestic affairs, including the education of their children, religious matters, cultural affairs, the care of their delicate and precious environment, and the local economy. Beijing would continue to be responsible for the conduct of foreign and defense affairs. This solution would greatly enhance the international image of China and contribute to her stability and unity—the two topmost priorities of Beijing—while at the same time the Tibetans would be ensured of the basic rights and freedoms to preserve their own civilization and to protect the delicate environment of the Tibetan plateau.

Here he revisits the vision of a truly autonomous Tibet in federation with the People's Republic of China, adding details to the visions already given in his previous talks in 1987 and 1988. Leaving defense and foreign affairs in the hands of the Chinese Federal Union is only practical, and since Tibet will be an unarmed zone of peace, border troops will become more and more irrelevant.

Since then our relation with the Chinese government has taken many twists and turns. Unfortunately, I must sadly inform you that a lack of political will on the part of the Chinese leadership to address the issue of Tibet in a serious manner has failed to produce any progress. My initiatives and overtures over the years to engage the Chinese leadership in a dialogue remain unreciprocated. Last September, I communicated through the Chinese Embassy in New Delhi our wish to send a delegation to Beijing to deliver a detailed memorandum outlining my thinking on the issue of Tibet and to explain and discuss the points raised in the memorandum. I conveyed that through face-to-face meetings we would succeed in clarifying misunderstandings and overcoming distrust. I expressed the strong belief that once this is achieved, then a mutually acceptable solution of the problem can be found without much difficulty. But the Chinese government is refusing to accept my delegation till today. It is obvious that Beijing's attitude has hardened significantly compared to the eighties, when six Tibetan delegations from exile were accepted. Whatever explanations Beijing may give concerning communications between the

Chinese government and myself, I must state here clearly that the Chinese government is refusing to talk to representatives I have designated for the task.

A year or two after this speech, preliminary, formally unacknowledged talks began between low-level representatives of the United Front, the Chinese agency that handles minority affairs, and the Dalai Lama's representatives—not of the Tibetan Government in Exile, which China does not recognize. However, for the Chinese these were never serious talks. They were merely stalling tactics, the kind of feint taught in Sun Tzu's *The Art of War*, in which one side distracts the enemy by raising hopes of a settlement without conflict while it quietly prepares the field for the final devastation.

The failure of the Chinese leadership to respond positively to my Middle Way Approach reaffirms the Tibetan people's suspicion that the Chinese government has no interest whatsoever in any kind of peaceful coexistence. Many Tibetans believe that China is bent on complete forceful assimilation and absorption of Tibet into China. They call for the independence of Tibet and criticize my Middle Way Approach. Others are advocating a referendum in Tibet. They argue if conditions inside Tibet are as the Chinese authorities portray them to be and if the Tibetans are truly happy, then there should be no difficulty holding a vote in Tibet. I have also always maintained that ultimately the Tibetan people must be able to decide about the future of Tibet as Pandit Jawaharlal Nehru, the first Prime Minister of India, stated in the Indian Parliament on December 7, 1950: ". . . the last voice in regard to Tibet should be the voice of the people of Tibet and nobody else."

This is the kind of strong statement the Dalai Lama ceased to make after the talks began in 2003, voicing the feelings of not only most Tibetans but also all China's Asian neighbors who see the Tibetans as the canaries in the mine shaft. If China feels it can get away with the assimilation and absorption of Tibetans and Tibet, what can other countries and territories expect when their turn comes, when the Chinese juggernaut wants their productive lands, trees, plants, and minerals?

While I firmly reject the use of violence as a means in our freedom struggle, we certainly have the right to explore all other political options available to us. I am a staunch believer in freedom and democracy and have therefore been encouraging the Tibetans in exile to follow the democratic process. Today, the Tibetan refugees may be among the few communities in exile that have established all the three pillars of democracy: legislature, judiciary, and executive. This year we have taken another big stride in the process of democratization by having the chairman of the Tibetan Cabinet elected by popular vote. The elected chairman of the Cabinet and the elected parliament will shoulder the responsibility of running the Tibetan affairs as the legitimate representatives of the people. However, I do consider it my moral obligation to the six million Tibetans to continue taking up the Tibetan issue with the Chinese leadership and to act as the free spokesman of the Tibetan people until a solution is reached.

He justifies his internationalization of his problem, since China pretends that its oppression in Tibet is its internal affair and therefore no one can take an interest in it without violating China's sovereignty. The Dalai Lama does so out of his Tibetan-born sense of etiquette and politeness. It is as if he is saying, "I'm so sorry, but I have to talk to these friendly people here in Europe about our mutual problem because you won't come face to face with me to talk it through!" And then he shows his pride in the Tibetan exile community's gradual development of democratic habits in governance, indicating that they, and not just he, have the responsibility to seek justice for their fellow countrymen in Tibet. He also asserts his responsibility to continue speaking out until the acceptable solution can be reached.

In the absence of any positive response from the Chinese government to my overtures over the years, I am left with no alternative but to appeal to the members of the international community. It is clear now that only increased, concerted, and consistent international efforts will persuade Beijing to change its policy on Tibet. Although the immediate reactions from the Chinese side will be most probably negative, nevertheless, I strongly believe that expressions of international concern and support are essential for creating an environment conducive for the peaceful resolution of the Tibetan problem.

This statement could easily apply to the intent of this book: Irritation and a negative response are to be expected when you appeal to someone to take steps to solve a problem that they deny exists. China may maintain, "There is no Tibet problem. There are no Tibetans, just minority Chinese who sometimes resist our commands, but we can do what we want with our own people. Nobody's business and no problem!" But the Dalai Lama and others who care about Tibetans' plight will continue to stand on the truth.

On my part, I remain committed to the process of dialogue. It is my firm belief that dialogue and a willingness to look with honesty and clarity at the reality of Tibet can lead us to a mutually beneficial solution that will contribute to the stability and unity of the People's Republic of China and secure the right for the Tibetan people to live in freedom, peace, and dignity.

This is his key solution again—friendly dialogue in place of violent confrontation. The People's Republic of China leadership might rethink the meaning of friendship in the light of all the ancient Chinese wisdom traditions. They should recognize that all those world leaders who come to China with smiling faces, catering to China's aggressive postures in order to gain profit from Chinese productivity and consumption, are not real friends of China. They are friends of China's money. The Dalai Lama has suffered directly from China's aggression and hostility, and has no motive to exploit China's economy, and yet he still wants dialogue and reconciliation instead of recrimination and vengeance. That is someone who is truly a friend of China. Isn't it inefficient to strain oneself by making an enemy out of a potential friend?

Madam Speaker, honorable members of the Parliament, brothers and sisters of the European Parliament, I consider myself as the free spokesman for my captive countrymen and women. It is my duty to speak on their behalf. I speak not with a feeling of anger or hatred towards those who are responsible for the immense suffering of our people and the destruction of our land, homes, temples, monasteries, and culture. They too are human beings who struggle to find happiness and deserve our compassion. I speak to inform you of the sad situation in my country today and of the aspirations of my people, because in our struggle for freedom, truth is the only weapon we possess. Today, our people, our distinct rich cultural heritage, and our national identity are facing the threat of extinction. We need your support to survive as a people and as a culture.

This is why he is concerned for China. In their quest for happiness, the Chinese leaders have caused great damage to others, including the Tibetans the Dalai Lama is responsible for. In the Buddhist view, the evolutionary effects of this action will blow back upon the Chinese, individually and collectively, with damaging consequences in one lifetime or another. That is why in Buddhist ethics one is as concerned for the welfare of the wrongdoer as much as for the welfare of the wronged.

When one looks at the situation inside Tibet, it seems almost hopeless in the face of increasing repression, continuing environmental destruction, and the ongoing systematic undermining of the culture and identity of Tibet. Yet I believe that no matter how big and powerful China may be, she is still part of the world. The global trend today is towards more openness, freedom, democracy, and respect for human rights. Sooner or later China will have to follow the world trend, and in the long run, there is no way that China can escape from truth, justice, and freedom. Since the Tibetan issue is closely related with what is happening in China, I believe there is reason and ground for hope.

Again a very dire prospect bravely faced, and again a call to the seemingly remote and imperially aloof leadership to recognize their connectedness to the Tibetan reality and to the world. He will not give up hope. He hints at his spiritual perception of the Chinese leaders as his long-lost relatives. They talk about being a "motherland" and Tibetans "returning to the motherland," while their treatment of Tibetans is anything but respectful. But the Dalai Lama actually meditates upon all of them as having been his dearly beloved mother in previous lives, and calls them to come back to true motherly affection toward him and his people.

The consistent and principled engagement of the European Parliament with China will accelerate this process of change that is already taking place in China. I would like to thank the European Parliament for the consistent display of concern and support for the nonviolent Tibetan freedom struggle. Your sympathy and support have always been a deep source of inspiration and encouragement to the Tibetan people both inside and outside Tibet. The numerous resolutions of the European Parliament on the issue of Tibet helped greatly to highlight the plight of the Tibetan people and raise the awareness of the public and governments in Europe and around the world of the issue of Tibet. I am especially encouraged by the European Parliament's resolution calling for the appointment of an EU special representative for Tibet. I strongly believe that the implementation of this resolution will enable the European Union not only to help promote a peaceful resolution of the Tibetan issue through negotiations in a more consistent, effective, and creative way, but also provide support for other legitimate needs of the Tibetan people, including ways and means to preserve our distinct identity. This initiative will also send a strong signal to Beijing that the European Union is serious in encouraging and promoting a solution for the Tibetan problem. I have no doubt that your continued expressions of concern and support for Tibet will in the long run impact positively and help create the conducive political environment for a constructive dialogue on the issue of Tibet. I ask for your continued support in this critical time in our country's history. I thank you for providing me the opportunity to share my thoughts with you. Thank you.

In response to this talk, the European Parliament set a deadline for China to begin meaningful dialogue with the Dalai Lama's representatives of the Tibetan Government in Exile. If these did not take place before the Dalai Lama's birthday (July 6) in 2003, they said that they would appoint a special coordinator in charge of monitoring the Tibetan issue. In early spring 2003, the People's Republic of China informally invited two representatives of the Dalai Lama to begin a series of informal meetings in Beijing, thus forestalling the European Parliament's promised action of instituting such a special coordinator.

At the time of the brutal crackdown by the Chinese authorities in March 2008, six rounds of such talks had been held, the last one ending inconclusively, even negatively. During these talks, the People's Republic of China government denied there were substantial negotiations going on and refused to recognize any such entity as the Tibetan Government in Exile in Dharamsala. Nevertheless, the exile government took many steps in connection with the worldwide Tibet support movement to make goodwill gestures toward the Chinese government, such as seeking to mute protests when People's Republic of China leaders traveled to foreign capitals. On their part, the People's Republic of China made no such goodwill gestures and instead took aggressive steps, such as installing super hard-liners to administrate Tibet, intensifying its anti–Dalai Lama campaign in Tibet, persecuting Tibetan monks and nuns, demolishing centers of learning, pursuing the Dalai Lama during his travels and teachings, and pressuring governments not to grant him visas.

The most recent assaults have been in Nepal and India, where the Nepalese government in the midst of its own constitutional crisis has been forced to persecute Tibetan refugees settled there, turning back new ones from escaping across the border—as a few thousand leave for exile every year in spite of the journey's tremendous hardships and dangers—and even blocking the American government from its humanitarian plan to accept five thousand unsettled Tibetan refugees. And the Indian government was bluntly told last year by the People's Republic of China's foreign minister that, if India wanted to be a friend of China, it would expel the Dalai Lama and all Tibetan refugees, many of whom have been born in India and have lived there for half a century.

While the oceanic Dalai Lama has been increasingly successful in achieving recognition of his people's tragedy and of his own eminence as a world teacher, the People's Republic of China's increasingly unmovable hard-line stance has caused great discouragement among Tibetans and their friends. The frustrations of Tibetans living in Tibet have built to a boiling point that occasionally erupts into violence, as occurred in Lhasa and elsewhere in Tibet and China in March 2008, in the run-up to the 2008 Olympics.

And that is why I have written this book. It is important for people on all sides to see the reasons why the Dalai Lama's nonviolent dialogic approach can succeed. In the next part we'll shift the focus to action steps that Chinese President Hu Jintao can make to help solve the China-Tibet problem in a way that satisfies both cultures.

PART II

THE SOLUTION FOR
CHINA AND TIBET

4

A MIDDLE WAY FOR CHINA AND TIBET

China's current president, Hu Jintao, is a central figure in Tibet's efforts to achieve autonomy. He holds immense power in the situation and also has a lot to gain by handling it to his advantage. This chapter speaks to the role he and the Chinese leadership could have, which the Dalai Lama outlined in an essay he wrote for the *Economist* in 2007. If President Hu is unwilling or unable to take advantage of this earthshaking opportunity, then whoever is his successor may be the one who joins Mao and Deng as a truly pivotal figure for China and joins the Dalai Lama, Jimmy Carter, Mikhail Gorbachev, Desmond Tutu, and Nelson Mandela as a planetary hero.

Few people know that President Hu Jintao was in charge of Tibet 1988–89, though he did not live there, as he had difficulty coping with the 12,000-foot altitude of Lhasa. He personally imposed the policy of so-called "merciless repression" on Tibetan demonstrators. He thereby no doubt attracted the favorable attention of the then supreme leader, Deng Xiaoping. The determination to be tough and hard-line on Tibet was a quality of cardinal importance for Deng in considering his successors in Jiang Zemin and Li Peng, and apparently still played a role in their passing things on to Hu Jintao. Holding on tightly to Tibet was a vital matter for Deng, who was himself from Sichuan province (part of which comprises most of the Kham province of Great Tibet), was the mastermind of the campaign to conquer Tibet, and considered its acquisition one of his greatest achievements.

So Hu Jintao was a loyalist to Deng's line by being tough on Tibet, which might not appear to bode well for Tibet's efforts to achieve autonomy. On the other hand, this very toughness of Hu in previous dealings on Tibet could be a source of hope. Just as it was the fervent anti-communist Richard Nixon who was able to open relations with Mao's Communist China, so it might only be the established hard-liner Hu who today could change China's unrealistic and self-defeating hard-line policy on Tibet.

At least President Hu has a firsthand idea of the toughness and resilience of the Tibetan people and should realize that no amount of oppression will destroy their sense of Tibetan-ness and dedication to Buddhism and the Dalai Lamas (including the decades-in-the-future Fifteenth Dalai Lama, whoever he or she will be). Since Hu himself could not adapt to Tibet's altitude, he might also realize that the population transfer, or genocidal strategy of submerging the Tibetan race in a sea of Chinese colonists, may not work on the Tibetan plateau because the lack of oxygen at that altitude will prevent hordes of Chinese settlers from developing a long-term livelihood there.

The year 2008 was a critical year for China. In particular, the Beijing Olympics, with their fantastic price tag of up to $40 billion, put China in the world's spotlight—though that amount of money is a drop in the bucket compared to the 1.4-trillion-dollar sovereign fund amassed from the country's huge trade surplus with the United States. With all the attention focused on Beijing for the Summer Games,

China was also given a unique opportunity to show the world its leadership abilities and humanity by dealing justly with Tibet.

As a backbone and preface for the recommendations I offer President Hu and his colleagues in the next chapter, I'd like to quote and discuss the Dalai Lama's recent essay of advice to the Chinese leadership, which he presented in the "World in 2008" issue of the *Economist*, Special Section on China.

In 2008, Be Nicer to Your Neighbors

From *The World in 2008* print edition of the *Economist* Reuters

As we face the challenge of ever-expanding populations, increasing demands for energy and food, as well as huge disparities in wealth, we have to embrace globalization and accept people from all countries as neighbors and collaborators, not rivals. In this interdependent world, war is outdated. Destroying other countries brings no benefit, but creates humanitarian suffering, trade disruption, and environmental problems that everyone must bear.

Not mincing words, instinctively adopting his prophetic role, the Dalai Lama says that the time for international conflict and superpower rivalry has passed. It is no longer sustainable, there are no victors, and it is merely self-defeating. The Dalai Lama here generally impugns the actions of many governments—the United States in Iraq, Israel in Palestine, Russia in Chechnya, Sudan in Darfur, and of course China in Tibet. He is in a prophetic role here, by which I mean in the tradition of the Hebrew prophets, who were less concerned to predict the future than to challenge the moral laxity and corruption of the rulers and high priests of the day. Once, shortly after he had written *Ethics for the New Millennium*, which I really liked, I asked the Dalai Lama, "Well now, is Your Holiness ready to become a prophet to the world, speaking truth to power and calling unethical leaders to account?" He laughed, and replied with an amused but emphatic, "No!" So I admit I am nudging him into this role.

His last sentence here concords perfectly with the brilliant analysis of Jonathan Schell's *The Unconquerable World*. War is no longer an effective method of achieving any goal today, since postmodern war is not as much a contest between armies and soldiers as it is an assault on whole civilian populations. Therefore, a war made on a country, even if it purports to target the leader or ruling clique, ends up destroying the country's infrastructure and its civilian families, and so stirs up hatred and desire for vengeance. Since the main purpose of war, according to the military philosopher Carl von Clausewitz, is to get the people of your enemy nation to bend to your will after you have defeated their armies in the field, any true victory in war today is impossible to achieve. The people have become so destroyed and embittered they will not bend to the conqueror's will but will endlessly resist. Therefore, war is obsolete. It is ethically bad, bad for business, and bad for the planet.

In 2008 there will be efforts to put an end to ongoing violent conflict in several parts of the world. The drive to achieve economic growth will also go on, while awareness of the perils of climate change and the need to protect ourselves from its unpredictable effects will become more acute. This will surely focus attention on the powerless and dispossessed, who will be the first to suffer and the least able to help themselves.

He is assigned here by the *Economist* in its crystal ball issue to engage in some predictions for the year, so he does make that effort, presenting some broad guesses based on common sense. He can safely predict effort to end violence everywhere, since violence is so destructive and costly, the intensification of economic striving, and the growth of awareness of the environmental crisis. The Dalai Lama shows his compassionate awareness of the miserable reality faced by the powerless and dispossessed of this world; this is the meaning of *Avalokita*, "the looking down compassionately on the suffering," of "a God," *Ishvara* (as opposed, I imagine, to a God who floats above, aloof in his own freedom and bliss). Skeptics who think the pressures for victory, prosperity, and environmental security will crowd out any concern for the dispossessed might reflect on how generously people gave assistance at the time of the Indian Ocean tsunami.

> *People need goods and services to meet the essential requirements of existence, not to mention those things that bring dignity and comfort to human life. Yet for all the innovation and creativity of our economic activity, we have not succeeded in securing these essentials for all human beings. The yawning gap between the "haves" and "have-nots" is going to create a great deal of suffering for everyone.*

The Dalai Lama once said to me as we rode in a limo back to his elegant hotel after a reception for wealthy patrons, through the better neighborhood of a city where he was teaching, "The concentration of wealth in the very rich is so huge, nowadays, even in China, and there is such poverty everywhere, what can be done? Last century there were revolutions and they took it all away from the very rich people, but it didn't do any good! The new leaders started to behave the same way, and maybe it got even worse. What can be done?" I remember saying what he himself would often teach in his Buddhist teacher mode: "Generosity! They should think of giving a lot of it away where it will do the most good!" But both of us in that moment felt that such a thought might be unrealistic, to judge from what is actually going on.

> *We watch, hear, and read every day about breathtaking manifestations of affluence alongside deaths due to starvation, poverty, malnutrition, and preventable or curable diseases. Shouldn't we ask ourselves whether something is wrong with our choice of goals or our motivation, or both? I believe we have to find ways of bringing compassion to bear in our economic activity.*

I am happy to say that people influenced by the Dalai Lama and other spiritual leaders are beginning to do this. Many movements among the wealthy are emerging to help the poor, from the high-profile acts of generosity by Bill and Melinda Gates and Warren Buffett to the philanthropic activities of Marc Benioff and the Salesforce.com Foundation, to the efforts of many US companies, such as the Google Foundation. The Chinese premier, Wen Jiabao, has on many occasions expressed concern for the excessive rich-poor divide in China and has been taking some preliminary steps to improve the situation.

> *Compassion and love are fundamental to relations between human beings. Therefore the interdependent society in which we live has to be a compassionate one, compassionate in its choice of goals, and compassionate in the pursuit of those goals.*

Who can argue with this? It springs from the Dalai Lama's perception of human mammalian biology: a being grows within its mother's body, the mother must allow that being to occupy her body, and in the first years of life, the being is utterly helpless and completely dependent on the kindness of others. *Compassion* for the Dalai Lama means "the wish that others do not suffer based on the sensitivity to their suffering." *Love* means "the wish for others to be happy," and loving someone means wanting them to be happy. Clearly for him, the ends do not justify the means, but rather the means must correspond to the ends. Society's goal is to minimize suffering for all and to maximize happiness, and the means to that goal should be chosen in such a way that suffering is diminished and happiness increased along the way.

This is where the Dalai Lama parted ways with Marxism, which has sometimes been attractive to Buddhists with its ideas of sharing and equality of classes, since generosity and empathy are cardinal virtues. But Karl Marx felt violence was justified in achieving the communist utopian future, and Vladimir Lenin and Mao took this even further; this was the fatal flaw that led to the many deaths caused by the Russian, Chinese, and Cambodian communist leaders. Although Buddhist ethical thought is pragmatic and contains a concept of exceptional, surgical violence, the Dalai Lama chooses not to compromise on the necessity of nonviolence.

Tibetans love their own culture and their way of life, but Chinese officials regard their urge to preserve their identity as a threat to the unity of China.

He explains that at the core of China's problem with Tibet, is fear. Why are the Chinese so afraid of the Tibetans' sense of identity and love of their culture? The answer is simple: *because the Chinese know full well that the Tibetans are not Chinese!* The Chinese leadership knows this historically and any Chinese people who have met any Tibetan people instantly know it in their bones. This fact conclusively contradicts the Chinese official claim that Tibet is an inalienable part of China. It is now conquered and occupied by Chinese troops, officials, and colonists, and it looks like it would be hard to get them out. But before 1950 there were virtually no Chinese people on the Tibetan plateau.

When we focus only on our own requirements and disregard the needs and interests of others, we are likely to provoke hostility. This is especially true when we view our own happiness and needs predominantly in terms of material wealth and power. All human beings yearn for freedom, equality, and dignity, and have a right to achieve them. Therefore, in today's shrinking world the acceptance of universally binding standards of human rights is essential.

The Dalai Lama is not focusing only on his own requirements. He is considering the needs and interests of the Chinese as well by seeking to free his people and country without any threats or violence. He is unprecedented, seeking to liberate his people by having them give themselves away to their oppressors! Essentially he is saying, "We are really free people of an independent country. You have invaded us and taken our country, but you cannot relax since you know the world will not agree with such aggression, and you cannot forgive us for not being yours, really. So what we propose is that we relieve you of this anxiety and strain by voluntarily joining in union with you. Then you need not worry that anyone could take us away from you again. But in order for that to be legitimate, you must liberate us internally in our own land, so that our joining will truly be voluntary! We have to be allowed to be ourselves to join with you of our own free will. And then we can live together in one real union, and you won't need to worry that we are ourselves, different from you—in fact, our difference will enrich you as your difference will enrich us!"

If the Chinese step back, begin to withdraw their colonists, remove their internal military, and allow real internal autonomy to the whole of Great Tibet, the Tibetans cannot fail to recognize that as an enormous achievement of the Dalai Lama, and an earthshaking gift by the Chinese. Then, the Tibetans will feel free, confirmed in the essential independence they always have had and always will have. They will begin to reflect on where they should invest it, where they should connect themselves. They can see that China can emerge as the most prosperous and stable power in the world, especially if it does not imitate the others and embark on world conquest. China's change of policy on Tibet would make the uncontestable statement that they do not intend such an atavistic approach to a world centrality that would naturally and effortlessly become theirs. So then, China would become the natural choice for union. Of course, Tibet would be free to connect nonpolitically with all its other neighbors, which it would certainly do. Tibet would become an integral connecter for the Chinese union, serving as a bridge to India and Mongolia, in particular, and to any other neighboring countries.

I do not see any contradiction between the need for economic development and the need to respect human rights. The right to free speech and association is vital in promoting a country's economic development. In Tibet, for example, there have been instances where unsuitable economic policies have been implemented and continued long after they have failed to produce benefits, because citizens and government officials could not speak out against them. And it is the same elsewhere.

This is very understated. Almost half of the estimated 1.2 million Tibetans who have died unnaturally due to the Chinese occupation died because of forced agricultural practices unsuited to the environment, such as the attempt to grow wheat on the high plateau, which leached out the delicate soil and made for several years of failed harvests and a nationwide famine.

The Dalai Lama titles the next section of his piece "A middle way for Tibet." Buddhists love middle ways, centrist positions. The middle way he proposes is midway between demanding absolute political independence on the one hand and, on the other, surrendering to all the pretend unrealities, repeating the lie that Tibet has always been part of China, abandoning his people and their culture, and urging his people just to give up and to assimilate themselves to becoming as Chinese as possible.

We praise diversity in theory, but too often fail to respect it in practice. If someone is different from us, we are inclined to interpret the difference in negative terms and perceive it as threatening. The Chinese government's attitude to the people of Tibet is a case in point. Naturally Tibetans love their own culture and their way of life as best suited to their distinct environment and situation, but whenever they show active interest, respect, or faith in it, Chinese officials regard their urge to preserve their identity as a threat to the unity of China. Such an inability to embrace diversity is a major source of dissatisfaction that can give rise to conflict.

The distinctiveness of the Tibetan identity need not mean that Tibetans could not be excellent citizens of a Chinese federation, just as a Massachusetts person who is a Red Sox fanatic and is in love with his Bay State can be a perfectly loyal US citizen. On the contrary, when the Chinese majority tries to remake a Tibetan into a secondhand Chinese, especially using force to try to do so, it only increases the Tibetan sense of estrangement from the Chinese. I remember the Dalai Lama once making a joke that it is like someone beating a person and saying, "You've got to love me!" Whack! "You have to love me!" Whack! This, of course, is ridiculous.

The Chinese leadership places great emphasis on harmony: an excellent goal. But in order to achieve it, there must be trust. Trust flows from equality and

compassion. Suspicion creates restraint and is an obstacle to trust. Without trust,
how can you develop genuine unity or harmony?

Harmony does not mean playing only one note. All voices and instruments forced to stick to one note cannot be harmonious, cannot be music—it is nothing but a drone. For there to be harmony, there must be different notes that blend in thirds or fifths and move in and out of dissonance to accent the sweetness of harmonious resonance at the right intervals. Trust comes from realizing the partner players also want harmony and not discord; one allows them to play freely so they can find the magic third of harmony. The Dalai Lama is urging President Hu and his colleagues not to create self-fulfilling paranoid prophecies by being suspicious of the Tibetans' intentions. The Tibetans have suffered and are upset, no doubt. But they are mainly spiritual people, relatively jolly by nature, and their amazing culture is based on the Buddhist enlightenment insight that vengeance is self-destructive, that true happiness comes from forgiveness and reconciliation. And this lesson is not only for China and Tibet. It is for all those nations and groups pitted in endless cycles of fruitless tit for tat. The United States and Russia, Pakistan and India, Israel and Palestine, Turks and Kurds, Azeris and Armenians, Sunni and Shia, blacks and whites—the litany is familiar to all.

I believe we can find a way for both Chinese and Tibetans to live together with
dignity, freedom, and in the spirit of good neighborliness. I am convinced that
we can achieve a middle way, if we engage in a process that respects our differ-
ences and acknowledges that we have the ability and the means to solve our
problems and help each other.

The middle way is of course the middle between the extremes of either totally absorbing Tibetans into the Chinese body by eradicating Tibetan culture and any sense of difference of personal, radical, religious, linguistic, and cultural identity, or breaking Tibet free from China altogether, returning to its age-old independent status all alone on the

Roof of the World. That middle way is to develop the plan for allowing the Tibetans to rule themselves in their own land while preserving and developing their land and society as they wish, with the help of China, and joining voluntarily in a Chinese union, in parallel with Hong Kong and eventually Taiwan.

In this light, it is interesting that the current UN Secretary General Ban Ki-moon espouses a dream of seeing all the nations of Asia joining together in an Asian Union and Asian common market, following the example of the EU and common market. China's natural leadership in such a mutually beneficial union would be cemented by its showing creativity in solving the problem of functional unity in the midst of diversity, by coming to a mutually acceptable arrangement with Tibet along the lines suggested by the Dalai Lama. As long as China does not step up to that opportunity, the country's efforts to achieve respect by measures such as hosting the Olympic Games will be overshadowed by its harsh behavior against human rights and freedom of speech and assembly, its suppression of ethnic and religious diversity, its harsh treatment of its neighbors and its own lower classes, and their disregard of the environment.

> In 2008 close attention will be focused on China as it hosts the Olympic Games. I feel strongly that as the world's most populous nation, with its long history and ancient civilization, China deserves this privilege and honor. However, we must not forget that the Olympics are a free, fair, and open contest in which athletes of all recognized nations, no matter how small, are welcome to compete on an equal footing. Freedom, fairness, openness, and equality are not only the principles enshrined in the Olympic games but among the highest human values, a measure against which all nations should be held to account.

Some feel the Dalai Lama should have joined the Falun Gong movement, the Burmese supporters, the Uighur supporters, and others in calling for a full boycott of the Beijing Olympics. Instead, he stated repeatedly—even in the face of the brutal Chinese response to the mostly peaceful protests in Tibet in the spring of 2008—that the Games are a force for peace and reconciliation in the world, and therefore, should go on. Pointing out how hard thousands of athletes from around the globe had trained over many years for their events, he offered his support, reiterating that they should not be penalized by a boycott of the competitions themselves. He did, however, state his support for the plans of some world leaders to refrain from attending the opening ceremonies if the Chinese government persisted in suppressing the Tibetans and refusing to meet with him in constructive dialog.

His characteristically Middle Way response has been unwavering with regard to the 2008 Olympics. From the beginning, he offered congratulations to the Chinese for their good fortune in being chosen to host the games and wished them well in the result. On that same positive basis, he continues to call upon the leadership to rein in the tendency to fear the people and suppress their freedoms.

The Dalai Lama's friendly warning to the Chinese leaders expresses a sentiment shared by many. Some observers suggested from the start that, while the Olympics would have been an incredible opportunity for China to boost its global image, things could easily go the other way. At the time of this writing, protests at the lighting of the torch ceremony in Greece and along the torch's route around the world are evidence that those being oppressed by the People's Republic of China will use the intense global publicity to advance their causes and embarrass the Chinese hosts. As one journalist opined, "All the great global PR will be ruined with the first truncheon blow on an unarmed protestor." Unfortunately, that sad day occurred early, when China's heavy-handed response to the March 10th inspired demonstrations in Lhasa and elsewhere resulted in the deaths of over one hundred unarmed Tibetans, many of them Buddhist monks.

Still, it is the Dalai Lama's hope, and many other people's, that China will yet use its opportunity in the world's spotlight to reverse its dismal track record on human rights and freedom, and instead set an example of humaneness, nonviolence, and ethical fairness.

Figure I. This is a satellite relief map of the vast Tibetan plateau—average altitude of 14,000 feet (3,400 meters)—the natural homeland of the six million Tibetan people. Tibetans are genetically acclimated to breathing half the oxygen the rest of us need. No lowland people ever even tried to live there long-term until the Chinese invaded Tibet and began to occupy it in 1949.

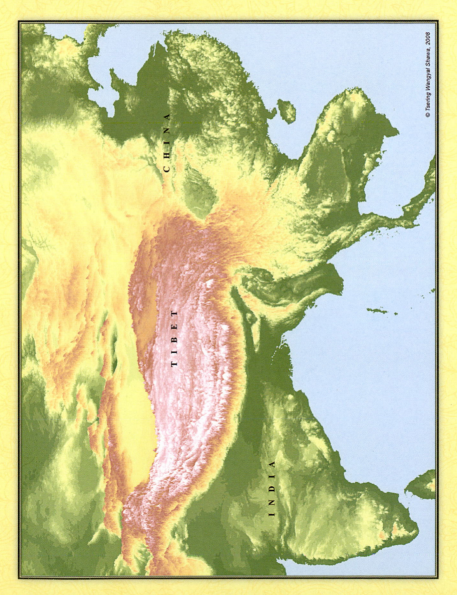

A

Figure 2. This ethnic map of Tibet as it was before the occupation—painted by a Tibetan artist in exile—depicts the traditional costumes of the people of each region and the distribution of wildlife in forests, grasslands, mountains, and deserts, when the land was pristine and the culture intact. Mythic guardians float in the skies, and a lama procession

of religious dancers descends the northwest boundary. Along the bottom (L–R), farmers plow with yaks, nomads travel, nobles picnic in an elegant tent. Some of Tibet's beautiful birds perch on a tree. In the lower center, the Potala Palace rises above Lhasa, and a few of the thousands of monasteries are scattered about the land.

Figure 3. The Tibet Autonomous Region (TAR) with the eleven Tibet Autonomous Prefectures (TAPs—where two thirds of the Tibetans live). The TAPs were divided off from the natural homeland by the Chinese in the 1950s, to create Outer Tibet and Inner Tibet. Reuniting the TAR and TAPs by the stroke of a pen, the Tibetan homeland becomes intact once again. To give a sense of scale, Lhasa to Beijing as the crow flies is 2,000 miles (3,219 kilometers).

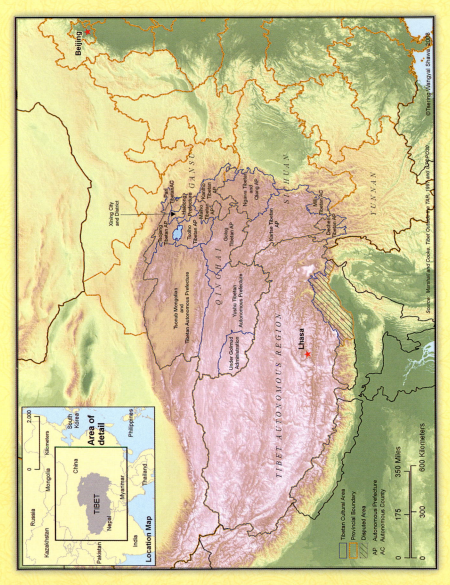

D

Figure 4. This satellite map shows the coincidence of the 13,000-plus-foot (3,000-plus-meter) altitude area and the Tibetan ethnic homeland. The extent of the Chinese deforestation of southeastern Tibet is demonstrated by the dramatic lack of dark green within the boundary; the forest of fifty years ago would appear like the dark green forest of Burma today. The great Asian river headwaters are also visible.

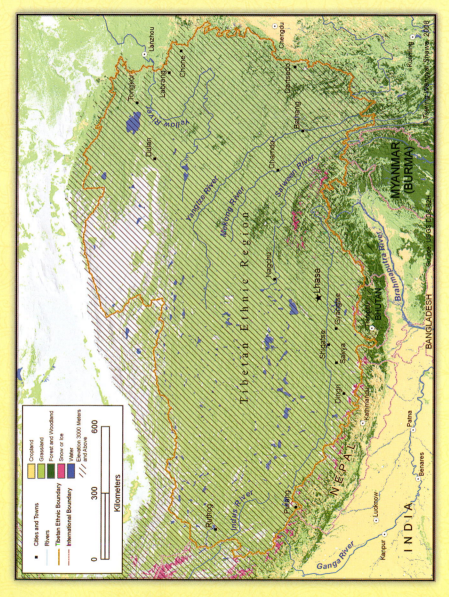

Figure 5. The smiling face of His Holiness the Dalai Lama brings a smile to the face of whoever sees it. Dr. Paul Ekman, the world authority on emotion revealed in facial expression, was unable to find the slightest trace of artificiality in the Dalai Lama's smile.

Figure 6. The Dalai Lama wears the yellow pandit hat (professor's hat used in the ancient Indian and modern Tibetan monastic universities) while reading prayers from a Western printed book during a formal teaching ceremony. It is the same kind of hat Lama Tsong Khapa wore when he founded the great monastic universities of Lhasa in the early fifteenth century, at the start of the Tibetan Renaissance.

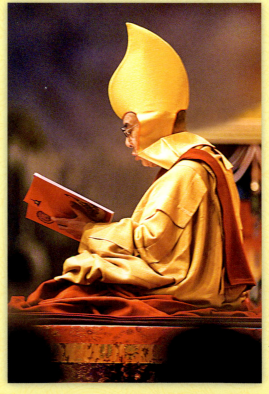

© Rajiv Mehrotra

Figure 7. His Holiness the Dalai Lama receiving the Nobel Peace Prize medal and diploma from Dr. Jakob Sverdrup in Oslo on December 10, 1989.

© Don Farber

Figure 8. The Dalai Lama showing the audience the Congressional Gold Medal awarded to him, October 17, 2007, at the Capitol Rotunda in Washington, DC, with (L–R) First Lady Laura Bush, an officer, Speaker Nancy Pelosi, Senator Robert Byrd, and President George W. Bush.

Figure 9. (Left) The Dalai Lama in discussion with the author in Bodh Gaya in 1980, preparing outlines for the first Inner (Mind) Science Conference, held later at Amherst College, as announced on the poster shown. (Below) The Dalai Lama and the author in a relaxed moment among friends during a visit to the United States in 2006. He is laughing at the way the cloth-wrapped Tibetan book peeks out of the author's jacket pocket.

Figure 10. A Tibetan pilgrim from northern Tibet resting and turning his *Om Mani Padme Hum* prayer wheel, while the tea water boils over his dried yak-dung cooking fire. He is on his way to Mount Kailash in southwestern Tibet, a sacred place to the Chakrasamvara Superbliss form of Buddha and the great Tibetan yogin, Milarepa (1040–1123).

Figure 11. In eastern Tibet (in the Ngaba TAP), a young nomad woman smiles as she churns her butter at the front door of her yak-felt tent, pitched high in the mountains near her summer pastures.

Figure 12. A Tibetan grandmother has her young charges share some bowls of noodles on the front step of a Tibetan tea shop in the poor Tibetan section of Lhasa.

Figure 13. A Tibetan girl in a group of village dancers shyly holds up a probably required picture of a young Mao Zedong in military uniform.

Figure 14. A sign advertises the construction of a tourist hotel in Lhasa, replacing rundown Tibetan houses in front of a Buddhist temple rebuilt in the 1980s.

Figure 15. A MIG fighter plane parked in front of the Potala symbolizes the conquest of Tibet. Popular pictures are shot of Chinese tourists sitting in the cockpit against the palace backdrop.

Figure 16. Chinese officials and tourists in Lhasa photograph each other sitting atop a yak, wearing Western style suits, while the Tibetan yak herder in traditional *chuba* robe looks on patiently.

Figure 17. (Clockwise from upper left) Filling the teapot from a frozen stream, Brahmaputra headwaters, western Tibet; an endangered black-necked crane (Tibetan *Trung-trung*) silhouetted against Shishapangma mountain (26,289 feet) in western Tibet; endangered snow leopard in southern Tibet; Tibetan blue bharal wild sheep in the Rongbuk Valley below Qhomolangma (Mount Everest); Tibetan owl (Tibetan *Ookpa*) on the Nangpa Pass, near Dingri, southern Tibet; endangered panda in southeastern Tibet; yellow poppy blooming in the Amnye Machen Range, northeastern Tibet.

M

Figure 18. Giant appliqué *tangka* icon of Shakyamuni Buddha, displayed on special occasion above Drepung Monastery. Tibetans create such huge images to commemorate legendary festival times when whole communities reported they all beheld visions of buddhas and deities in the sky.

Figure 19. A Tibetan nomad pilgrim in western Tibet prays before a pile of scattered *mani* stones, stones inscribed with Buddhist prayers and traditionally neatly stacked in sacred walls.

N

Photograph courtesy of SacredSites.com

Figure 20. (Above) Mount Kailash (22,027 ft.) in western Tibet, a remote site sacred to billions of members of four religions. (Below) Pilgrimage by full prostration around Mount Kailash.

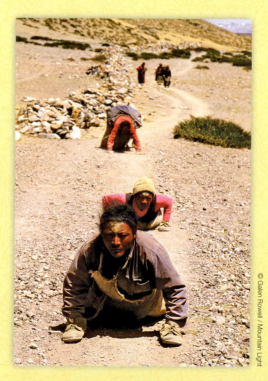

© Galen Rowell / Mountain Light

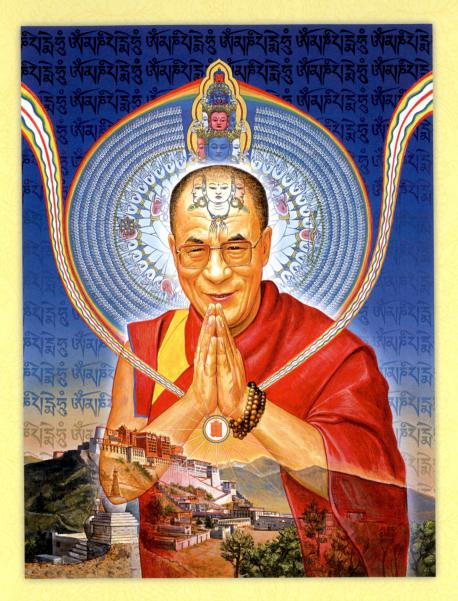

Figure 21. Artist Alex Grey's vision of the Dalai Lama as the incarnation of Avalokiteshvara, shown in his eleven-faced, thousand-armed form, at home before Lhasa's Potala Palace. He stands under a sky filled with mantras, with rainbow rays of light for world peace emanating from his heart in the future Tibet, finally released by an enlightened Chinese leadership.

Additional maps and images available at www.DalaiLamaMatters.com.

P

5

A Plan for President Hu and the Dalai Lama

The President and the Lama Each Takes Five Steps

Here now, in this moment of crisis and great opportunity, after "seeking truth from facts," from intelligent recognition of these dangerous trends and amazing opportunities, President Hu Jintao can take a breathtaking stand. He can make history for China, for himself, and for the world by taking five courageous and really simple steps, which we'll explore in this chapter.

For China, he can truly and uncontestably achieve the international respect his government seeks through its long-term fifty-billion-dollar-effort to host the Olympic Games, but will fail to achieve if it continues to support repression in Tibet, Xinjiang, Mongolia, Hong Kong, Taiwan, North Korea, Burma, and Sudan; irresponsible resource extraction in Indonesia, Africa, South America, Canada, Siberia, and elsewhere around the world; and uncontrolled polluting industrial practices at home in the frantic race to gain wealth supremacy and super power status. Tibet is where China can begin to reverse field.

For himself, he can obtain the Nobel Peace Prize in the international arena, and nationally and historically, he can realize a stature as supreme leader greater than Mao or Deng or Jiang, gaining the legitimate acquisition of Tibet and virtually solving the Taiwan problem.[1]

For the world, he can set an example of an ethical policy that would give a moral authority to China that could eclipse what was once enjoyed by the United States from its victory over fascism in World War II and its generous rebuilding of Europe and Japan by the Marshall Plan. This could inspire Russia and the United States to follow suit, and the real promise of the twenty-first century would become attainable by the world's major powers working together cooperatively on the world community's real objectives: preventing global warming, stopping overpopulation, preserving resources, minimizing the gap between the rich and poor, and avoiding war.

President Hu can please China's one billion Buddhists by following the example of the ancient Indian Mauryan Emperor Ashoka, the great reforming Emperor Wudi of the Han Dynasty of China, and many other visionary leaders. They are all fondly remembered for their breakthrough achievements that succeeded by abandoning the errors of preceding rulers. With his politburo lined up behind him, he can proclaim himself no longer bound to follow his predecessors' erroneous and ineffective policies, while still acknowledging his debt to them for their positive contributions. In China's effort to recover from centuries of imperialistic oppression, previous leaders did some things that in fact imitated the behavior of the imperialists. This is why many nations still fear and dislike China and why China cannot reach the height of glory it deserves.

So he, President Hu Jintao, can make a change. This change is not a loss of face or surrender of any sort of prestige, as weaker leaders always fear may be the case if they change an ineffective policy in favor of a new approach. For example, Deng Xiaoping in his good days changed the failed policies of Mao and made a complete about-face to embrace state capitalism and the rational quest of wealth while beginning the process of modernizing China's economy. This was not a loss of face for Deng, but his greatest source of fame and honor. (When Deng grew older and implemented the crackdown on the student protesters in 1989, he lost that good face dramatically, and eventually history will judge him harshly for that action.)

Of course to take this dramatic step, President Hu needs first to assure himself of the support of his colleagues in the politburo, and together they must bring the People's Liberation Army generals into conformity with the new policies and campaigns. Understandably, this is not so easy, but it is within President Hu's ability at this moment in time.

Thus, with all these considerations in mind and prerequisite conditions at hand, President Hu can proclaim his determination to solve the problem of Tibet. He would be able to enlist the goodwill of the Tibetan people at last and remove all the issues surrounding Tibet as major irritants that spoil China's good relations with the world. He can wake up to the truth that the old policy of suppressing the Tibetan people is not working and realize that the Dalai Lama is not a bad person. If the relationship is mended, the Dalai Lama can become an enormous asset for China.

A FIVE-STEP PLAN FOR CHINA'S SUCCESS

The Dalai Lama is the key, since President Hu can easily, ethically, and economically secure his friendship and the Dalai Lama can easily realize China's most important goals. Tibet is the most easily solved of China's previously caused problems; a resolution can be effected swiftly by President Hu by taking the following five steps. Taking these five steps will, in terms of the great culture of ancient China, usher in the time of Great Tai, "Magnificent Peace," hexagram number 11 in the *I Ching* classic Chinese book of oracles.[2]

STEP 1: REINSTATE THE GREAT TIBET AS THE BÖD AUTONOMOUS REGION (BAR)

First of all, he issues an edict that designates all eleven of the Tibet Autonomous Prefectures (TAPs) in Qinghai, Gansu, Sichuan, and Yunnan provinces to be part of the Great Tibet Autonomous Region (TAR),[3] or more easily the Böd Autonomous Region (BAR), so that the whole population of the Tibetan Minority of China is unified under one administration, and decisions can be made that consider all of them. To accomplish this administrative reorganization, President Hu makes sure that the governors of these prefectures obey the edict, reassuring them that they can continue to serve within the new reporting structure. A three-year program is launched that will ensure that the minority area status of these regions is respected according to the People's Republic of China constitution, article 51, and that excessive Han Chinese in-migration is prevented or, if already present on the ground, reversed. It is unlikely that the current chief administrators of the TAR will be able to serve effectively in the new structure, since they have staked so much of their reputation on enmity with the Dalai Lama and have incurred the resentment of the Tibetan population, so it is likely they will have to be transferred to positions in the capital or in other provinces.

STEP 2: ESTABLISH A ONE-COUNTRY, TWO-SYSTEMS ARRANGEMENT

President Hu offers a One-Country, Two-Systems arrangement to the newly constituted enlarged BAR regional government, to be implemented over a period of several years. The arrangement is formalized by a working commission based on the Democratic Constitution of the Tibetan Government in Exile developed since the 1960s in exile, fitting it together with the constitution of the People's Republic of China.

The seventeen-point agreement between the People's Republic of China central government and the Tibetan Regional government of 1951 and the current system in place in Hong Kong serve as background for this new arrangement, the main points of which are set down in the proclamation President Hu prepares to cover the entire new plan. This arrangement made with the Tibetan minority nationality within the People's Republic of China Union is openly declared to serve as a model for similar arrangements to be made, each according to the special characteristics of each case, with the Uighur people of Xinjiang, the Mongolian people of Inner Mongolia, the Manchu people of Manchuria, and the Taiwanese and Chinese residents of Taiwan. Thus no one can protest the plan by saying that such an arrangement with Tibet becomes the first domino to fall that starts a cascade of similarly-minded dominos. The Tibet arrangement clearly aims to avoid the danger of losing Tibet and leads the way in uniting the peoples of the minority nationalities by fully respecting their diversities.

Step 3: Reassign Chinese Settlers and Soldiers

President Hu begins a gradual process of reassigning the majority of Han Chinese settlers in Tibet, including internal military personnel but not including temporary, environmentally responsible workers. This process is carefully planned and supervised in consultation with the existing regional government of the BAR, now augmented by inclusion of the administrations of the various TAPs of the provinces of Qinghai (almost the whole province), Gansu, Sichuan, and Yunnan. Under the People's Republic of China constitution minority provisions, this means that all Chinese colonization and resettlement must cease in those minority areas. This saves the People's Republic of China government huge sums of money currently wasted in unsustainable population transfer onto the high plateau. Some of that money can be spent on revitalizing the areas of China whence the settlers came, and some can be devoted to repairing Tibetan environmental and infrastructure damage.

President Hu reassigns all the People's Liberation Army (PLA) and People's Armed Police (PAP) units currently deployed and maintained within Tibet for the purpose of controlling the Tibetan population (another huge expense for the People's Republic of China government) back to their areas of origin, except for garrisons along the borders of Tibet, which can be kept indefinitely. There is a huge savings in the People's Republic of China military budget as a result of this redeployment. This may have to be gradual while Tibetan police are organized to take their place to maintain law and order. There will be no need for any Tibetan military, as Tibet is slated to become a demilitarized peace zone. But the Tibetan people will no longer have to fear internal military control exercised by Han Chinese authorities. All political prisoners and nonviolent criminals are released in a general amnesty.

STEP 4: MEND RELATIONS WITH THE DALAI LAMA

President Hu invites the Dalai Lama to Beijing for a formal presentation, where the two leaders co-sign a charter implementing the new policy. The event, totally transparent to international media, is attended by heads of state and foreign ministers of all major nations and the UN. The proclamation contains apologies to His Holiness the Dalai Lama for the recent persistence of negative rhetoric directed against him for years. He is presented officially with an honorary citizenship of the People's Republic of China, along with membership in various People's Republic of China governing bodies.

This will ideally take place while China is basking in the international media glow of the Games, hopefully unmarred by further human rights protests, which are no longer called for because of China's new, more humanitarian stance toward Tibet, Darfur and Burma. The Dalai Lama gives an internationally televised speech to thank the People's Republic of China leadership, greet the Chinese people, and usher in the new era in Asian history marked by this great turnaround. In attendance are appropriate officials from Taiwan, both the Koreas, and the whole ring of Asian neighbors. The Uighurs, the Mongolians, and the

Manchurians are recognized as the key minority nations that they are, and a similar process of self-determination and transnational union is promised to them as well in due course.

Step 5: Prioritize Environmental Issues

President Hu proclaims the creation of the largest environmental preserve in the world, essentially the whole of the new BAR. This step picks up on the current world focus on global cooling, shows China's good faith in making powerful efforts in the direction of environmental preservation, and follows on a number of large-scale environmental preservation actions already underway.

Five-Step Response from the Dalai Lama

In return for the seemingly extraordinary but actually only reasonable measures implemented by President Hu and the Chinese leadership, the Dalai Lama, on behalf of the Tibetan people, can reciprocate by taking the following five steps I envision for a peaceful future:

Step 1: Tour Tibet

During the autumn of whatever year, the Dalai Lama would come to Beijing and participates with President Hu and other Chinese leaders in the auspicious Great Tai signing ceremony in Tiananmen Square. The following year, once internal soldiers and most settlers have been reassigned, the Dalai Lama will tour Great Tibet—the newly designated BAR—in a triumphal procession that begins an ongoing dance of joyful celebration for the Tibetan people. He will be accompanied at key venues by President Hu Jintao and Premier Wen Jiabao or, if those two do not avail themselves of the opportunity, other People's Republic of China leaders. His message to the Tibetan people will be in celebration of the enlightened policy of the People's Republic of China, letting bygones be bygones, and the joyful facing of a new future of national self-determination within a truly harmonious and legitimate United States of China. A commitment can then be made to organize a vote, with international observers invited, allowing the ethnic Tibetan people of the newly reunited BAR to determine their own future. The Dalai Lama and all major Tibetan Buddhist and Bön Lamas and Tibetan Muslim Imams can pledge to campaign energetically for the Tibetan people to vote to join the Chinese Union under firm and realistic guarantees of true internal self-determination and autonomy. This vote cannot be considered fair and genuine until internal military is withdrawn, Chinese settlers have begun to move off the plateau into lowland China, and a full BAR regional government has been organized along the lines of the "One-Country, Two-Systems" principle.

STEP 2: REWARD THE CHINESE LEADERSHIP AND RESTORE THE TIBETAN CULTURE

The Dalai Lama and all his friends around the world nominate President Hu Jintao for a Nobel Peace Prize, perhaps to share with his colleagues in the politburo (as Al Gore, the 2007 recipient, shared it with the UN Intergovernmental Panel on Climate Changes). Even though this would not at all be President Hu's driving motive for his magnificent transformative act in solving the Tibet issue and, through it, most of China's nagging foreign policy issues, he would surely receive it. The Dalai Lama can re-establish his main residency in Lhasa at the Norbulingka, with occasional ceremonial occasions at the Potala and the Jokhang, and other official residences at the Yonghe Gong in Beijing and at Wu Tai Shan in Shansi. (His long-term exile home at Dharamsala would still be kept as a place of spiritual retreat and continued teachings to the people of India.) He's likely to preemptively abdicate all political roles in the Tibetan BAR government for his reincarnate successor, though when the Tibetan people vote for a new constitution and regional government structure, it is very possible they will vote to reinstate ongoing Dalai Lamas in at least ceremonial positions of leadership. The Panchen Lama designated by the People's Republic of China will join the Dalai Lama–designated Panchen

Lama (provided he is available) in sharing the leadership of the Tashi Lhunpo Monastery, if they so desired, or some other generous accommodation. A comprehensive plan for the rebirth of Tibetan culture in its liberated modern form will be developed.

Step 3: Increase National Unity and Spiritual Well-Being

The Dalai Lama tours China, giving initiations and teachings, attending meetings with Buddhist leaders, contributing to a rebirth of Chinese Buddhism, and participating with the development of Buddhist universities in the tradition of Great Nalanda University in India, all in the atmosphere of tolerance and patronage of Confucianism, Taoism, Christianity, Islam, and secular humanism. He will also visit other minority areas of China, especially the other three small stars on the People's Republic of China flag (Uighurs, Mongols, Manchus), and work to implement similar solutions to increase national unity and harmony among the minorities.

Step 4: Urge Tibetans to Join with China

The Dalai Lama will proclaim his goal that Tibet formally become part of China, providing his people agree in the vote. He invites Uighurs, Mongols, Manchus, and Taiwanese to voluntarily join the union as well, now that the fear of being forced to do so has been removed. He travels to Mongolia and Russia—including to Mongolian areas of Russia—this time to present China's goodwill and friendliness, rekindling Buddhist culture in those areas and promoting positive relations with China.

Step 5: Become a Goodwill Ambassador for China

The Dalai Lama's occasional service as a goodwill ambassador and special envoy of China, include traveling back and forth to India and effectively participating in a final negotiation to settle the China-India border disputes, resolving them so China and India can start a new level of friendship without the tension involved in these lingering disagreements. India might well decide to offer the Dalai Lama honorary citizenship. A demilitarization of the Himalayan frontier will save both governments huge sums of money, trans-Himalayan trade will greatly improve the economies of Tibet and the mountainous border regions of India, Nepal, and Bhutan. The resulting détente will go a long way in calming the Indo-Pakistani confrontation. Nalanda Buddhist University in India could hold a special dedication, and branches in Tibet and China will surely be initiated. The Dalai Lama will address the UN, presenting President Hu and his plan to make the Tibetan plateau an environmental preserve, effectively joining Al Gore by becoming China's Global Cooling Campaign leader to preserve Tibet's glaciers and China's river headwaters. The Dalai Lama can then visit the new American president with President Hu and would enlist the US government finally in the Global Cooling Campaign.

PUTTING TO REST LINGERING DOUBTS

Each of these two world leaders taking each of these five steps accomplishes the definitive solution to the Tibet problem and turns China away from its anachronistic path toward being an aggressive superpower and to its new path of inviting all its neighbors into a prosperous, stable, harmonious Asian Union or United States of Asia.

In fact, there is no good reason for them not to take these steps. Some might think that President Hu is having to do more, and so is unlikely to move. It is easier for the Dalai Lama, because he is in so much a worse situation and his people are suffering so much more. This is actually a misperception. True, President Hu seems to have much more worldly power. He has more money, military, manpower. But he is also under much more pressure. Maybe three hundred million party elite and burgeoning middle-class Chinese people are prospering materially at the moment, but there are also at least one billion hungry, angry, and dissatisfied people in his own country. He is feared and hated by anti-communist and anti-Chinese people all over the world. He is also constantly pressed by close associates, rivals, and envious competitors who would like nothing better than to see him fall and take his place. The Dalai Lama on the other hand is liked by almost everyone in the world. His own people adore him. He jokes that he is particularly loved by Tibetans in Tibet, since he has not had to govern them and so be associated with unpopular orders, but stands pristine as a symbol and spokesman seeking their liberation from the Chinese oppression. He is older than President Hu, but he has already made his mark in history and has global positive recognition. Even if he dies before President Hu, he can happily reincarnate and continue his work. President Hu does not believe in reincarnation, but in case there is some sort of continuity of consciousness anyway, when he also eventually passes away, no one will be there to help him—except perhaps his unexpected good friend, the Dalai Lama!

Similar doubts in both leaders' minds might be as follows: President Hu might worry that once the Tibetans are free of the presence of the Chinese military, are reunited in the restored BAR, and see crowds of Chinese colonists leaving the plateau, they will use the occasion of the free vote to declare their wish to be independent; China then could only reassert control with supreme embarrassment. The Dalai Lama might worry that once he is in Tibet within physical reach of the People's Republic of China government, they can simply imprison him in some comfortable but incommunicado location, pretend to allow autonomy as they already do on paper, hold a rigged vote, and show to the outside world a false result of Tibetans voting to remain as part of China.

In fact both negative outcomes are possibilities. Even if President Hu and the Dalai Lama do not give in to these fears and decide to trust each other, each of their follower camps might be full of people with such worries who might attempt to short circuit the successful execution of the plans. But trust should prevail for both sides. The Tibetans will still have the rail link with China and Chinese troops on their borders. They know that China, if hard-line elements feel they have been betrayed, could brush aside what they would characterize as an overly idealistic President Hu and reinvade Tibet without caring for the public image. However, Tibetans know that China is the most plausible partner for reconstruction of Tibet's environment, and they love Chinese cooking! Why would they vote dangerously for an insecure full independence from China, breaking the wishes of their beloved Dalai Lama? It is unthinkable. Similarly, why would China, spending tens of billions of dollars on the Olympic Games, seeking respect and cordial relations with a world ready to fear and fight them as they emerge as a superpower, miss the huge savings accruing to abandonment of a nonviable massive colonization of the highest region on earth, miss the opportunity of having the most popular man on earth as an ally and spokesperson, and miss having the president and his governing council receive a Nobel Peace Prize? It is also unthinkable.

And finally, both sides, as any parties to any treaty or international agreement, can imagine there might come a time or circumstance when they would go back on their intention. In a time of war or chaos, Tibetans might decide to try to break away under the protection of some other patron. The Chinese might decide they need to re-militarize Tibet in order to attack enemies in South Asia. The military-industrial system can have its last fling in a bang-up World War III. Anything can go wrong. The world can be imperfect. But for the moment, in the dawn of the twenty-first century, this Great Tai Magnificent Peace event is too good to pass up. It is too beneficial for too many, at too little a monetary cost, not to move forward.

But let's dig deeper and think still more about the reasons why people think this great solution cannot be accomplished and will never happen.

Some may say that President Hu will not do this because it would make him have to change his policy, it would make him seem weak, and he would lose face.

Nixon changed a lifelong anti-communist policy by visiting China, and it is his greatest legacy in an otherwise blemished career. Gorbachev changed policy and received a Nobel Peace Prize and began a process that is leading Russia toward real prosperity. Deng radically changed communist China's policy to capitalism with Chinese or socialist characteristics, and he is revered for that, and China has prospered mightily, with perhaps too much sacrifice of the health of the people and of the environment. Mandela changed the policy of the African National Congress from violence to nonviolence, and the process began by which apartheid was dismantled. So it's a sign of realism and efficiency to change policy when an old one is not working, and the courage shown is appreciated by everyone, even down through history.

These steps would not at all make President Hu seem weak. They would prove his strength. Among the many wrong things Winston Churchill said was the famous statement, "Democracy is the worst possible form of government—except for all the others." But the very best form of government is benevolent autocracy; that is, rule by one person who is intelligent, good-hearted, and able to do what's right. The reason we moved away from autocracy is, of course, that all too often malevolent persons become the autocrats, and malevolent autocracy is certainly the worst form of government. But when an autocrat gets the right idea about something, he or she can implement it easily, without major bureaucratic resistance and parliamentary delays and dilutions. President Hu ruled Tibet and declared martial law and enforced it harshly when he was younger. He cannot be accused of being soft on Tibetans. So when he says he knows the Tibetan spirit, he knows their will, he knows the harshness of the Tibetan environment, he is certain there is a better way to handle first the Tibetans and then all China's neighbors, he has to be believed. So when he puts his foot down and says, "I abandon the unworkable oppression policy and move to an open cooperation policy. I will turn this problem into an asset," the matter is settled.

Finally, concerning the matter of losing face, President Hu is certainly capable of adapting to a stressful situation by taking responsibility and making changes in himself and his attitudes.

Not only that, he could become an international superstar, empowered by the Dalai Lama's influence on him and personally boosted by being in league historically with other great innovators. He would certainly eclipse Jiang, equal Deng as a major innovator, and in the long run be considered far greater than Mao. If Mao would end up in the category of the Chin Shi Huangdi emperor, brutal founder of a dynasty that lasted less than two decades, Hu could be put in the category of the Emperor Wudi, key early emperor of the great Han dynasty that lasted four centuries. Hu would be hailed as the leader of China that brought it into the postmodern era as a responsible, moral, realistic, creative superpower, paralleling America in the role it once had as winner of WW II and subsequently defender of the free world.

Mao defended against the Japanese and drove out Chiang Kai-shek but deeply ruined his legacy by irresponsibly causing the deaths of tens of millions of his own and neighboring peoples. Deng liberalized the economy and negotiated back Hong Kong but also spoiled it all by engineering the Tiananmen crackdown and persisting in colonialist policies outside the Chinese heartland. Jiang presided over the return of Hong Kong and built up business, basically continuing Deng's work, but supported the Burmese generals and the North Korean dictator, made a mess of the Panchen Lama selection, and perpetrated atrocities on the Falun Gong members.

What kind of legacy will President Hu Jintao leave for history? By implementing the solution presented here for Tibet, Hu Jintao becomes the first Chinese to get the Nobel Peace Prize, settles Tibet favorably by acquiring it legitimately by the will of the Tibetan people, secured simply by treating them right, saves Burma, stops the genocide in Sudan, restores the relationship with Taiwan, brings China to a new level of twenty-first century world leadership, and begins to restore the environment.

If President Hu Jintao does not want this wonderful result, this glory will belong to the next supreme leader of China, the fifth since the founding of the People's Republic of China. Whoever he is, by then, he will have still more evidence of how unworkable China's current hardline neo-imperialist behavior is, and he will surely not pass up this golden opportunity. And the Dalai Lama will still be standing there, patiently holding the key to the solution.

ENDNOTES

1. Taiwan is the second biggest problem that looms in the mind of China's leadership, after Tibet. In casual comments of Chinese leaders, from Jiang Zemin to various ministers, the common theme is, "The Dalai Lama has to say that Tibet *and Taiwan* have always been an inalienable part of China—then we will talk to him." Taiwan was the island where Chiang Kai-shek and his Nationalist government escaped in 1949 when Mao conquered mainland China. Taiwan calls itself Republic of China, and formally considers the People's Republic of China to be illegitimate. When the Red Army invaded Tibet in 1949–1951, Taiwan held China's seat in the UN and confused matters by saying that Taiwan did own Tibet, so it was an internal matter—even though the communists were doing the invading and America was defending Taiwan against them!

Of course, this stance is obsolete today and Taiwanese businessmen are major investors in the mainland Chinese economy. But the continued independent existence of Taiwan is a sore point with Chinese leaders, who threaten invasion should Taiwan ever declare independence and seek recognition as a separate nation. As a capitalist society, Taiwan generated huge wealth during the long, dry decades of Mao's rule, and the Chinese want to possess Taiwan, as they possessed the formerly free Hong Kong in 1997. The Taiwanese don't trust the communist leadership to not smother their democracy and expropriate their wealth, since they lost everything once before when Mao took over. The way Beijing has handled Hong Kong has not reassured the Taiwanese that their way of life would be safe under communist dictatorship, and Taiwanese thinkers point to the treatment of Tibet as an example of what could happen to them under the power of the Beijing politburo.

Therefore, if China's leaders make a turnaround of their colonial policy in Tibet, release the Tibetans into the freedom of true internal autonomy—with a local democratic government and as a demilitarized zone of peace without Chinese colonists— then the Taiwanese will surely rest easier. They could consider their fear of a closer union with the People's Republic unnecessary, and reunification can easily follow in the new era of One Country, Many Systems, or better, a United States of China.

2. The *I Qing* is the ancient Chinese book of oracles, collected by Confucius, containing sixty-four basic readings that stimulate reflection and impart wisdom in making important decisions in life. Tai, the eleventh hexagram, Magnificent Peace, is composed of six lines, three broken lines above, standing for the earth, and three solid lines below symbolizing heaven. Adapted from the Richard Wilhelm translation, "The Judgment" reads:

"The small departs, the great approaches. Good fortune. Success." The commentary continues: "This hexagram denotes a time in nature when heaven seems to be on earth. Heaven has placed itself beneath the earth, and so their powers unite in deep harmony. Then peace and blessing descend upon all living things. In the world of man it is a time of social harmony; those in high places show favor to the lowly, and the lowly and inferior is an end to all feuds...." Finally there is "The Image": "Heaven and earth unite: the image of Tai—Peace. Thus the ruler divides and completes the course of heaven and earth, and so aids the people." And in commentary: "Heaven and earth are in contact and combine their influences, producing a time of universal flowering and prosperity. This stream of energy must be regulated by the ruler of men. It is done by a process of division. Thus men divide the uniform flow of time into the seasons, according to the succession of natural phenomena, and mark off infinite space by the points of the compass. In this way nature in its overwhelming profusion of phenomena is bounded and controlled. On the other hand, nature must be furthered in her productiveness. This is done by adjusting the products to the right time and the right place, which increases the natural yield. This controlling and furthering activity of man in his relation to nature is the work on nature that rewards him."

The wisdom of Confucius and the oracle is very moving here, and totally appropriate to what could be accomplished by President Hu and the Dalai Lama working together at this moment in history. The Chinese character for Tai is most appropriate in form, and a pavilion inspired by it might be designed by an architect like Frank Gehry or Rem Koolhaas, in which the Magnificent Tai Accord between China and Tibet could be signed in Beijing and Lhasa to mark the auspicious occasion, as suggested by my wise friend Joost Elffers.

3. The Tibetan name for Tibet is Böd, pronounced *Boeu*. To avoid confusion between "Tibet Autonomous Region" (half of Tibet) and the full region encompassed in Great Tibet that will be formed by reuniting the TAPs and TACs with the current TAR, I have chosen to begin to use the indigenous name internationally (as in the change of Peking to Beijing, Bombay to Mumbai, Calcutta to Kolkata, and so on), by using the Tibetans' own name for their land. So the restored and reunified Tibet is here called the Böd Autonomous Region, giving the felicitous acronym BAR. Of course, this change will be up to the Tibetans when the time comes, and I am only using the name in this book, interchangeably with Great Tibet, as a good omen.

PART III

TIBET SOLVED,
FREED, RESTORED

6

ENVISIONING THE GOAL

There is a short but famous Universalist (Mahayana) Buddhist scripture called "The Teaching of Vimalakirti" (in Chinese, *Wei-mo Ching*) that begins with a story about the Buddha. Outside the great city of Vaishali, five hundred young seekers come to salute and listen to the Buddha. In offering, they place five hundred jeweled parasols in a heap before him. He then performs a magical feat of forging that heap of jeweled parasols into a giant canopy over the entire assembly, in which they see reflected the entire interconnected natural universe, like a fabulous planetarium show. Astonished and delighted by this display, they declare verses of praise and appreciation. Then they ask him a big question: "Oh Divine Lord, we five hundred are already embarked on the quest to unexcelled perfect enlightenment; what we now need to know is, how do we perfect the buddhaverse, the world that best works for the evolutionary development and enlightened happiness of all beings?"

The Buddha responds by describing how the vast evolutionary progression of the bodhisattva to buddhahood involves developing so many other beings in the same positive direction over so many lives that when they finally become perfect buddhas, all the beings and their land have become constituted entirely of virtue. Hearing this, the Buddha's most distinguished monastic disciple present thinks to himself, "Well, if the land becomes perfect when a bodhisattva becomes a perfect buddha, what happened to this land since this former bodhisattva is now supposed to be a perfect buddha?"

The Buddha reads his mind and teases him about how it's his perception that is imperfect and not the buddhaverse or buddha-land of Shakyamuni Buddha. The chief god present, Brahma, the Indian Creator God, also chimes in to scold the poor monk, who then begs everyone's pardon, though of course he still sees the world as highly imperfect.

The Buddha then performs a second piece of performance art to demonstrate. He ceremoniously raises his right foot and places his big toe on the ground, and suddenly everyone sees the world as if it were the utterly perfect place for them to be, each one in the ideal situation for their optimal evolutionary, physical, and spiritual development.

"Now what do you see?" asks the Buddha, and the monk and everyone agree that it is utterly perfect. Then, the Buddha lifts up his toe, and everyone's perception switches back to seeing the ordinary scene. The remainder of the scripture focuses on this paradox between the world as perceived by the enlightened and the world as normally experienced by the unenlightened.

My point is this: In this book we are envisioning how wonderful and positive the world of Tibet, China, and the catastrophically overheating planet could be, if those responsible would see the enlightened vision and then act in an enlightened manner. They don't have to attain full enlightenment, though the Dalai Lama may be there already; all they have to do is *act as if* they are enlightened. In other words, "Buddha is as Buddha does!" But first seeing or imagining the enlightened, best of all possible worlds is what inspires us all to strive to build it. So let us carry on with imagining the positive, replacing the thought "These good outcomes just aren't possible!" with positive images of how indeed they are always possible, in as specific detail as we can manage.

THE DALAI LAMA PUTS HIS BIG TOE ON THE GROUND

The Dalai Lama sets an example for us in the context of imagining an ideal Tibet-China situation. Everything he says, does, and thinks comes from his vision of how possible it all is. The secret of his not getting discouraged, remaining patient and determined and even joyful in the midst of not looking away from the misery is related to this as well. So let us support him by letting ourselves imagine how easily President Hu, his colleagues, and their successors could take the momentous five steps presented in the last chapter as the most realistic solution to all their major problems, and how easily the Dalai Lama and the Tibetan people could reciprocate with their five steps.

What will Tibet become once the Tibet Autonomous Region (TAR) and the Tibet Autonomous Prefectures (TAPs) are reunited as the "Böd Autonomous Region (BAR) of the People's Republic of China (PRC)"? What will it look like when Tibet is at last granted real internal political freedom corresponding to the historical, moral, and spiritual freedoms the Tibetans once did enjoy and, actually, have never ceased to enjoy? The Dalai Lama has said that he needs—and, in fact, sees—an internally demilitarized zone of peace and nonviolence, an autonomous internal multi-party democratic government, and for the entire plateau to become an environmental preserve. Fulfilling these needs could free the PRC central government from the necessity of continuing to station, pay, feed, and maintain the approximately two hundred thousand internal People's Liberation Army (PLA) and People's Armed Police (PAP) troops they have in Tibet. They can simply move a sufficient number to their border garrisons and bases, and send the rest home downstream. Soon, after the neighboring countries behold this historic agreement and transformative change of the PRC's widely feared expansionist policy, there will be no fear from India or anyone else south of China's borders. The amount of money saved by abandoning the military occupation of Tibet and shifting any remaining military to border defense will more than make up for the costs of redeployments under this world transforming agreement.

On the economic level, the BAR, will be managed by Tibetans much more economically, sustainably, and profitably, both for "Mother China" as well as, of course, for the Tibetans themselves. Running Tibet as a *de facto* colony in this day and age is not economical; it involves a huge waste of money, the loss of international prestige, the danger of revolt and disrepute in the future, an enormous environmental disaster, and a waste of China's human resources. Perhaps certain military businesses—China's very own Halliburton-type war profiteers—are gaining from the current arrangement, but the bottom line for the national government is deep in the red. This deficit is not noticed now because it is hidden by the trade surplus and the boom in China's economy, but it will be recognized eventually. Modern militarism has utterly bankrupted first the USSR and now the USA; why should the PRC be different in the end if it goes down the same misguided path? Far better for China to become the exception to the rule of the inevitable bankruptcy that comes from trying to maintain superpower status in the twenty-first century, and for the Chinese leaders to prevent it from happening by changing course beforehand. Let China be the visionary leader in this new century and voluntarily forget about its old-fashioned, military-industrial, territorial aggrandizement plan and become a new kind of superpower—the number one moral, cultural, and eco-economical superpower.

A HISTORICAL PERSPECTIVE

Chinese people often talk about their thousands-of-years-old grand ancient culture and civilization, a major reason for their right to be a great power again today. They talk of almost two hundred years of being at the mercy of Western and Japanese imperialist forces and of their right to be free of such interventions. Everyone agrees about that right and about the wonder of the emerging new China today. Still, we and they all should look carefully at what the ancient great Chinese civilization was. It called itself the Central Land, thinking of itself and its way of life as superior to all nations under heaven. It built a Great Wall to keep out barbarians. It did not need to conquer neighbors, though it allowed them to come and pay tribute and receive gifts to remain harmonious on the frontiers. Often toward the end of dynasties, a ruler who had lost touch with the Central Land core vision embarked on a program of expansion and neighbor conquest. This inevitably bankrupted the country and started the process of the fall of that dynasty. In the last eight hundred years, at least four foreign nations from outside of China intervened in Chinese life: the Mongolians, the Manchurians, the British, and finally the Japanese, with a smattering of other Western empires, such as the Soviet Union and the United States, which played a minor role through ideology and forcible trade more than through occupation. With independence since 1911, first under the nationalists and then the communists, the Chinese began to take back control of their own land, their Central Land.

But then confusion set in. The Mongols and the Manchus had their own homelands outside of China and also had conquered other non-Chinese nations and territories. Both nations were conquerors from outside, just as much imperialists as any Western powers or the Japanese. The Mongols had conquered all the way to Europe, bypassing India on the way, and the Manchus had contented themselves with Tibet, Mongolia, and East Turkestan, as well as receiving regular tribute missions from Thailand and Nepal and other countries. So, first the Nationalist and then the Communist Chinese, both regimes heavily influenced not so much by ancient Chinese civilization as by different versions of Western colonialist culture, had to liberate their homeland from Manchu imperialism. The Tibetans expelled the Manchus first, then the Mongols and the Uighur Turks joined the Chinese in revolution, thinking they too would be liberated from Manchu domination. But after ridding themselves of the Manchu emperors, the leaders of each Chinese government, one after the other, decided they should own the Manchu empire they had just liberated themselves from! The nationalists didn't mind being imperialists, as that was what they considered to be modernization along military-industrial-complex-driven lines, but the communists envisioned themselves as part of a revolutionary movement against all imperialism. They have been caught in this double bind vice-grip ever since, going about imperialistically "liberating" their neighbors from imperialism.

This was the inner contradiction that ultimately caused the demise of the Soviet Union and the rebirth of Russia. But the Soviet Union's fate is what Chinese leaders from Deng to Hu have been so desperately afraid of. And this is what drives the Chinese leaders' irrationally harsh policy in Tibet—the fear that if they do not fill it up with Chinese immigrants, they will ultimately lose it, just as the Soviets lost the Ukraine, the Baltics, Kazakhistan, and so on. Yet ironically, that same contradictory policy is what will ultimately cause them to lose Tibet, as the Tibetan plateau itself defies all attempts at long-term conquest by non-Tibetans, as history has demonstrated. So, if they really examine the reality of the situation and move beyond stubborn denial, there is no alternative but to make friends with the Tibetans themselves, then to make sure the Tibetans are so well treated they decide to join in an equal union or at least become the best of neighbors.

A NEW KIND OF GOVERNANCE

Now, in this all-important moment of China's reemergence as the Central Land civilization, its leaders have to return to the moral task of gaining what Confucius so insightfully called the "mandate of heaven." They have to rule in such a way, with such a spiritual (which means nothing more mysterious than altruistic) motivation, that it makes their own land and culture so harmonious and beautiful that they have no need to conquer or suppress anyone, but all will flock to enjoy the magnificence of their ancient civilization reborn. These leaders should not be fooled into trying to reproduce the military-industrial imperialist lifestyle in their quest to outdo Japan and the West. They should rather understand that such a lifestyle ultimately defeats itself, now that our technologies of information, transportation, and warfare have brought us into the unprecedented situation of postmodern global society ("post" in the sense of beyond the nineteenth- and twentieth-century fantasies of materialist utopias).

The Western military-industrial imperialist culture has proven its self-destructiveness, bringing the whole planet closer to devastation than it has ever been in all recorded history—through overpopulation, mutually assured destruction via military overdevelopment, soil and water pollution, and global warming due to uncontrolled greed for energy. The more China reproduces this military-industrial culture, the more its huge size magnifies its effect far beyond the planet's tolerance. But instead, China now has the opportunity to abandon this futile and self-destructive superpower competition, return to its more peaceful and harmonious pattern of high civilization, reopen the gates of its people's spirituality—deeply rooted in a noble, if distant, past—and show the community of nations a truly viable way of living sustainably in balance with neighbors and with nature. Tibet is the key point, the pivot where this turnaround can best begin.

The transformative agreement envisioned here for China can only come through facing the fact that the People's Republic of China's covert, but not hidden well enough, intention and overt behavior in Tibet has been straightforwardly colonialist. Once the long-term futility of that colonialist project is understood, a visionary leader of China can realize that the hard-power approach is no longer needed and is, in fact, counter-productive and self-defeating. Then, the creative, earthshaking turnaround can be accomplished as the natural thing to do. As Confucius and Lao Tzu used to say, "The sincere leader merely needs to face the south, and all under heaven will be at peace."

SOME CHALLENGES IN IMPLEMENTATION

Admittedly, President Hu or his successor will have to overcome real implementation challenges in order to establish a *truly* autonomous region consisting of the whole BAR. Fortunately for this situation, the autocratic power and authority of the Chinese Communist Party (CCP) and its president and his politburo standing committee is sufficient. This revolution from the top can be implemented over the objections of various levels of bureaucratic and military officials, who may be personally comfortable in their situations within the present unsustainable and self-destructive colonialist regime.

REASSIGNMENT OF CHINESE SETTLERS

The first major challenge is the reassignment and removal of Chinese settlers from the BAR, mainly those now living anywhere above the 10,000-foot (3,000-meter) altitude line. There may also be some nonviable settlements at lower altitudes, though below 10,000-feet we can assume for the most part that the settlements are sustainable, and those settlers may need to be accepted as permanent residents of the BAR. The Dalai Lama will inspire his people to restrain any sort of urge for ethnic cleansing. From the satellite map of the 10,000-foot line, seen on page E, it is clear that these are relatively small areas anyway.

Whatever degree of challenge the reassignment and removal poses, however, it is far less than the difficulties that arise due to the damages and dangers of high altitude, heavily populated settlements. The main one is the massive environmental destruction that is causing and will cause untold damage eventually not only to Tibet but also to China's downstream provinces and other downstream countries of South and Southeast Asia.

One stunning example is Yamdrok Mother Lake in south central Tibet, which is being steadily drained down giant tubes that drive huge turbines, its pristine glacial waters joining the silted flow of the Tsangpo (Brahmaputra) River far below. It is as if the heart of the Tibetan ecosystem is bleeding to death. Its eventual desiccation threatens central Tibet's agricultural heartland and breadbasket. Chinese administrators want the electric power in order to support a huge new urban concentration of Chinese immigrants in the region, even bigger than that in the already overcrowded city of Lhasa, who could not possibly live sustainably in a Tibetan rural condition without the amenities that power on this scale will provide. It is a huge expense that is doomed to failure, as the low-altitude people cannot tolerate the long-term lack of oxygen. And it will deal a death blow to the ecological balance and livability of Tibet for the Tibetans.

This first challenge is therefore only a difficulty because Tibet's development thus far has been mainly for the benefit of Chinese settlers. The colonization creates an artificial community and economy of occupiers who require preferential treatment and large subsidies to induce them to leave their native downstream regions and live in the much more uncomfortable highland environment, where they will ultimately be unable to adapt physiologically in any case. The government can put the money saved by ending the enormous subsidies to this artificial community toward settling and improving the lot of these Chinese citizens in their home regions. With proper planning and preparation by those in charge, itinerant merchants and laborers could return downstream in a short timeframe of, say, thirty days, and with the bulk of Chinese settlers able to return home within three months or so.

REASSIGNMENT OF TROOPS

The second apparent challenge is reassigning and removing PLA and PAP troops from positions of internal domination and control, for until they leave, the Tibetans will have no sensation of autonomy and will feel too intimidated to assume responsibility for the management of their own affairs. The Dalai Lama and other lama leaders cannot return safely to a Tibet still policed by PLA and PAP personnel due to the Tibetans' long-repressed emotions that would likely surface. Once emotional crowds are excited by the Dalai Lama's long awaited presence, if remaining Chinese soldiers were to react fearfully and forcefully, it would create a temporarily chaotic and unstable situation, working against the

Dalai Lama's vision for acceptance by the Tibetan people of the five-point plan for becoming an autonomous region within China. It is clear that only the complete removal of these dominating and controlling Chinese personnel and institutions would begin the true condition of internal autonomy; without their removal, it would only be a paper autonomy.

In the Basic Law of Hong Kong, there are provisions for defense garrisons of the PLA in the Hong Kong Autonomous Region, and the same would apply for the BAR. As in the Hong Kong case, these troops would be forbidden to act against BAR citizens, and their garrisons would be restricted to locations in the frontier areas. Internal police units would be constituted exclusively of Tibetans, chosen by the BAR interim government. Some of the present internal Chinese troops could be shifted to expanded border garrisons. But by diminishing by at least half the overall number of the estimated two hundred thousand PLA and PAP troops in Tibet, the especially high cost of maintaining troops in the high plateau would be saved, and any troops not needed on the borders or in their home regions could be demobilized for another substantial savings. Certain troops and other Chinese residents with special skills could remain for specified periods of time to, for example, help clean up environmental damage.

GIVING TIBETANS GOVERNMENTAL CONTROL

The third apparent challenge involves turning over control of governmental administrative and economic affairs to Tibetans. Those Tibetans now working in, or who have recently worked in (but may have been recently purged over religious or loyalty issues), the TAR and TAP governments would be put in charge of forming the BAR administration. They would be free to appoint other Tibetans to fill vacancies of posts essential to the complex process of reassigning the troops and settlers. Once the Central Government has demonstrated its changed intentions, policies, and practices by actually removing troops and settlers, the Tibetans' confidence in the truth of the new autonomy would increase, and Tibetan exiles so inclined would be free to return to take up responsibilities in the new administration.

It is reasonable to expect that the transformation process of the TAR and the TAP from occupied colonies into the unified BAR would be managed by the gradually and truly liberated Tibetans with tremendous care and self-restraint. They would surely avoid any tendency toward recriminations and retaliations, under the active inspiration and direction of their beloved leaders, the Dalai Lama, the Ganden Tri Lama, the Karmapa, Drigung, and Drukpa Kagyu Lamas, the Sakya Trizin Lama, the Nyingma Lamas, and the Bön head lama. For those who doubt that Tibetans can be left to police and govern themselves under the ethical guidance of their leaders, consider that recently tens of thousands of Tibetans in Tibet gave up their valuable furs at the Dalai Lama's mere suggestion that killing animals for their pelts was un-Buddhist and inhumane. Any properties in the cities that are now owned by Chinese investors would be secured, the facilities systematically protected during the time it would take to find and train Tibetan partners, managers, and workers, with the assistance of the interim government.

The Dalai Lama has called for an interim regional government to prepare to hold a vote for Tibetans to choose whether they will voluntarily join with the Chinese Union under the guarantee of a robust internal autonomy and to draw up a new democratic constitution for self-rule within the BAR under the remote control of the China Central Government and the Chinese Communist Party. The proposed system would share with Hong Kong Region a "One-Country, Two-Systems" regime, though the Tibetan system would differ quite markedly from the Hong Kong one. To avoid undue concern and worry in the Central Government about the final decision of the Tibetan people, the Dalai Lama could state from the outset his personal decision to vote to join the Union under the true autonomy and the One Country, Many Systems guarantees, and even request his people to make some symbolic indication of their promise to follow his example. The other leaders of the Tibetan Buddhist orders and the Bon Lamas as well could be asked to indicate their choice in advance. The Central Government and the Chinese people could thus be assured that as long as the true internal autonomy is there, the vote to join the Chinese union is there.

Those Tibetans who cannot envision any sort of meaningful autonomy short of independence should be free to campaign before the vote that the people should vote no to joining the union, but they would have to campaign against the Dalai Lama and other spiritual leaders, and the vote would doubtless go against them. There are some who will say that the voting would be conducted under duress, due to the presence of the Chinese army on the frontier, but nothing in this world is perfect. The Tibetans could still vote not to join, and the Chinese would perhaps be too embarrassed to have to reoccupy the plateau by force in the face of such a vote, so there will be the element of risk that goes with free choice.

Since China's physical power is dominant in this relationship, it must take the first step by removing the settler population and military forces whose presence automatically prevents true autonomy. This requires trusting in the moral power of the Tibetan people to reciprocate when given the freedom to act voluntarily. And of course, the transformative change accomplished by the Central Government leadership, president, and politburo standing committee will be instantly seen *planet-wide* as monumental, moving, and historically creative, thus inspiring all parties to live up to what the ethicists call an "ultra-obligatory" standard of behavior.

The very first act of the interim BAR government under the Central Government eco-revolutionary provision in the initial Beijing Accord signed by the president and the Dalai Lama will be to proclaim the entire BAR as China's and the world's largest nature preserve. The rules of further resource development and extraction will thus be radically changed, in that *green* or ecological principles will be paramount in all projects. This nature preserve will not result merely in what some call a

Paper Park but will build upon the Thirteen National Nature Preserves already existing on paper in the TAR and will bring the whole system under a strict naturalist management that will truly serve as a model to the whole world.

In this single stroke of the pen and subsequent march of many feet, China's reputation will be established as leading the way in a 180-degree turnaround from having been a major polluter and contributor to global warming to leading the way to a truly sustainable future. The country will have made a Herculean beginning in turning its process of economic development toward the new direction that every other nation must inevitably adopt, in the context of the clear and present danger of global warming. This twenty-first century way of winning the global superpower competition is China's magnificent opportunity to establish itself as the truly great Central Land, Zhongguo, civilization that it can easily be, rising to fulfill its destiny with the help of its key friend, His Holiness the Dalai Lama.

7

THE BÖD AUTONOMOUS
REGION INTERNAL SYSTEM
OF GOVERNMENT

The Chinese government in its "White Paper on Tibet,"[1] specifically repudiated any suggestion of offering a Hong Kong–exemplified "One-Country, Two-Systems" arrangement to Tibet. But that is unrealistic and shortsighted. Even the Seventeen-Point Agreement for the Liberation of Tibet, imposed under duress and therefore reflecting China's style of unilateral decision-making, included provisions for noninterference with the independent "local government" of Tibet.

To get an idea of how an autonomous Tibet government would function, let's turn to the Dalai Lama's words from a speech he delivered in 1994.

Guidelines for Future Tibet's Polity and the
Basic Features of Its Constitution

When Tibetans inside and outside Tibet realize the joyful occasion of their reunion, Tibet shall become a nation made up of all its three provinces and shall be a nation based on the principles of freedom and democracy, upholding the creed of love and compassion, guided by the teachings of Lord Buddha. Its policies shall be based on the principles of justice and equality.

It is quite moving to me that in this political document, the Dalai Lama begins by looking forward to the joyful occasion of the reunion of all Tibetans with each other and with himself, in a climate of freedom caused by the reversal of the Chinese oppression under whatever arrangement. There are several things to notice here: The Dalai Lama does not mention either independence or autonomy, but talks of "reunion" of all Tibetans. He urges the adoption of democracy, which he has spent decades in exile developing with the virtual nation comprised of the international exile community, which is spread out around the globe. Love and compassion, wishing others happiness and freedom from suffering, are the operative principles of what the Buddhists call "realistic livelihood." He mentions the guidance of Lord Buddha, but does not state that Tibet will be a Buddhist theocracy, as he is a long-term advocate of the separation of church and state, having long ago foresworn playing a political role in the new government of a free and autonomous Tibet.

Tibet shall be a zone of peace where there shall be full protection of the environment. The legislative, the judiciary, and the executive organs of the Tibetan government shall be independent and vested with equal power and authority. Tibet shall be a multi-party parliamentary democracy. In line with this system of parliamentary democracy, a duly elected citizen of Tibet shall become the supreme head of the country and shall assume the ensuing responsibility.

The Dalai Lama specifies the entire BAR as a "zone of peace" and an environmental nature preserve. He adopts the tripartite division of powers necessary to a democracy: legislative, executive, and judiciary. He further prefers a multi-party model to either the Chinese Communist single-party rule, or the American two-party rule. Finally, he clearly abdicates his ruling position as any sort of head of state, giving that responsibility to a duly elected Tibetan citizen.

The Basic Law of the Hong Kong Autonomous Region is much more strongly placed under the authority of the Beijing government and the Chinese Communist Party than what the Dalai Lama envisions for Tibet. Laws passed by the Hong Kong Assembly must be approved in Beijing, and so forth. In the case of the BAR government, there is no mention at all of any subordination to the Beijing government or the Chinese Communist Party, and a multi-party democratic system means that the Tibetan Communist Party, which would surely come into existence, would have to compete for votes with other parties. In his address and in the plan below, the Dalai Lama makes no provision for the vote, which he has often mentioned elsewhere as part of his Middle Way Approach. So what follows can be considered the Tibetan ideal structure and process whose final form will result from negotiation with the Chinese Central Government.

As I have always said, Tibet belongs to the Tibetans, especially to those who have remained in Tibet. That being so, in the future democratic Tibet, those within Tibet shall, in general, bear the main responsibility of its democratic government. In particular, those Tibetan officials who are presently serving under the Chinese occupation, because of their experience and knowledge, shall have greater responsibility in the running of the government. As such, it is important that these officials should eschew all feelings of uncertainty and doubt, and dedicate themselves to regaining the freedom of Tibet, while at the same time making efforts towards improving the quality of administration.

Here the Dalai Lama reaches out to those Tibetans who have served under the Chinese occupation officials, respecting their experience and the knowledge they have gained regarding how things operate in a Tibet much changed from the days he lived there. Unfortunately, since this address in 1994 many Tibetan officials have failed their loyalty tests in the eyes of the Chinese by not denouncing the Dalai Lama with sufficient vehemence, not vowing loyalty to the Chinese-selected Panchen Lama, not pledging sufficiently intense devotion to the Chinese Communist Party, and so forth. Or even if they did do so, as the Dalai Lama always told them they could, the hard-line Chinese officials began to suspect them of disloyalty and fired them during the various Strike Hard campaigns. This kind of ideological cleansing campaign that communist societies engage in to root out enemies of the state—are people who do not conform to party standards with sufficient zeal—fill the reform-through-labor prison camps all over China that contain some criminals but mainly political prisoners. Many former Tibetan officials, then, will have to be retrieved from whatever camps they have been imprisoned in or occupations they have taken up since being removed from office.

Some Tibetans have had to say or do things against their wishes under coercive Chinese influences. However, I see no purpose in inquiring into their past activities. What is vitally important is the happiness of Tibetans as a whole. To this end, all must stand united.

There will be no measures or reprisals taken against any Tibetan officials under the taint of having been collaborators. The past will be ignored as much as possible and all Tibetans will work together toward their better future. If it turns out that there are a large number of grievances by Tibetan citizens against Tibetans who worked in the secret services or in the police or prison system, then a reconciliation process, such as that presided over by Bishop Desmond Tutu in post-apartheid South Africa, could be very naturally implemented.

All Tibetans must assume common responsibility to transform the present total-itarian system in Tibet, which actually guarantees no freedom to the people, into a genuinely democratic federal system in accordance with the choice of Tibetans as a whole.

The Dalai Lama is clearly telling his people that he is not making their decisions for them, but wants them as much as possible to step into their responsibilities as citizens of a democratic country. On the other hand, the Chinese leaders can safely assume that the Tibetans as a whole will support a democratic system of internal self-rule as envisioned by the Dalai Lama. Their choice favorable for China will emerge from the vote held to ratify a new constitution and to join the union with China under conditions of full internal autonomy. Those on the Tibetan side who are skeptical of internal autonomy, as the Chinese will not be forced to keep their promises but can break them without impunity as they did so many times before, are not sufficiently considering the constitutional and voting processes envisioned by the Dalai Lama. Holding an internationally secured vote can only emerge from a Chinese acknowledgment of the historical freedom of the Tibetan people and so, in itself, is an admission of their right to self-determination. Once their free choice has been made, the international community will have been the witnesses of the conditions under which the choice to join obtains. If the Chinese break their promises and interfere subsequently, then international disapproval would be registered. Of course, there is always a danger that brute force will be employed by future actors. No one is going to come to Tibet's aid with counterforce. That is the risk of the nonviolent approach; but it may not be as great a risk as that of the violent approach, where forceful measures might fail anyway, bringing even greater force down upon the oppressed.

The Chinese side has not already accepted the Dalai Lama's recommendations because it is still hoping that the past will be transformed to fit its propaganda and that the natural and historical independence of Tibet will disappear. Then everyone will think the Tibetans are Chinese. That is why they shout that the Dalai Lama really only wants independence. What they mean is that, if they seriously deal with the

Dalai Lama and the Tibetans, then they will have admitted that Tibet is and always has been independent! So the anti-autonomy people should cheer up. The mere opening of a sincere conversation in front of the world about the possibility of the BAR's autonomy is, in and of itself, a dramatic reversal of China's hundred-year-long pretense that Tibet has always been just a part of China. That is why China is so afraid to take that step.

> *I have already decided not to accept any political status in the government of future Tibet on the basis of the traditional system. This is not without reason, for it is well known that Tibetans as a whole place great faith and hope in me, and that, for my part, I have an unflinching determination to be of benefit to the Tibetans, both politically and from the religious point of view, in line with my past karma and prayers.*

In the traditional Tibetan context, the Dalai Lama's stepping down is a revolutionary step, a voluntary change from his 366-year-old position as the reincarnated head of the Ganden Palace Government that held sway in Tibet from 1642 to 1959 and has been a government in exile in India ever since. By saying that it "is not without reason," he means that he has not made this decision to step aside from a government leadership role without giving it deep and penetrating thought. He acknowledges the great faith all Tibetans have in him, and he indicates that changing his role from that of a formal political ruler to spiritual head and teacher is not an abandonment of his people.

> *In future, without holding any political status in the government, I shall remain a sort of public figure who might be able to resolve some of the particularly difficult problems which may not be resolved by the existing political mechanism. Also, in order that Tibet shall be able to stand as an equal member in today's community of nations, it is highly important that it should not depend on one single person but reflect the collective consciousness of the Tibetan people.*

The Dalai Lama shows that he intends for Tibet to be recognized by the world as an existing nation, independently relating to all outside nations except in foreign policy and defense, and therefore requiring that its leadership be legitimized by having a popular electoral mandate.

This requires the Tibetan people to take responsibility for their own political destiny. Hence, it is in both the immediate and future interest of the Tibetan people in general, and for a multiplicity of reasons of crucial importance, that I have come to this decision. Therefore, Tibetans need not worry that I have slackened in my sense of responsibility for the common good.

This reflects his long effort to get the Tibetans actually to depend less on him personally and more on taking responsibility for their own governance. And he reassures them again that he is not abandoning them in the slightest.

Once Tibet regains its freedom, following the withdrawal of the oppressive Chinese regime, there will be a transitional period before the finalization of its constitution, during which the existing Tibetan administration in Tibet shall continue to function with the same Tibetan officials shouldering responsibility. During this transitional period, a president shall be appointed as the interim head of state. He shall be vested with all political powers which are currently held by me. Simultaneously, the Tibetan Government in Exile shall be deemed to have automatically ceased to exist. All the officials of the dissolved administration shall bear the same responsibility in respect of the affairs of Tibet as any other Tibetan.

The Dalai Lama talks simply of freedom, without specifying either absolute or only internal, and this is after he has presented his Middle Way Approach, asking the Chinese government only for real autonomy, foregoing the demand for full independence. But it is as if he does not consider this important, as true internal autonomy subsequent to the "withdrawal of the oppressive Chinese regime" is tantamount to freedom, as indeed it would be. So he is not hiding any secret intention of separatism as the Chinese accuse him constantly. He is openly saying that genuine internal autonomy is the freedom his people need and deserve based on their independent history and their cultural distinctiveness; and yet he is confident that they will invest that freedom in choosing legitimate—voluntary—union with China.

He states below that he personally would appoint the interim president, either from a slate of seven candidates nominated by representatives from all over Tibet or just from his own choice if such an election were too cumbersome in the transitional period. This is only practical at first, since the Dalai Lama's approval would be critically important for the interim president to have legitimacy in Tibetans' eyes. The Dalai Lama's statement that he would then dissolve the Tibetan Government in Exile came as a shock to its present officials, but it is clearly logical to release any members of that government who wish to return to Tibet to run for office in the new government.

Though members of the Tibetan Government in Exile shall not be officially entitled to any special privileges by virtue of their positions, they may, according to their desire and qualifications, voluntarily accept positions which may be assigned to them and for which they may be thought fit in the transitional administration. The main responsibility of the transitional government shall be to set up a Constituent Assembly to finalize Tibet's constitution. This Assembly shall be comprised of members representing the whole of Tibet. These members shall take on the responsibility of the Constituent Assembly and shall finalize Tibet's constitution on the basis of the draft constitution prepared here in exile by the Tibet Constitution Redrafting Committee, which was appointed by me, with the assent of the interim president.

Under the provision of this draft constitution, the executive head is empowered to directly set up certain independent bodies, the majority of which shall, after the election of the new government, be constituted in accordance with the law. At the same time, an Election Commission shall immediately be created, headed by an individual appointed by the interim president in accordance with the law. A comprehensive draft democratic constitution for a free Tibet is under preparation. The power to finalize it shall be vested in the Constituent Assembly of a free Tibet consisting of representatives from the whole of the country.

For the purpose of creating awareness and as a basis for the formulation of opinions as to what kind of democratic government Tibet is going to have, I am hereby announcing the guidelines for the framework of the Constitution of free Tibet.

The following guidelines are more specific and detailed in their prescriptions. This section requires little comment as it simply specifies what is mentioned in general in the preamble above. Since it repeats in legalistic language most of the points the Dalai Lama already made in the preamble above, I will skip some of the details of implementation and only quote and comment on a few of the more remarkable selections from the constitutional framework guidelines. Though there are other points in the agreement itself, the most pertinent ones, below, highlight the desired future of Tibet's Switzerland-like role in the future of Asia:

2. Nature of Polity: Tibet shall stand for the benefit and well-being not only of itself but also of its neighboring countries and the whole world. Based on the principles of nonviolence, it shall be a free, social welfare—oriented, federal, democratic polity, based on principles of the Dharma. It shall ensure full protection of the environment and form a zone of peace.

The Dalai Lama clearly sees Tibet becoming a light unto the nations. Releasing Tibet from being a colonial "zone of misery" and allowing it to manifest its Buddhist culture in a free polity that embodies enlightened principles, this will also empower China to go beyond just making cheap light bulbs for the nations and shine its own unique "light unto the nations." The principles of the Dharma can be summarized as: 1) individualism, as a Dharmic society is founded on its highest aim, which is to support the evolution and liberation of its individual members;

2) nonviolence, as all life and especially human life is precious and so not to be wasted by violence; 3) evolutionary educationalism, as the supreme aim and purpose of human life is a total mind-body-spirit education toward perfect enlightenment; 4) social altruism, as all have universal responsibility for all, and; 5) egalitarianism, in that every human (and animal) has the buddha-potential, and so should have equal access to life, liberty, and the pursuit of the happiness of enlightenment.[2]

The next set of recommendations, below, follows from such principles.

3. Fundamental Government Policy: The Tibetan Government shall observe and abide by the UN Universal Declaration of Human Rights and shall seek to advance the moral and material well-being of its people.

5. Renunciation of Violence and Use of Force: Tibet shall be a zone of peace based on principles of nonviolence, love, and compassion, and shall be a center for environmental protection. Tibet shall be neutral and avoid the use of violence for any purpose.

The Dalai Lama in his prophetic role of speaking truth to power has long called for the total demilitarization of the planet, which many, especially those who still think that they are benefiting from war and will benefit even more in the future, consider impractically idealistic. More knowledgeable thinkers have realized the futility of war in the age of overwhelmingly destructive technology that can be wielded by individuals as well as states, and which therefore assures that there is no such thing as a stable victory or conquest any longer.[3] According to them, the shifting of the vast multi-trillion-dollar yearly expenditure on war and violence into peaceful activities—for example, the building of health, education, and welfare facilities around the world—is highly realistic and is the only way to save the planet from destruction by military-industrial humans and bring our global human society back into a healthy balance.

6. Fundamental Rights: All citizens of Tibet shall be equal before the law, and shall be entitled to the enjoyment of all rights and privileges under the law, irre-

spective of sex, race, language, religion, color, status, and whether he/she is lay
or ordained.

Here is the Buddhist principle of egalitarianism of all beings, including human beings.

7. *Other Fundamental Rights: All Tibetans shall have the right to life, liberty, and
property, the right to freedom of expression, to buy, sell, or own land and property,
to form associations, the freedom of the press and the publication of periodicals, and
the rights of employment in the Government or in an agency thereof.*

The right to private property and the ownership of land goes against
the communist ideology of everything belonging to the people, which
has been in practice in Tibet for the last fifty years.

8. *Right to Election and Nomination: All citizens of Tibet, irrespective of sex,
shall have the right to nomination and election in accordance with the law.*
9. *Ownership of Land: The entire territory within the confines of Tibet shall
be distributed and used for the benefit of the people and for their habitation,
having due regard to the environment. In providing land to the citizens of Tibet
for the purpose of residence, agriculture, animal husbandry, building, manufacture, or business or private occupational purposes, the government shall pay
due regard to the requirement of the individual, restricting the concentration of
wealth in a few hands. All land not privately owned shall be controlled by the
government.*

The Dalai Lama here shows his intention to balance elements of
market capitalism with welfare socialism, all within an environmental
low-impact use policy.

10. *Economic System: Tibet shall have a unique economic system which, without
falling into the extremes of capitalism or socialism, shall be in accordance with
its requirements. Taxation shall be based on income criteria.*

This will be fascinating to see, how the enlightenment-oriented (not simply enlightened, as some might wish to misread me) Tibetan Buddhist culture will elaborate an economic middle way between the two extremes of laissez-faire capitalism and state-monopolized industrial socialism. A progressive taxation system is promoted for the redistribution of accumulated wealth.

11. Education and Culture: Since the progress of society and moral integrity of the citizens depends basically on the standard of education, efforts shall be made to provide appropriate facilities for providing education at all levels, whether higher education, professional institutions, or for technical, scientific, and research purposes, by way of implementing a sound education policy.

Here is the Buddhist social principle I have called educationalism, for want of any indigenous word in English. It means that, due to the Buddhist biological notion of individual evolutionary responsibility in a sequence of lives, the most important thing a person can do in a lifetime is to learn, to expand her or his awareness of reality, wisdom, and scientific insight and to develop the corresponding more evolved qualities of empathy, compassion, altruism, generosity, and so forth. Thus the ideal life is one of lifelong education of the total human. Therefore, society should provide the facilities for any people who recognize that and want that ideal life. This was the source of Tibet's unique mass-monastic social structure. How this evolves into a modern form, without being suppressed by the communist materialist theory and practice, will be fascinating to see.

12. Health: A public healthcare system shall be established aimed at providing appropriate community health services and medical care.

Tibetan rulers, incarnations of bodhisattvas all, by popular demand or myth, have always established public health systems, beginning with the dynastic emperors from the sixth to the ninth centuries and continuing with the Dalai Lamas and their Tibetan medical institutions. Modern natural medicine institutes in the new free Tibet will oversee the restoration of the pristine environment they need for supplying their natural herbal remedies, while combining the natural approach with the best of the modern industrial medicine's analytic and therapeutic insights and techniques. The Dalai Lama intends to make Tibet's natural medicine traditions available to the world as Tibet's favored industry, so Tibet will be poised to make a major contribution to the growing worldwide holistic or integrative medicine movement.

13. *Legislative Power:* Legislative power shall be vested in the two chambers of the Tibetan National Assembly and the president. Laws passed by the upper and lower chambers of the assembly shall have to obtain the assent of the president. The lower chamber of the Tibetan National Assembly shall consist of representatives directly elected by the citizens within their respective constituencies, as demarcated in accordance with population distribution. It shall be the highest law-making body. The upper chamber of the Tibetan National Assembly shall consist of members elected by their provincial assemblies and those nominated by the president.

14. *Executive Power:* 1. Executive power shall be vested in the president and the vice president elected by the upper and lower chambers of the Tibetan National Assembly in accordance with the law; 2. The prime minister shall be elected from the party or any group constituting the majority of the members of the lower chamber of the Tibetan National Assembly actually present. However, should this recourse fail, the prime minister shall be elected by the entire members of the Tibetan National Assembly. The power to exercise executive powers shall rest primarily in the cabinet set up by the prime minister.

15. *Judicial Power:* An independent Supreme Court of Tibet shall be the highest appellate court of justice. The supreme court shall be the head of the judiciary, which shall safeguard and decide by interpreting the provisions of the constitution all matters brought before it concerning alleged violation of law, whether by the government or by citizens, so as to ensure correct and equal dispensation of justice.

Note that there is no reference to the involvement of the Central Government of China, or of the Chinese Communist Party for that matter. This makes these constitutional guidelines much more radical than the Basic Law of the Hong Kong Autonomous Region, which further demonstrates that the Dalai Lama's vision of autonomous self-rule is a robust form of freedom within a union.

> To sum up, Tibet, which is located in the heart of Asia and on the Roof of the World between India and China, and whose people are endowed with inborn qualities of honesty, peace, and a sense of moral integrity, shall in the future be a nation committed to peace and non-violence, based on free democracy, and the health and life of its people shall not be endangered by pollution. Tibet shall be fully equipped to safeguard the integrity of its environment.
>
> Tibet shall have no offensive forces or bases for weapons of destruction, but shall be a nation of peace and harmony. Today, in some parts of the world, while there are all kinds of material benefits, human values and freedoms have suffered such a degradation that people have virtually become a slave of machines.
>
> In general, in most countries, the people lack even basic necessities and are impoverished. Tibet shall be free of these two extremes and its economic system shall provide for the needs of its people. It shall plan for a just development, fulfilling all the basic needs of its people.
>
> Tibet shall not be influenced or swayed by the policies and ideologies of other countries but remain a neutral state in true sense of the term. It shall maintain harmonious relationships with its neighbors on equal terms for their mutual benefits. It shall maintain a cordial and fraternal relationship with all nations, without any sense of hostility or enmity. Such an ideal state of affairs requires that all right-thinking and loyal Tibetans must strive to achieve it with a joyful sense of dedication and determination.

In these noble principles, we see a sketch for an ideal Buddhist-inspired but not Buddhist-dominated polity. Clearly China would always have the military might to re-enter Tibet and stop any policy or practice that it considered threatening to its own interests, so China need not fear that this blueprint for a free Tibet means it will be independent from China entirely. But in normal times, the Dalai Lama and the Tibetans clearly prefer to run their own affairs in their own way. These guidelines also do not mention the holding of the vote for self-determination, in which, under the agreement, the Dalai Lama is pledged to campaign for the Tibetans to vote to join China legitimately, under guarantees and the realities of genuine autonomy. So these matters would have to be spelled out carefully in negotiations beginning with the key agreement.

The next step is the naturalistic one: to restore and preserve the precious environment of the plateau.

ENDNOTES

1. "White Paper on Tibet," *Regional Ethnic Autonomy in Tibet*, 2004, one of a series of propaganda efforts by China to promote its line on Tibet, in response to US State Department White Papers on human rights problems in Tibet, and indirectly in response to resolutions of the US Congress declaring Tibet an independent country under Chinese occupation.

2. For more detail on these principles, see my *Inner Revolution: Life, Liberty, and the Pursuit of Real Happiness* (Riverhead, 1996).

3. For example, Jonathan Schell, *The Unconquerable World: Power, Nonviolence, and the Will of the People* (Owl Books, New York, 2004).

8

THE DEDICATION OF TIBET
AS A NATURE PRESERVE

In roughly the past ten years, the Chinese government has accelerated its designation of large areas of the Tibet Autonomous
Region (TAR) as National Nature Preserves. Unfortunately, this
appears to be mostly on paper, as people say that animals are still
being hunted, herbs unsustainably harvested, trees logged too inten-
sively, and grasslands mismanaged and abused. These Chinese actions
are likely part of its propaganda campaign to show its worthiness as
possessor of Tibet. Even so, it is also an example of how even remote
dialogue spurs response, since the Dalai Lama has been talking to a
wide public about environmentalism for years.

But until the Tibetans themselves are empowered by internal
self-rule and assume responsibility under the beloved spiritual and
ethical leadership of the Dalai Lama, the dream of preserving what's
left of Tibet's fragile high-altitude environment and restoring it for

the healing of Asia's entire water and weather system will never be realized.

According to a recent book, *Across the Tibetan Plateau*,[1] presently 40 percent of TAR's land surface is in conservation. The following information on the reserve's thirteen parks comes from that beautiful book.

1. The Changtang National Nature Reserve

A huge area in the northwest of the TAR, this reserve covers a great deal of the TAR portion of the northern plain (in Tibetan, *Jangtang*), with a size of 115,028 square miles (298,000 square kilometers). It was created in 1995 to save the wild yak and the Tibetan antelope. The American naturalist George Schaller was a driving force behind it. It is the third largest nature preserve in the world, after Saudi Arabia's Empty Quarter and Denmark's Greenland. It can be considered a reserve mainly in intention and on paper. Since the funding for managing personnel and equipment is inadequate, the government and outside NGO-sponsored effort to control poachers' hunting of antelopes for their coveted shatoosh wool and the yaks for their meat is not at all up to the level necessary to be effective.

2. The Se-lin-cuo Black-Necked Crane Breeding Ground

Two small areas above Peku Lake in central Tibet.

3. Yaluzangbu River Middle Reaches Black-necked Crane Winter Transient Ground Nature Protected Area

Two small areas not far above Bhutan were the Phobjika Valley, famous for its black-necked crane winter sanctuary.

4. The Qomolangma National Nature Preserve

A large area around Mount Everest (Qomolangma) in the counties of Dingri and Dingjie, it runs along the border with Nepal; created in 1994, it contains 13,986 square miles (36,000 square kilometers), populated by 320 villages. An ambitious program stimulated by outside nongovernment organizations working with local authorities recruits villagers as helpers (in Tibetan, *pendeba*). This involves the villagers themselves in conserving the environment and protecting the snow leopards, kyang (wild asses), blue sheep, and gazelles.

5. Yaluzangbu River Great Canyon National Nature Protected Area

6. Chayu's Cibagou National Nature Protected Area

7. Mangkang Snub-nosed Monkey National Nature Protected Area

8. Riwuchi Chang-mao-ling Red Deer (Regional) Nature Protected Area

9. Bajie Giant Cypress (Regional) Nature Protected Area, Linzhi

10. Gongbo Regional Nature Reserve
These five areas are now included in Reserve Number 13, discussed below.

11. Lhasa's Lhalu Wetland Nature Protected Area
A wetland area west of Lhasa of 1,650 acres, created to preserve the common red-shank bird, as well as to assist black-necked cranes, also serves to purify Lhasa's water supply, a critical need in the vastly expanded city.

12. Namtso Wetland Nature Protected Area
An area north of Lhasa around the beautiful Namtso Lake, one of Tibet's largest.

13. Four Great Rivers Nature Preserve
This recently approved area of 87,120 square miles (225,700 square kilometers) basically includes and hugely augments areas 5, 6, 7, 8, 9, and 10.

It is said to contain 800,000 people, 5,000 plant species, forests estimated to constitute one-seventh of China's total timber resources (and
the government is engaged in heavy replanting in the headwater valleys of
the Yangtse, Mekong, and Salween rivers), 450 species of birds, approximately 90 species of mammals, and an unknown number of aquatic
creatures. It is located in the TAR prefectures of Chamdo and Linzhi.

The authors also say that all endangered wild animal numbers are
increasing, deforestation rates have decreased by more than 80 percent,
there is more "environmentally friendly geothermal and hydroelectric generated energy," and that local people are working with government and
scientists cooperatively. During the period from 1959 to 1989, the first
thirty years of naked occupation by Chinese Communist military and
party officials, the book states that the TAR's and the TAP's environment
and flora and fauna were pillaged to such an extent that clear-cut forests
resulted in major silting of river upper reaches and terrible floods throughout Western China. Animal and bird species were hunted to near extinction, and wild growing medicinal herbs considered precious on the huge
Chinese herbal medicine market were harvested to near depletion.

From these past disasters we can learn how to avoid them in the
future. The creation of the above-mentioned reserves is a very important
initiative and demonstrates some sort of response to the thoughts
expressed by the Dalai Lama and his colleagues in talks and presenta-
tions they give. With the historic agreement we are recommending, the
entire Tibetan plateau ecosystem will become one of the largest nature
preserves on the planet, giving China the credit of voluntarily taking a
major step toward combating global warming.

THE DALAI LAMA'S HOPE FOR THE ENVIRONMENT

The Dalai Lama is genuinely interested in and objectively knowledgeable
about environmental preservation. I remember once in the early 1990s

having the pleasure of accompanying him on his first trip to Costa Rica and being impressed by his knowledge of nature.

He amazed the scientists at the National Botanical Garden in San José by demonstrating his detailed knowledge of orchids, even reciting their botanical names in Latin, as he enjoyed the great variety they had there. When they offered him some cuttings to take home and cultivate in his own greenhouse in Dharamsala, he declined, saying he had previously tried to cultivate such exotic species after having been given them on visits to other tropical regions, but that they had always failed to grow and thrive in the mountainous altitude of his home.

When the Dalai Lama had an afternoon off from his usual grueling schedule of talks and conferences, he requested a visit to an active volcano. When we reached the summit we all got out of our jeeps and began walking with him—who was wearing a floppy, wide-brimmed sun hat—toward the main crater. Suddenly, with a whoop of glee, he leaped off the roadway and across a ditch, giving his security detail a panic that he might fall, and clambered up the opposite embankment to where a tall plant was growing. He examined the plant carefully and then proclaimed that he had the same plant in Dharamsala, but that this one was two or three times bigger. He then asked to be photographed holding out a leaf of the plant. He stood there in his goofy hat, grinning from ear to ear, with a hunter's sense of triumph, holding the broad, long leaf. Once photographed, he clambered back, security men helping, and as he came up to where I stood, he looked at me intently and said, "Next life I will be a naturalist!" It was an utterly surprising and charming moment.

To illustrate the Dalai Lama's thoughts about the Tibetan environment, I'd like to quote and elucidate his speech "Hope for Tibet's Environment," given at the Endangered Tibet Conference in Sydney, Australia, on September 28, 1996.

I am very happy and feel especially honored to be speaking to a group of people who are really dedicated to environmental problems in general and the Tibetan

environmental problems in particular ... Now, environmental problems are
something new to me. When we were in Tibet, we always considered the envi-
ronment pure. For Tibetans, whenever we saw a stream of water in Tibet, there
was no question as to whether it was safe for drinking or not. However, it was
different when we reached India and other places. For example, Switzerland is a
very beautiful and impressive country, yet people say, "Don't drink the water
from this stream, it is polluted!"

He certainly does not mean he has not studied environmental problems or that he doesn't know about the rape of Tibetan forests, herbs,
animals, and mineral resources that the current crop of Chinese environmental scientists admit took place in Tibet from the late 1950s until the
late 1980s. He means "new" to him in the sense that he hasn't confronted
environmental problems that immediately in his own experience.

Gradually, we Tibetans gained the knowledge and awareness that certain
things are polluted and cannot be utilized. Actually, in India, when our
settlements started in some places, large number of Tibetans fell ill with
stomach problems as a result of drinking polluted water. So through our own
experience and by meeting scientists, we have become better educated about
environmental issues.

When we look back at our own country, Tibet, it is a big country with
vast land area, with high altitude and a cold and dry climate. Perhaps these
things provided some kind of natural protection to Tibet's environment—keep-
ing it clean and fresh.

According to the Tibetan naturalist and scholar, Tsultrim Palden
Dekhang,[2] "The Tibetan Plateau is the biggest and highest plateau on
Earth, an area well over a million square miles (more than 2.5 million
square kilometers), with average altitude of almost 14,000 feet (4,000
meters). It has all fourteen of the world's 8,000-meter (over five miles
high) peaks, yet also has a great variety of landscapes ranging from the
Himalayas in southern Tibet to lush tropical forests in eastern Tibet."

In the Northern pastures, the rocky areas, the forested areas, and the river valleys, there used to be lots of wild animals, fish, and birds. As a Buddhist country there were certain traditional laws in Tibet concerned with a complete ban on fishing and hunting.

It is well documented that before the 1949–1951 Chinese invasion, Tibet was teeming with wildlife. The Dalai Lama himself, in his previous incarnations, applied the Buddhist principle of nonviolence to the care of wildlife and nature. The Great Fifth Dalai Lama was enthroned in 1642 as the supreme spiritual and political leader of Tibet, the first Dalai Lama to be requested to assume political responsibilities along with his spiritual ones. He began the practice of promulgating, in the tenth lunar month of every year, a Decree for the Protection of Animals and the Environment. This continued until the 1940s, though of course not all Tibetans heeded the decree to the letter, and there were definitely hunters, trappers, and others who lived off the trade in furs and skins. But these were exceptions, and in general, hunting was disapproved of. Fishing was prohibited quite effectively, as it was thought that the destruction of fish would cause great harm to the water system spirits— the *Lu*, or dragon-serpent beings who could bring good fortune to the society, or, if provoked, spread diseases and misery. As a result of these attempts at a Buddhist low-impact land use and wildlife preservation policy, the plateau was full of animals.

The British explorer, Francis Kingdon-Ward, who visited Tibet before World War I, said, "I have never seen so many varieties of birds in one place, one great zoological garden." And in the 1940s, the American adventurer Leonard Clark reported, "Every few minutes we would spot a bear, a hunting wolf, herds of musk deer, kiang (wild ass), gazelles, big horned sheep, or foxes. This must be one of the last unspoiled big game paradises."

Even today, the Tibetan plateau is rich with plant and animal life. Dekhang states, "In the so-called Tibet Autonomous Region, there are 2,307 species of insects, 64 species of fish, 45 species of amphibian,

55 species of reptiles, 488 species of birds and 142 species of mammals. There are 163 rare, endangered, and valuable species, which consist of 74 species of mammals, 79 birds, 4 reptiles, 2 amphibians, 2 fishes, and 2 insects. There are over 5000 higher plant species and 280 families. Among them, woody plants total over 100 families and 300 species. The Tibetan Plateau contains all the large ecosystems of the terrestrial ecosystem: forest, scrub, steppe desert, and aquatic formations. Such ecosystems are usually fully displayed only on a continental scale." Its unique ecosystem is yet another reason why Tibet should be designated as a nature preserve.[3]

> *I remember in Lhasa when I was young, some Nepalese did a little hunting and fishing because they were not very much concerned with Tibetan laws. Otherwise, there was a real safety for animals at that time.*

Tibet's wildlife is diverse and remarkable. According to Dekhang, "The [widespread] distribution of animal species on the Plateau is abundant, with 40 endemic mammals, such as giant panda, red panda, takin, musk deer, Tibetan antelope, wild yak, kyang, Himalayan marmot, Himalayan mouse-hair or pika, Tibetan woolly hare, vole, and so on, up to 60 percent of China's total endemic mammals, 28 endemic birds, such as tragopan, Tibetan eared pheasant, Himalayan monal, snowcock, Tibetan sand grouse, and so on, 2 endemic reptiles, and 10 endemic amphibians."

> *There is a strange story. Chinese farmers and road builders who came to Tibet after 1959 were very fond of meat. They usually went hunting birds, such as ducks, wearing Chinese army uniforms or Chinese clothes. These clothes startled the birds and made them immediately fly away. Eventually these hunters were forced to wear Tibetan dress (roar of laughter from the audience). This is a true story! Such things happened, especially during the 1970s and '80s when there were still large numbers of birds.*
>
> *Recently, a few thousand Tibetans from India went to their native places in Tibet. When they returned they all tell the same story. They said that about*

forty or fifty years ago there was huge forest cover in their native areas. Now all these richly forested mountains have become bald like a monk's head. No more tall trees. In some cases the roots of the trees were even uprooted and taken away! This is the present situation. In the past, there were big herds of animals to be seen in Tibet, but few remain today. Therefore, much has changed.

According to all authorities, including Chinese scientists, the devastation of the wildlife in Tibet from the 1950s to 1990s was incalculable. Upwards of sixty formerly plentiful birds and animals are now on the endangered species list, including the Tibetan antelope and the giant panda—two of China's 2008 Olympic mascots![4]

A friend of mine, a longtime student of Tibet, told me that he went to visit the plateau as soon as it opened up in the early 1980s, during the time when one could travel most everywhere without much supervision. One early morning as he was camped on the southern shore of Lake Manasarovar (Tibetan *Mapham*), he and his girlfriend were awakened by the sound of machine gun fire nearby. Peeking nervously out of their small tent, they saw a group of Chinese soldiers fifty yards or so down the beach. They had set up a machine gun on its tripod and were calmly doing target practice on the flocks of birds floating around in the lake, mowing them down without mercy. They had no hunting dogs and were making no effort to recover carcasses for food—just enjoying the target practice, as if they were in a fairway shooting gallery. Fortunately, my friend had a camera with good lenses, so he surreptitiously recorded this mindless slaughter to prove his story. One day soon, with the Dalai Lama's preservation ideas instituted, such meaningless atrocities against wildlife will be a thing of the past.

The large-scale deforestation in Tibet is a matter of great sadness. It is not only sad for the local area, which has lost its beauty, but for the local people who now find it hard to collect even enough fuelwood. Relatively, these are small problems; looking from a wider perspective, deforestation has other extensive negative consequences. Firstly, many parts of Tibet are high and dry. This means that it takes longer for the land to recover compared to lower regions with humid climate, and the negative effects therefore last much longer.

The Tibetan Environmental Watch (TEW) website compiled Chinese government statistics (which, admittedly, are not usually very reliable) to report that "Tibet's total forest cover declined from 25.2 million hectares in 1949 to 13.57 million hectares in 1985, which represents a 46 percent destruction up to a time over twenty years ago." It is conservatively estimated that over a hundred billion dollars worth of lumber was extracted from the primeval Tibetan rainforest in the 50 years of the Chinese occupation. Dekhang mentions the story of Tenzin, a middle-aged farmer of Markham village in Kham, eastern Tibet, who told the *New York Times* correspondent Nicholas Meysztowics in April 1990, "In the time it takes to drink one cup of tea, fifteen Chinese trucks loaded with Tibetan logs pass by."

I can personally testify to this, having swallowed the dust of hundreds of lumber trucks passing per day, always eastward toward China, while touring on the roads during a dozen trips to central and eastern Tibet from the mid-eighties even up to today. In eastern Tibet in the early nineties, I saw river headwaters in the Sichuan TAPs literally choked with tree trunks being floated downstream.

"The chaotic commune-period (1956–1981) initiated by the government of China caused an unprecedented destruction of Tibet's forest," says Dekhang. "During this period local villages became production brigades during which mountains in Tibet were stripped of their forests to feed inefficient steel furnaces, in the madness to produce enough steel for China to advance rapidly to the ranks of the advanced nations!"

Secondly, many of the rivers which flow through large areas of Asia, through Pakistan, India, China, Vietnam, Laos, and Cambodia, rivers such as the Yellow river, Brahmaputra, Yangtse, Salween, and Mekong, all originate in Tibet. It is at the places of origin of these rivers that large-scale deforestation and min-

ing are taking place. Any pollution of these rivers has a drastic effect on the downstream countries.

The TEW website highlights the importance of these waterways: "The water system in Tibet is formed by inner and outer river systems. The inner rivers and streams form lakes and ponds in the basins of the plateau, which has more than fifteen thousand lakes." The major lakes are the huge Kokonor lake in the northeast. Namtso lake north of Lhasa, the Yamdrok "Mother" lake, essential for the southern farm belt near Gyantse and Shigatse (nowadays being drained down into the Brahmaputra river through huge power-generating turbine tubes), and Mapham (Manasarovar) Lake in the far west. Tibet is also the headwater source of the eight major rivers of Asia: the Tsangpo (Brahmaputra), the lifeline of Bengal and Bangladesh, the Sutlej and Indus, the lifelines of Pakistan and the Indian Punjab, the Yangtse and Yellow rivers, the lifelines of China, the Salween, the lifeline of Burma, the Karnali and Ganga, the lifelines of central India, the Mekong, the lifeline of Thailand, Laos, Cambodia, and Vietnam, and numerous other streams flowing down off the plateau. These rivers and their tributaries sustain the lives of billions of people, comprising about half of the world's total population. In light of this information, it's easy to see why it is vital to keep these waters healthy. (See figure 4.)

In sum, Tibet has been aptly called, the "water-storage tower" of Asia. The very low impact, low population density traditional Tibetan habitation pattern of the plateau was ideal for the preservations of these all-important water sources. It is impossible of course to return the plateau to such a best-use, no-use management pattern, but it is certainly possible to minimize environmental degradation due to mining, deforestation, grassland desertification, by empowering the Tibetans themselves to return to some aspects of their traditional custodial function.

According to Chinese statistics, there are 126 different minerals in Tibet. When these resources were discovered by the Chinese, they were extensively mined without proper environmental safeguards, resulting in devastation of the environment. As a result, deforestation and mining are causing more floods in the lowlands of Tibet.

Actually, there were such devastating floods in western downstream China in the 1980s and 1990s, each one causing so much loss of life and so many tens of billions of dollars of damage, especially in the Yangtse basin, that the Chinese government itself began to try to stop the clear-cutting of the headwater forests. It has made some progress in replanting certain areas, though the effect will take decades to be felt. Since the time of the Dalai Lama's speech, there have been many more gigantic mineral discoveries, and Chinese mining plans have vastly expanded. This makes it all the more important that the plateau be placed in conservation, as this will assure that Chinese or other foreign mining concerns will be bound by strict environmental rules to maintain the most up-to-date and sophisticated safeguards against pollution.

The deforestation of the Tibetan plateau, according to experts, will change the amount of reflection from snow into space (forested areas absorb more solar radiation) and this affects the monsoon of the next year, not only in Tibet, but in all surrounding areas. Therefore, it becomes even more important to conserve Tibet's environment.

Although the research is still imprecise, it seems to be well accepted that the deforestation of the hills and the desertification of the steppes by overhunting and unskillful sedentary (using fencing) grazing patterns creates a powerful thermal reflection from the Roof of the World into the stratosphere. This blocks the normal flow of the westerly jet streams and complicates the El Niño patterns in the southern Pacific, making for powerful weather disruptions in Tibet's latitude the whole globe around, including the United States and Europe, not to mention downstream China. The Chinese meteorologist T. Zhang wrote, "The Qinghai-Tibetan Plateau is a harbinger of climate change due to its early and accelerated warming. It represents the largest high-elevation region on the globe … Observational evidence indicates that impacts related to climate warming are well underway on the Tibetan Plateau and involve increasing air temperature, vegetation degradation, the cumulative negative mass balance of glaciers, thickening of the active layer, and increases in permafrost temperature. The Qinghai-Tibetan Plateau … provides a crucial link for the water resources for most of the Asian continent, thereby impacting the livelihood of over 3.7 billion people. Climate change in this part of the world is arguably of heightened importance due to the plateau's far-reaching impacts across Asia, the northern hemisphere, and the globe."[5]

In his article he also states that intensive land exploitation has occurred in the region as a result of urban expansion and changes in agricultural and industrial practices. Tibet's population has tripled over the last forty-five years, entirely due to China's efforts to populate the plateau, and the new China-to-Lhasa train line will cause a dramatic influx of more people—residents and tourists alike. Human activities and needed infrastructure will have an impact on the land. Plus, the presence of more people has contributed to early snow thaws, which compromise the soil. Then there's the problem of livestock overgrazing: "severe land degradation and desertification are happening at an alarming rate, rendering the land unusable for agriculture and grazing."

"The pastoral society residing on the Qinghai-Tibetan Plateau was in equilibrium with its ecosystem for thousands of years, practicing seasonal moves to sustain the productivity of the land." As thousands were forced to settle and large numbers of immigrants arrived, the land was overgrazed, then replaced by cropland, and eventually in many places became barren ground. "It can be hypothesized that it is these land surface changes that are responsible for the reported climate change on the Qinghai-Tibetan Plateau," the article states. Vegetation changes led to less soil moisture, which raises temperatures. Higher temperatures dry out the land and change precipitation patterns, which further reduce vegetation and moisture. And on it goes. "There is thus a complex chain of events that have led to the current state of the ecosystems over the

Qinghai-Tibetan Plateau. The land degradation also affects the socioe-conomics of the region, which will have significant repercussions in the future, if current trends indeed accelerate as anticipated."

I think the climate change in Tibet will not affect Australia immediately. So your concern for Tibet is a genuine altruistic one. Concern from China and India may not be genuine as it directly relates to their own future.

In fact, it might affect the weather in Australia, causing unusual monsoon patterns that may well contribute to drought conditions there. So there may be self-interest in Australia's concern after all!

To quote Mr. Dekang, from the TEW website: "Tibet is 70 percent grassland and the health of these extensive grasslands is fundamental to the survival of about one million people consisting mainly of nomads and about 70 million population of domestic animals, such as sheep, goat and yak, and a countless number of wildlife.

"Leonard Clark, the American adventurer, in 1948 returned from Tibet with valuable botanical samples. He wrote, 'Surprisingly, our scientists estimated that among the basic foundation stones of ... [the vibrant nomadic economy] is grass, strong grass converted into excellent animal flesh—among the finest in the world. I was taking grass samples and seeds, hoping to transfer its power to the pastures of America and Europe.'"

Overgrazing by nomadic herders is not the culprit behind grassland degradation: "In fact many cases of grassland devastation are related to extensive use of nomadic pastures for Chinese military encampments and installations. In the Machu district in Amdo (Qinghai), one-third of over 10,000 sq. km., of Tibetan grasslands have been fenced for exclusive grazing of horses and cattle belonging to the Chinese army."

The loss of grasslands has been significant. Mr. Dekang goes on to say, "The principle pasture lands of Amdo (Qinghai) regions of Tibet before 1949 [i.e., before China's occupation of Tibet] grew to an average height of 20 cm, covering 75 to 90 percent of the area. Today, the grass grows to maximum height of only 10 cm while the percentage coverage of pasture lands has fallen considerably and grass yields are estimated to have fallen by approximately 50 percent....

"A widespread and economically very costly phenomenon has been the extinction of the four principal rat predators: foxes, weasels, cats, and owls. This had led to local outbreaks of massive rat infestation with ratpacks destroying crops in the daytime. For example, rat outbreaks damaged previously productive pastures in the Tibetan province of Amdo (Qinghai). In the late 1970s some 8 million hectares of pastures were affected (one eighth of the province's total), and the annual loss of dry grass reached 2.5 million tons, enough to feed more than 5 million sheep ..." These details exemplify the interconnectedness of this ecosystem and show how degradation in any form can have widespread ramifications throughout the whole.

> The Tibetan environment is very delicate and it is very important. Unfortunately, as you know, in the Communist world, in countries such as the former Soviet Union, Poland, and the former East Germany, there were many pollution problems in the past resulting from carelessness, simply because factories are growing bigger and production is rising with little regard to the damage this growth causes to the environment. The situation is the same in the People's Republic of China. In the 1970s and 1980s there was no awareness of pollution, although now I think some awareness is developing. So I think the situation was initially to do with ignorance.

With all the excitement about the intense growth of Chinese industry, since 2000 there has been a growing awareness of the tremendous impact the polluting factories and coal-powered power plants have had on the air quality all over China. This pollution has not affected Tibet much but has palpably affected Hong Kong, and more remotely Japan, Korea, and the west coast of North America, as the winds tend to be westerly. Articles recently published in the *New York Times*, *Time*, and *Newsweek* report how China Inc. bought entire old-fashioned smoke-belching steel mill complexes from the Saarbrücken area in Germany and shipped them piece-by-piece and set them up operationally in China, in all their polluting glory. It boggles the mind.

According to some information, it seems that during the Cultural Revolution (1966–1976), temples in China proper suffered less destruction than in other areas. This may not be due to government policy, but rather may be the result of discrimination by local officials. So it seems that Chinese officials have neglected the environment in the places where ethnic groups are living.

It has become clear that, while soldiers and workers from downstream China may have been more destructive in Tibet, a land they do not naturally identify as their own when they are actually there but feel as foreign, the intense pursuit of wealth throughout China has caused great ecological damage everywhere.

Another story comes from the Dingri region of southern Tibet. Five years ago a local Tibetan told me about a river that all the villagers used for drinking. There were also Chinese living in the area. The Chinese residents belonging to the People's Liberation Army (PLA) were informed not to drink the water from the river, but local Tibetans were not informed. Tibetans still drink the polluted water. This shows that some form of negligence is going on, this obviously is not because of lack of awareness, but due to other reasons. In this light, any concern from other human brothers and sisters for our unfortunate situation, unfortunate people and their environment is very gratefully received and very important.

This is a sad illustration of the genocidal tendency the Chinese have in their "final solution" to the Tibet problem.

Then talking about the environment more generally, it comes to mind that one key factor in the future is human population. Look at India and China, there are so many people. The standard of living is very low. It is very difficult to explain or educate the masses about the environment when their most pressing concern is survival.

The Dalai Lama shows his more global concern for overpopulation, one of the disasters caused by the military-industrial development model of limitless growth that holds the world economy in its grip.

For example, in our second home in the Kangra valley (Himachal Pradesh, India), the local Indian villager's survival depends on cutting wood and slate mining. On the eastern side of Dharamsala we have large-scale slate quarries. Some of my Indian friends told me that I should speak out about the huge environmental damage that these quarries cause, but it is very difficult, for at least a few hundred families' livelihoods depend solely on these activities. Unless we show them new ways of earning their livelihood, it is very difficult to stop them. Therefore, the population explosion is ultimately a very serious matter. So family planning is crucial, especially in the developing world.

China does get congratulations for limiting families to one child per family, on paper, and at least somewhat in practice. Traditional Tibet kept its population in check by the unusual social institution of mass monasticism, taking 20 percent of the males and perhaps 10 percent of the females out of the reproduction process. The exile community shows the continuing strength of that Tibetan institution by maintaining similar percentages of monastics even under the sparse economic conditions of exile, begun as destitute refugees.

Then there are industries such as the meat industries, where killing of animals takes place on a large scale. This is not only cruel, but it has very negative effects on the environment. There are industries that produce constructive machineries. There may be some justification for their existence. But those that produce destructive things, such as war machines, do great damage.

Some companies and governments actually make profit from these activities, but the nature of their production is a destructive one. For example, a bullet is designed to kill a person, not as a decoration piece! All these war machines look very beautiful. When I was small, these machines seemed beautiful to me, even small toys like tanks and machine guns seemed very beautiful, very smart, don't

*you think? The whole military establishment, their uniforms, their discipline,
everything seems very striking and very impressive, but the very purpose of this
organization is to kill. So we must think of these matters if we are to be truly
concerned about the environment, not only for this generation, but for future
generations as well.*

The Dalai Lama from his own perspective touches the theme so dear
to the heart of the European and American 1960s generations—and
now a generation of their children—based on the awareness that the
worldwide war industries constitute an inordinately huge part of the
global economy, trillions of dollars circulating through it. Were those
trillions instead put to use cleaning up the environment, improving the
livelihoods of the masses, educating families on family planning methods, creating infrastructure to conserve water and energy, and so on, the
world would look very, very different even in a few years, with a real rise
in standards of living everywhere for all classes of people in all nations
and continents.

*I think all these things are interrelated. As I mentioned earlier, family planning
should be encouraged. From a Buddhist perspective it is quite simple. Each
human life is very precious. From this perspective it is better to avoid any control
of birth, but today there are 6.5 billion precious lives—too many precious lives!
As a result it is not only one or two precious human lives that are at stake, but
the question is of the survival of humanity at large. So therefore the conclusion
we arrive at is that we must take family planning very seriously, if we are to
save the prosperity of entire humanity, preferably through nonviolent means, not
through abortion or killing, but by some other means. I often half jokingly say
. . . more monks and nuns [roar of laughter]. That is the most nonviolent and
effective method. So if you can't become a monk or a nun then practice other
nonviolent methods of birth control.*

*Then there is the question of how to reduce military establishments. The
groundwork we must do is to promote nonviolence. But this is not enough
because we have so many conflicts in this world. So long as humanity remains,*

so will conflict. One way of promoting nonviolence against warfare and the production of weapons is to promote ideas of dialogue and compromise, and the spirit of reconciliation. I think we must promote these ideas at the family and community level. It is much more practical to solve problems through dialogue rather than through confrontation.

Here he broaches the idea he first put forward in a globally prophetic way in his speech to the Nobel Peace Prize committee, developed further in his book *Ethics for the New Millennium*, and delivered in the 9/11 time of crisis in his European Parliament speech in 2001, as quoted earlier in this book. The United States and the Soviet Union avoided direct and all-out conflict for over forty years of the Cold War. They had to dialogue with each other when push came to shove because the weapons were too powerful for either side to be the clear victor in any all-out war. Yet in cases like the Israeli-Palestinian conflict, the American and Iraqi conflict, and countless smaller conflicts, the more powerful side thinks it doesn't need to talk to the weaker side, and so the wars continue. The Dalai Lama offered, before the second American invasion, to join other Nobel Peace Prize laureates and go all together to Iraq and dialogue with Saddam Hussein and bring his concerns back to the American President and Congress. But other laureates were unwilling to go and the Dalai Lama felt his impact would be insignificant all alone, a nonbelieving Buddhist in a Muslim country.

So the concept of dialogue must begin at the family level. As individuals we must look within, investigate, analyze, and then try to overcome contradictory ideas. We must not lose hope or despair of the irritating conflict we find inside ourselves. So these are some of the ways in which we can ultimately solve environmental problems.

Just as Confucius did, the Dalai Lama looks to home to solve problems abroad, looks within to solve the problems outside. First educate and harmonize your inner self, then your family will be harmonious. Once the family is harmonious, the community will be harmonious. Once the community is harmonious, the nation will be harmonious. The Dalai Lama always says, "World peace through inner peace."

> *Finally, I want to tell you that self-confidence and enthusiasm are the key to a successful life and to succeed in any activity one is engaged in. We must be determined and must have an optimistic outlook; then even if we fail, we will have no regrets. On the other hand, lack of determination and effort will cause double regret. Firstly because the objectives were not realized, and secondly because you feel guilty and regret at not having made full effort in the realization of the objectives.*

This couldn't be a better description of what I am trying to accomplish in this book. We need to restore, not only in those who don't care anyway, but also in those who are friends of Tibet the confidence that this problem of the Chinese exaggerations and destructive policies in Tibet can be stopped. The Chinese people and leadership can and will come to see that they are self-defeating, and can and will adopt a more reasonable, effective, and enjoyable policy and practice. How can we work with full enthusiasm and dedication for Tibet's freedom if in our hearts we think it is a lost cause? To achieve success, we need positive thought—it is a cardinal principle in Buddhist psychology. Negative thought is actually despair. Despair only leads to violence, either futile and ultimately self-defeating lashing out at the enemy or internal self-destruction by impotently nursing hatred and bitterness.

> *So therefore, whether we commit ourselves or not it is an individual choice. Once you have made up your mind, you must go forward with a single-minded devotion in spite of the obstacles. This is very important.*

The Dalai Lama here describes his own determination and commitment. He is outstanding in his own example that his recommendation of such determination toward the positive carries a powerful force. This is just how he manages not to waver in his pursuit of a positive solution to the problem between his people and the Chinese occupiers of their land.

Finally I would like to express my deep appreciation to all participants and those who organized this conference. I very much appreciate it. I would also like to express my deep appreciation on behalf of the six million Tibetan people whose lives are very much in danger due to pollution. Some children are already suffering from illness because of air pollution. There is tremendous anxiety and suffering, and their voices may not be heard widely. They simply express their grievances within the confines of their small homes. I would like to express my deep appreciation on behalf of all these innocent people. Thank you!

The bodhisattva Avalokiteshvara is often iconically represented by an image of a deity with ten heads stacked up three to a tier, with a single fierce head on top of the stack, and a thousand arms branching out from an inconceivably powerful heart, chest, and shoulders, with each hand having an eye in its palm. This form of the divine bodhisattva is saluted by the verse: "With the thousand arms of the thousand world emperors, and the thousand eyes of the thousand buddhas of this good eon, to you, who manifest whatsoever educates whomsoever, the teacher Avalokiteshvara, I bow!" The Dalai Lama concludes with this reference to the million small children present in Tibetan homes under Chinese occupation, often bereft of grandparents, without much future, poor. Their mothers are likely employed in manual labor and their fathers are likely unemployed. They are malnourished, with no prospect of a Tibetan education and little prospect of the Chinese education necessary to survive in the Chinese colonial economy, exposed to pollutants in the overstrained water system and in the air due to polluting energy sources, combustion engines, and cooking fires of millions of Chinese settlers and soldiers.

We might hear this and consider it just a cliché, or read it quickly as a light human touch. But if we have gained a sense of who and what the Dalai Lama is, we realize that he feels the situations of these children and their homes. His thousand eyes are constantly aware of their lives as they experience them, his thousand arms reach out to them to remove the obstacles to their lives as best he can, and his gentle but booming voice naturally rises to speak for them. The phrases about how they are anxious and how they suffer, and about how they can only cry and complain within their little rooms where they are confined give us the picture that he sees, even though he is far away in Australia giving a talk to a cheerful, delighted audience. But the Dalai Lama speaks to the Australians on behalf of his small and suffering people, does not leave them out, reveals himself as the emissary of the powerless and meek. It is overwhelming.

ENDNOTES

1. R. L. Fleming Jr., Dorje Tsering, Liu Wulin, *Across the Tibetan Plateau: Ecosystems, Wildlife, and Conservation*, W. W. Norton, 2007.

2. Most of the information in my commentaries in this chapter comes from the Tibet Environment Watch (TEW) website (www.tew.org), from information compiled by Tsultrim Palden Dekhang.

3. In the eastern Tibetan region of Kham (now mostly divided into TAPs), there are "giant pandas, white-lipped deer, takin (a rare, deer-like animal), musk deer, and goral sheep. There are also unique indigenous birds, such as the Himalayan monal, the snow cock, the satyr tragopan bird, the Tibetan partridge, and the blood pheasant. Mr. Dekhang quotes the Chinese biologists, who found in just the northeastern Amdo province (now divided into the Qinghai TAPs) an estimated ten million birds belonging to two hundred species. Tsongon (Kokonor) lake in Amdo alone hosts ten out of fifteen duck families on record worldwide. Chinese statistics claim that the total fish catch from the lake from 1957–1970 was approximately 128,500 tons." It is hard to imagine how this count could be accurate, but we can certainly imagine the huge salt lake had a lot of fish, as the locals had not been catching them for centuries before the Chinese came. "According to the Chinese botanists Wu and Feng (1992), on the Tibetan Plateau there are over 12,000 species of 1,500 genera of vascular plants, accounting for over half of the total genera found in China. There are over 5,000 species of 700 genera of fungi, accounting for 82.4 percent of the total kinds of mushroms found in China; 210 species belonging to 29 families of mammals, accounting for 65.90 percent of the total families found in China."

4. The endangered list includes four varieties of the rare takin, the Tibetan wild yak, the ibex wild goat, the serow goat, the white-lipped deer, the red deer, McNeil's Deer, Pere David's deer, the Himalayan tahr, three types of musk deer, the red goral, the Tibetan argali sheep, the Tibetan antelope (an Olympic mascot!), the blue bharal, the giant panda (another Olympic mascot), the red panda, the Oriental small-clawed

otter and the regular otter, the lynx, the clouded leopard and the snow leopard, the stone marten, the Siberian tiger, the black bear, the Tibetan brown bear, the kyang or Tibetan wild ass, the golden snub-nosed monkey, and the Assamese, Rhesus, and Tibetan macaques. Listed among endangered birds are the wood snipe, the black-tailed godwit, the spoonbill, the Tibetan sand grouse, the Rufous-necked hornbill, the Golden eagle, the Long-legged boteo, the Saker falcon, the Lammmergeier bearded vulture, the Pallas's fishing eagle, the Brahmany kite, the red-breasted hill, the Rufous-throated, the snow, and the Tibetan partridges, five kinds of pheasants, the Himalayan and the Tibetan snowcocks, the Blyth's grey-bellied, the Satyr, and the Temminck tragopans, the demoiselle and the black-necked cranes, the Koslow bunting, the long-billed calandra lark, and the red-headed trogon.

5. "Perspectives on Environmental Study of Response to Climatic and Land Cover/Land Use Change over the Qinghai-Tibetan Plateau: an Introduction." Tingjun Zhang, Chinese Academy of Meteorological Sciences, China Meteorological Administration, Beijing 800081, China.

9

FREEING TIBET: A GREAT WIN FOR CHINA AND TIBET, ECOLOGICALLY AND ECONOMICALLY

As China's greatest environmental preserve, 100 percent of it, an internally autonomous or Böd Autonomous Region (BAR), will do justice to the Tibetan people, begin to restore the land of the high plateau—the water tower of Asia—bring enormous prestige and honor to China, and jumpstart a powerful trend on the planet that might yet save it from various doomsday scenarios—military-political, ideological-religious, racial-nationalist, and environmental. But it will also be much more highly profitable to China, not only better for Tibet itself. Pure resource extraction, as occurred pell-mell from the 1950s to the 1990s and still continues in many areas more quietly today, has gone about as far as it can without various inputs that are not there, and the side effects of the environmental damage wrought is costing more than the profit gained by the use or sale of the resources. Consciously or unconsciously, colonialist management of a complex and delicate ecosystem, such as Great Tibet's, is not only morally indefensible and environmentally destructive but it can never be efficient, much less sustainable. On the other hand, with continuing investment and technical inputs from downstream China and from all around the world, left to their own instincts and ingenuity and the joy of freedom, the Tibetans themselves can manage a much more sustainable and profitable economy.

This free Tibetan economy can be based on:

1. A much more restricted, high value–added tourism
2. A Switzerland of Asia–style global finance and banking industry
3. Sustainable, nonpolluting mining
4. Sustainable forest management
5. Sustainable medicinal herb harvesting
6. Luxury, or designer, water bottling
7. Environmentally beneficial agricultural products
8. Exotic and high-value salt products
9. Fine tea, exotically marketable
10. Sustainable, high-quality wool production and value-adding carpet-weaving
11. Other assets the Tibetans themselves will undoubtedly think of

We will go through each of these sources of income one by one and envision them thriving in the new Tibet. It will demonstrate how having Tibetans be the principals in these endeavors will make them more profitable in addition to more sustainable.

Before that, though, it bears repeating that eliminating the enormous cost of subsidizing Han Chinese in-migration, or better perhaps up-migration, to the high plateau is the first earning of the win-win scenario, right off the bat. It was the Tenth Panchen Rinpoche in 1987 who wondered why there was such a rush to colonize Tibet when it cost four times as much to settle and support a Han Chinese there as it did to do the same in her or his low altitude home territory. Then there is the saving of the huge military equipment and personnel costs, not needed to defend any frontiers, as no one has ever attempted to cross the nearly impenetrable Himalayan wall barrier, but needed to suppress the Tibetan people chafing under occupation (just as the Han Chinese people chafed under Western and Japanese colonialists). Then there is the saving of the future huge costs of repairing the great environmental damage being wrought there by the intensive population the fragile plateau never can support sustainably. Add to that the incalculable costs of downstream damage and threat to life due to disturbance of the river systems and monsoon weather patterns flowing and blowing into China. Finally, there is the saving of the immense propaganda costs of trying to persuade the world that China is not an aggressive, expansionist would-be military-industrial superpower when it is indeed behaving as one. It's so much cheaper and easier just not to behave that way.

The great thing holding back progress in all these industries, such as they exist at the moment, is that their market is restricted to mainly Chinese customers, so the money coming in is simply recirculating within China. Foreigners (e.g. the world market) not believing in the government's propaganda about how happy and liberated Tibetans are revulsed by the garish shopping malls, discotheques, and brothels, will not return to a high-altitude colonial country with a subject people miserably held down under occupation. Therefore, the goods produced in Tibet currently cannot be successfully marketed internationally, and the tourism is increasingly becoming simply internal Chinese tourism. The minerals cannot be exploited very well either, since foreign companies are hesitant to enter Tibet for business because of the human rights stigma attached to it in their home societies.

New Tibetan Industries

Tourism

First let's consider the tourist industry. After the monumental turn-around decision of the Chinese leadership makes lasting headlines the world over, there will be intense international interest in Tibet. It will be able to return to being a magnet for international tourism, as it was briefly during the eighties, when under Deng Xiaoping and Hu Yaobang the Chinese were focused on restoring their economy after the long Mao catastrophe and were temporarily a bit more hands off with Tibet. Existing Han Chinese investment, from either People's Liberation Army businesses or private investors in transportation networks, hotels, restaurants, and so forth will be secure under the agreement, of course, but there will be a both immediate and gradual process of training and employing Tibetan tourist workers in place of migrant Han Chinese. Brothels and discos will be removed and cleaned up, as the removal of internal military forces will reduce their clientele, and high-value tourists are repulsed by them.

The state-run Chinese Xinhua newspaper claimed that in 2006, four million tourists visited Tibet, which is probably exaggerated. The new train supposedly brought in almost two million, and airplanes perhaps the rest. Only a few hundred thousand of these were international, and certainly none of them will want to repeat such a crowded, low-quality experience. The hotel and transport infrastructure for such a horde of people is not adequate; the health centers alone can not handle so much altitude sickness as would result among such a number, and the monuments to be visited could not sustain such a constant crowd.

The solution to these problems is to reduce the number by 75 or 80 percent, to less than a million in the entire BAR, and to raise prices by four times. High-value international visitors will want to visit with the internally free Tibetans, who will be dancing and singing with joy under the new autonomous government, free of the oppressive presence of Chinese soldiers and police. They will go to the Tibetans' own unconstrained spiritual and holiday festivals, visit their reborn monasteries, study Buddhist Dharma teachings and meditation with their returned high lamas, such as the Dalai Lama and the head lamas of other orders, and travel with the proudly indigenous people to the many adventure and eco-travel destinations.

A Chinese and international high level of investment can upgrade the accommodations to a more luxurious standard, and the restriction on the number will make it an even more prestigious destination, following the pattern that has been so successful on a smaller scale for Bhutan. The investors can make much better money in high value–added adventure, eco, health, and spiritual tourism, and the Tibetan marketing mystique will attract large numbers from Europe, Japan, India, Russia, Australia, and the Americas. This tourism will be sustainable, as many people will come back again and again, developing friendships among the free Tibetans, and the money will come as foreign exchange, which will be highly welcome for China's overall economy after the current export trade surpluses have diminished due to world-wide recession and consumer collapse.

FINANCE

This one might surprise you. The Dalai Lama loves Switzerland, and it is only fitting that Tibet become the Switzerland of Asia, sharing that honor with Bhutan, potentially Nepal, and the Indian Arunachal, Sikkim, and Ladakh regions (such a prosperous zone of peace might even inspire India's Kashmir and the Himalayan sectors of Pakistan, such as Swat, to join in spirit if not formally). Let us remember that this honored position will still be—and even more important legitimately, be—part of China. It will be, after all, China's creation through China's turning away from the conquer-and-colonize empire approach toward the liberate-and-invest commonwealth approach. So its flourishing will be China's flourishing. The world will see that first the Tibetans themselves are lifted out of poverty into an internationally acceptable standard of living, and then no one will begrudge the Chinese investors and businesses the long-term money they will make in partnership with the joyously willing Tibetans.

Now, since the Basic Law of Tibet, in accordance with the Dalai Lama's preliminary sketch for a democratic constitution for an internally autonomous Tibet, will be much more autonomous than that of the Hong Kong Autonomous Region, Tibet can be accepted by the global financial industry and private financiers as a truly independent banking haven, not under the intrusive control of China. Such a highly autonomous Tibet can then pass plausibly secure privacy laws (a sector of the Tibetan banking economy could be declared formally immune to scrutiny from the Chinese government to assure account holders' privacy) that could attract international capital and financial accounts from all over the world.

China will be the ultimate beneficiary of the prosperity this will generate, as, based on the vote, it will have legitimate sovereignty with regard to Tibet, as long as the genuine autonomy is respected. Nevertheless, the privacy laws could convince sophisticated clients, perhaps mainly Asian, that their records there would be secure even from China, these being strict laws that could not be passed and credibly maintained in huge economies like China's. Today, Swiss banking thrives, which is seen as advantageous for its independence and neutrality in many circumstances, even by big European central banks. The 1.4 trillion dollar sovereign fund China now holds in depreciating dollar assets cannot be easily invested elsewhere in the world economy as many countries consider its huge investments to be political acts, a sort of financial invasion that they cannot tolerate. Therefore, channeling these funds through the technically autonomous Tibetan financial institutions, the investments could enter non-Chinese economies much more freely, not only being perceived as, but actually being, non-threatening.

Of course, the same can be done through Hong Kong to a certain extent, though high-level financiers do not yet fully trust the "One-Country, Two-Systems" approach still alive in Hong Kong, but under pressure from a Basic Law that evinces direct subordination to the Beijing government in almost every provision. Establishing a similar but far more autonomous pattern in the reborn Tibet could persuade these financial heavyweights that China is learning to play by truly non-colonialist rules, and so can be trusted not to interfere with their accounts located in Tibet, the Asian Switzerland. The example of noninterference set up for Tibet could bring the great prize of Taiwan finally into another "One-Country, Two-Systems" arrangement on the basis of trust established by the Taiwanese people witnessing the astoundingly innovative, courageous and fruitful Tibetan arrangement.

MINING AND ENERGY

The mining and energy industries could at last be upgraded by inviting foreign and international operators to work freely in Tibet, of course under strict green principles as supervised by the Tibetans themselves as custodians of their own environment. But since the Tibetan autonomous government would be their hosts, they would no longer experience human rights and environmental advocates lobbying against them worldwide. The Tibetans would be their partners, along with the Chinese, so the international community would see their work there as part of developing the Tibetan economy for the Tibetans in an exemplary, environmentally responsible way. And the partnership with Chinese individuals and businesses would have no impediment and will be far more profitable and sustainable than it could ever be under the present colonialist arrangement.

TIMBER

Environment-destroying logging practices like large-scale clear-cutting are decreasing now that people understand the cost of the devastating floods caused by the previous forty years of colonialist clear-cutting. With massive restoration of denuded areas, which will be a long and painstaking process due to the high altitude, scientific management of the remaining stands of primeval rainforest at sustainable level could still support a profitable industry.

ALTERNATIVE MEDICINE

The Dalai Lama has a particular personal interest in this industry. Twenty-seven years ago, in an interview for a documentary, I asked him how he saw a free Tibet in the future. What would its main industries be? How would it relate to the outside world? He very strongly resisted my questions, saying that he just wanted to see his people free and out from under their oppression, and was not scheming as to what to do with a Tibet reborn. But I persisted, urging that expressing whatever he could imagine would be inspiring to the friends of Tibet who would then more strongly share his goals. I was not surprised when he mentioned his desire to be like Switzerland, but I was surprised when he mentioned the aspect of Switzerland that is its many sanatoria, its health resorts, and its phyto-pharmaceutical industries.

He knew that I had studied Tibetan Medicine when I was a monk, so he leaned into his love for the Traditional Tibetan Medicine, its lifestyle practicality and nutritional wisdom, the special medicinal smell of its herbal compounds, the sophistication of its various therapies. His eyes glowed as he thought of Tibet's economy being sustained by her peoples' cultivated and Buddhist compassion-inspired vocation of offering healing to the sick people of the world, who would turn to Tibet's fresh air and unspoiled nature, its mineral baths, its world-class sanatoria, and its originally plentiful and Asia-wide famous Himalayan herbs. In this moment of enthusiasm, he specially mentioned the region of Kongpo, where I had not yet visited, which had very beautiful areas at not too high an altitude, very like some of the places he had visited in Switzerland. Then he suddenly turned sad, his voice trailing off as he remembered that he had heard that Kongpo had been extremely heavily logged and maybe it was no longer as he remembered it.

Under the current, and obsolete, system of Tibet colonialism, many billions of dollars worth of the precious and potent Himalayan medicinal herbs, already treasured in all Asian medicines and eventually highly valued in the rest of the world, have been extracted unsustainably. They've been sold off in the downstream Chinese market at prices much below their world value because they cannot be marketed effectively internationally as Tibetan herbs, since China's reputation of mercilessly repressing Tibetans and exploiting Tibet is so widespread. Under the new arrangement for the autonomous free Tibet to be reborn, an indigenous Tibetan medicinal herb industry combined with world-class destinations and restorative spiritual spas will be a huge money earner. A sincerely green and spiritually impeccable Tibetan marketing mystique would make this industry a worldwide success; it would become a leader in the burgeoning international holistic health industries, fulfilling another aspect of the Dalai Lama's Switzerland of Asia dream, while abundantly enriching Chinese public and private sectors, and offering authentically compounded and spiritually empowered traditional healing medicines to the Chinese people.

LUXURY BOTTLED WATER

Everest, Kailash, and K-2 are mountains that could lend their illustrious names to precious luxury waters, the Evians and Pellegrinos of Tibet, crystal glacial Himalayan water. Manufactured and bottled in crystal bottles with the most stringent modern chemical standards of purity while yet retaining unique Tibetan healing mineral content, they could be prayed over by teams of medicinal healing monks and nuns. Advertised with authentic Traditional Tibetan Medicine chants of blessing, these would be a major export from the country where the headwaters of all of Asia's major river systems originate. Volume would not need to be so huge as to endanger any local water supplies; as an exotic and precious water, it could be sold at luxury and medicinal prices far above normal drinking water prices, so the volume would not have to be so great. The dedication to environmental preservation of the entire country would instill confidence in the product, while not endangering the flow of water down to the various neighboring countries of south and southeast Asia, as well as downstream China.

HIGH-VALUE AGRICULTURE

China's autonomous BAR could further commercially exploit its instant image as the ultimate organic farm country for certain specialty products, in addition to the medicinal herbs. Whatever can be grown in high altitude—barley, goji berries, special grasses, exotic legumes, tubers, and sprouts, untouched by the modern chemical and biological meddling of most of the global economy, can be profitably marketed. Products with *Tibetan* on the label, exported from the proverbial land of purity, will fetch wonderful prices and be considered immensely valuable worldwide.

This will not have to endanger local food supplies for the Tibetan population, who are presently found by NGO medical studies to be malnourished due to the colonization and preferential treatment given to Chinese immigrants. With the restoration of Tibet's rather more sparse population density, the greenhouses and other agricultural facilities left by the Chinese will easily be able to support the much smaller indigenous population. A freed-up, sustainable, traditional Tibetan agricultural industry will restore the grasslands, maintain the farmlands, and bring them back up to their natural sufficiency. After all, there was no recorded famine in Tibet in the last, at least, eight centuries, until the Chinese intervened.

EXOTIC SALTS

Salt used to be a major export of the independent Tibet, trading across the Himalayas to India and Nepal and also down the plains to western China. Coming from the dried beds of the ancient Tethys Sea that existed before the Indian tectonic plate collided with the Asian plate and lifted Tibet to its double altitude, the Tibetan salt industry can rival Israeli and Jordanian Dead Sea salts with its exotic and healthful qualities. It is a product of the most ancient sea, prior to the formation of the continent of Eurasia, long before any pollution by humans. It can become immensely valuable, based on a green and clean and humanly benevolent marketing image, the latter achieved by China's gracious and world-transforming leadership action of freeing the Tibetans in a true internal autonomy that at last wins China the trusting allegiance of the fiercely independent-minded Tibetans.

TEA

Chinese, Indian, and Sri Lankan teas are the most well established and famous around the world and are likely to stay that way for a long time. However, specialty Tibetan brands are likely to do very well due to their exotic image as well as excellent taste. The fine tea from the Yigong Tea Estate mentioned in *Across the Tibetan Plateau* is just one example.

WOOL

Along with salt, wool traditionally has been perhaps Tibet's greatest export, due to the exceptional richness and vastness of the Tibetan high altitude grasslands, which have been sustainably maintained for thousands of years by the amazing yak (the word in Tibetan refers only to the male) and his female partner, the dri. The yak and dri are browsers, not grazers, which means their rough tongues lick the grass blade off its root, so they do not bite into it and do not pull up the root, as grazing animals tend to do. Sheep, goats, horses, and cows do graze, and so in large numbers they are destroying the huge high-altitude steppe of northern Tibet and the high-altitude steep mountain slopes even in the south. It is only the yak and dri that have made Tibet livable for Tibetans over the millennia by preserving the grasslands while turning its abundant energy into reliable and sure-footed transport, wool for felt and woven fabric, the richest milk of any bovine animal, leather, meat, bone implements, and dung for fuel. Yak wool is incredibly durable—yielding a tightly woven cloth lasting for centuries, warm and strong—while the under neck and chest hairs can be soft and delicate as cashmere. Yak wool should be emphasized, as the yak is the least ecologically damaging of the browsing and grazing animals.

It is also a fact that the Tibetan weaving industry has great potential. The relatively small number of Tibetan exiles in Nepal have turned their rug-weaving industry into Nepal's largest and most profitable export industry. Given the much greater numbers and resources within Tibet itself, the rug industry can become a national treasure, sending a sturdy and beautiful product around the world and enriching the Tibetans themselves, as well as their Chinese brothers and sisters.

Finally, there will be other creative entrepreneurial enterprises that the liberated and educated Tibetans will think of and initiate. The establishment of a UN branch headquarters there, an Asian Geneva, where conflict prevention and peacemaking studies and practices could be centered, would generate considerable local economic benefit. Perhaps the Dalai Lama could simultaneously continue his emulation of the Swiss and go back to one of the hobbies of his youth by returning to timepieces, beginning a Tibetan watch industry, a fine outlet for the abundant talents of Tibetan craftspeople. An autonomous Tibet would have unlimited options.

CONCLUSION

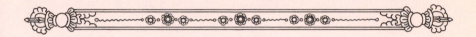

The miraculous display we all need to experience is the vision of Great Tibet, the Böd Autonomous Region, as the restored home of the unique Tibetan people, with their genetically high-altitude-adaptive lungs, their nitric-oxide-saturated oxygen-transporting bloodstreams, their culturally Buddhacized sharp, rational intellects, and their kind and friendly hearts. We need to see how they are already, even under brutal pressure, mostly free in their minds, free in their connection to their high plateau, and free in their sense of their own myth and history as a people and a civilized nation. I am confident the Chinese will awaken to this and save themselves by saving Tibet, honoring their other neighbors, and restoring their own environment.

Every one of us can participate in this reality for Tibet through our conviction that this hopeful picture is possible. Since the positive vision of one is a powerful thing, so much more so the shared vision of many.

Chinese people themselves, though consciously misinformed by their government, are subliminally aware that Tibet is not China. They see the ancient treaty made between the Tang Dynasty and Tibetan emperors in the ninth century, that "Chinese will be happy in China and Tibetans happy in Tibet." They sense they are invaders in Tibet, they are hyper-sensitive about anyone mentioning the fact that their possession of Tibet is not validated by history or international law. They are relying on time to make people forget about Tibet, including new generations of sino-cized Tibetans, and the eventual triumph of their propaganda. I am confident that they will see the futility of this and change their course quite soon—and I am not alone in my hopeful beliefs.

The Dalai Lama knows that Tibet is a free country and that he is a free man and Buddhist monk with a right to live there. Based on that profound confidence, he has inspired people and institutions worldwide to let them know that Tibet certainly does exist; merely its surface is occupied by China. Everyone can easily see what China is doing in Tibet, so the more the Chinese stick to their propaganda campaign, the more hostility they show toward the Dalai Lama, and the more they negate the very existence of the Tibetans' rights, the more ridiculous they appear in the eyes of a world they are trying to impress with their Olympics and their skyscrapers. I am confident they will get the clear picture of this and will desist, sooner or later.

The Dalai Lama is a Nobel Peace Prize Laureate and an honorary citizen of India, Canada, and the United States, where in October 2007 he received the Congressional Gold Medal, the highest honor the United States can bestow on an individual. He is friends with almost every major world leader, and he also very much wants to be friends with the great leaders of China. They could take advantage of his friendship and receive his blessing and assistance if they would simply face reality, disown the errors of their predecessors, and allow the Tibetan people their right of self-determination. I am confident that President Hu or his successor will seize this opportunity.

The Dalai Lama already does determine his freedom, and yet he looks at the situation and decides that since he is free, he can throw in his lot and that of his people with their nearest, most deeply concerned big neighbor. So he has signaled the Chinese leadership that although he and his people naturally prefer absolute freedom to being under anyone at all, they have to be dependent on their bigger neighbors. Since there are many Chinese now in the lower altitude, eastern parts of Great Tibet, some of whom might actually be willing and able to stay on even under post-occupation arrangements, he considers it wise and most propitious for himself and his people to vote to join China in a legitimate union, as long as their genuine internal autonomy is real and uncompromised. I am confident that this will begin the long and arduous restoration of Tibet as a free and well-supported prosperous homeland for Tibetans and a central land of Dharma.

This is confusing to many of the Dalai Lama's friends who think there is no such thing as a genuine autonomy; as long as your country is under some other country, they think, you are not autonomous but subject to that country. The Dalai Lama acknowledges their fears and their feelings as well as their reasonable historical arguments, but he nonetheless persists in proposing his Middle Way path for Tibet—midway between the extremes of outright independence that Tibetans have always had and still emotionally want and the absolute subjugation by China under which they presently suffer. I am confident that this confusion will soon be over.

The Chinese military businesses have made a lot of money in Tibet and intend to make a great deal more. The Chinese Government has been wasting equally great sums of money by paying the military to be there to suppress the Tibetan people and by subsidizing a mass colonization that will not last, due to the physical impossibility of large numbers of Chinese people successfully acclimatizing to the high altitude as medical research has shown. The more they spend on trying to make Tibet livable for non-Tibetan people, the more money they are wasting.

The Chinese leaders did pursue a final solution for the Tibetan people, which was mass extermination from the 1950s through the 1970s, and which now is merciless repression and a slow extermination through assimilation into the masses of Chinese trying to settle on the plateau. I am confident they will see that it will no longer work for colonists to behave like the Europeans did by committing genocide of the native people of North and South America, and still get away with it in the eyes of the global community.

The current situation is all very bad for Tibet and the Tibetans, but also very bad for China and the Chinese. China is doing well economically in conventional industrial terms, and if the Chinese used their money wisely and equitably, they could accomplish their material goals for their people. Their people have so many needs at home they really can't afford this nonviable colonization project any more than the United States can afford its overextended military adventures around the world. China's leaders would be strangely megalomaniac if they thought they would emerge as the military-industrial superpower on the planet and embark on a twenty-first century worldwide empire along the nineteenth-century British lines. I am confident insightful Chinese thinkers will see how they have to change course very soon, and how they could lead the rest of the nations to change the world system from military-industrial to conversational, ecological, spiritual, and more naturally peaceful.

There is a real need for China and the world to get along harmoniously. In order to gain the world's trust, China needs to have trustworthy deeds to point to, and the easiest and most trustworthy deed to point to would be its voluntary and enlightened liberation of Tibet. At the same time, thanks to the key player, the Dalai Lama, and his nonviolent peacemaking, China would gain the Dalai Lama as an ally. With his help, China would have a near 100 percent chance of acquiring the genuinely autonomous free Tibet legitimately through an internationally monitored vote in which the Dalai Lama would campaign for the Tibetans to join in a federal union with China. I am confident this deal could go through and could work out well for all concerned, if those in power, who stand the most to gain if they could see far down the chain of consequences, would just do it.

Chinese leaders now see the Dalai Lama as their enemy, disgracing themselves by pouring vitriol on possibly the most admired person on the planet. Chinese leaders are thinking that the death of the Dalai

Lama is the end of their problem—the illegitimacy of their possession of Tibet. But the opposite is the case: the Dalai Lama himself is the solution. The Dalai Lama has a benefit for everyone involved. He is the win-win bodhisattva. I am confident that this becomes more and more evident the more contact one has with him, through meeting, reading, or listening.

I wrote this book to kindle a vision in the mind of everyone who loves Tibet, who loves China, who loves the world and wants to see it all restored to balance to sustain many generations in the future. I don't pretend to speak for either the Dalai Lama or any Chinese leaders. I am just tired of people feeling that Tibet is doomed, China is hopelessly destructive and self-defeating, and even the whole world is wobbling on its axis, the last days having come upon us. Once we lose hope in that way, we withdraw into a passive sadness, or numb our emotions in frenetic rounds of distractions and entertainments. Some may consider this win-win solution to be science fiction or irrelevant to their worries. If so, may it not trouble their minds. I am confident they will enjoy it later.

I only ask that all admit, once and for all, that leaders in these positions could change their policies and their paths in these ways, and if they did, conditions would undoubtedly be better for many people. They may not, but they could. Therefore, though it might not happen, that is no reason to see it as impossible and to give up deep inside. We must be creative in seeing the various angles of the solution's close possibility, so as to be inspired to work for it, against all odds if necessary, and without ever giving up.

AFTERWORD

TEN POINTS OF HOPE

1. It is not true that the world always has to be a mess and vale of misery. It can be beautiful and meaningful, and the human life form is a wonderful opportunity to reach the highest fulfillment imaginable.
2. The Buddha's Noble Truth of Suffering means that life dominated by misknowledge will always be unsatisfactory, but that is not a final destination; it means that we can develop wisdom to eliminate misknowledge and then live free in bliss and share that bliss with others.
3. War and violence are not at all inevitable. When leaders and their people recognize this precious nature of human life in particular and all sentient life in general, they can definitely improve the nature of a society, can live sensibly and in harmony with nature and with one another. Being civilized means being wise, gentle, loving, and happy, and a society that enshrines those qualities is truly a civilization. There are definite examples of societies that have successfully cultivated a higher degree of gentleness, such as those of ancient India, Tibet, Mongolia, and China in certain flourishing periods.
4. The time we now live in is a unique moment when, due to science, technology, and the teachings of all the great religions, human beings could awaken to their true potential in larger numbers than ever before, and we really could realize the ancient dream of peace on earth, goodwill to all beings (not only humans).
5. Tibet is a special land, the highest "roof of the world", and it is a shining example of what spiritual heights some members of a society can achieve when supported by a people who, in the main, have limited their greed for wealth and abandoned any admiration for violence and militarism. They once were successful militarists, and they became a peaceful people. They prove it can be done.
6. China has both sides in its history; it reached high points of civilization at times, and at other times it switched back into predatory savagery toward

its own people and its neighbors. It was frequently violently conquered and then tended to imitate its conquerors. It is now caught up in imitating the Western ideological imperialism of Marxism, the physical imperialism of the Manchu empire, and the economic not-quite-post-colonial colonialist mentality of the not-quite-post-colonial Euro-American empires. It is also in the process of returning to its own soul, a soul of balance and harmony with humanity and nature, as it relearns its own deep ancient civilizational vision.

7. Therefore, it is not impossible that China, the waking giant, will quit its path of conquest empire and not seek to be a violent superpower, but will instead turn its great strength toward healing the overheated planet. It can listen to the Dalai Lama as one of the planet's clearest voices of reason, peacefulness, and the wise intelligence we need to overcome the crisis we are in. It can free his people and return Tibet to being an environmental sanctuary, the water tower of Asia, the Switzerland of Asia. In turn, the Dalai Lama, now and in future incarnations, and his capable and creative free people can help the Chinese rekindle their spiritual energies and restore their civilized lives of harmony and fulfillment.

8. It is not that this or that leader will do it just now or just then. No one can be sure. But cultivating the vision of the possibility, how easy it would be, how beneficial to all sides it would be, this is one way of keeping hope alive and creating a powerful resonance that will eventually reach the hearts of those empowered to effect such positive change.

9. In our lifetimes, the Soviet Union withdrew from its imperial behavior and liberated Eastern Europe and even the Ukraine without a shot being fired. The South African apartheid regime gave up that vicious and miserable racist life without any further violence. Who can say realistically that China will not see its enlightened self-interest fulfilled in truly freeing Tibet from its cumbersome occupation and impractical and destructive colonization?

10. Therefore, it is our duty and obligation to cultivate hope. We can free our imaginations from being stuck in the expectation of failure. We can free any enemy from expecting that he or she cannot become a friend. We can follow the Dalai Lama and never give up. We live in hope, as the realistic way to live. We live therefore without bitterness, joyfully and happily, while vigorously opposing violence and injustice. It is our duty to strive to live so happily, that even if someone kills us, we will die happy!

RESOURCES

FURTHER READING

H. H. Dalai Lama. *My Land and My People.* New York: Potala Publications, 1983.
————. *Freedom in Exile: The Autobiography of the Dalai Lama.* New York: Harper Collins, 1990.
————. *Ethics for the New Millennium.* New York: Riverhead Books, 1999.
————. *The Universe in a Single Atom: The Convergence of Science and Spirituality.* New York: Broadway Books, 2005.
————. *Collected Statements, Interviews, and Articles.* Dharamsala: DIIR Publications, 1986.
H. H. Dalai Lama & Jeffrey Hopkins, translator. *Kindness, Clarity, and Insight: The Fourteenth Dalai Lama, His Holiness Tenzin Gyatso.* Ithaca, New York: Snow Lion Publications, 1984.
H. H. Dalai Lama & Galen Rowell, photographer. *My Tibet.* Berkeley: University of California Press, 1990.

Adhe, Ama & Joy Blakeslee. *The Voice that Remembers: A Tibetan Woman's Inspiring Story of Survival.* Somerville, MA: Wisdom Publications, 1999.
Beer, Robert. *The Encyclopedia of Tibetan Symbols & Motifs.* Chicago: Serindia Publications, 2004.
Arpi, Claude. *The Fate of Tibet: When Big Insects Eat Small Insects.* New Delhi: Har-Anand Publications, 1999.
Avedon, John F. *In Exile from the Land of Snows.* New York: Knopf, 1984.
Bell, Sir Charles. *Portrait of a Dalai Lama: The Life and Times of the Great Thirteenth.* Somerville, MA: Wisdom Publications, 1987.
Fleming, Robert L., Dorje Tsering & Liu Wulin. *Across the Tibetan Plateau: Ecosystems, Wildlife, and Conservation.* New York: W. W. Norton & Company, 2006.
International Commission of Jurists. *The Question of Tibet and the Rule of Law.* Geneva, 1959.
Iyer, Pico. *The Open Road: The Global Journey of the Fourteenth Dalai Lama.* New York: Knopf, 2008.
Khétsun, Thupten. *Memories of Life in Lhasa under Chinese Rule.* New York: Columbia University Press, 2007.

Laird, Thomas. *The Story of Tibet: Conversations with the Dalai Lama*. New York: Grove Press, 2007.

Marshall, Steve. *Tibet Outside the TAR*. Washington, D.C.: International Campaign for Tibet, 1997. CD-ROM.

Norbu, Jamyang. *Shadow Tibet: Selected writings, 1989 to 2004*. New Delhi: Bluejay Books, 2007.

Norbulingka Institute. *Choyang* (Journal of the Institute). http://www.norbulingka.org.

Pachen, Ani & Adelaide Donnelley. *Sorrow Mountain: The Journey of a Tibetan Warrior Nun*. New York: Bantam Doubleday, 2000.

Schell, Jonathan. *The Unconquerable World: Power, Nonviolence, and the Will of the People*. New York: Metropolitan Books, 2003.

Shakabpa, Tsepon W. D. *Tibet: A Political History*. New York: Potala Publications, 1984.

Smith, Warren W., Jr. *Tibetan Nation: A History of Tibetan Nationalism and Sino-Tibetan Relations*. Boulder, CO: Westview Press, 1996.

———. *China's Tibet?* London: Rowman & Littlefield, 2008.

Thurman, Robert. *Inner Revolution: Life, Liberty, and the Pursuit of Real Happiness*. New York: Riverhead Books, 1991.

———. *Central Philosophy of Tibet: A Study and Translation of Jey Tsong Khapa's Essence of True Eloquence*. Princeton: Princeton University Press, 1988.

———. *Essential Tibetan Buddhism*. San Francisco: Harper San Francisco, 1996.

Tuttle, Gray. *Tibetan Buddhists in the Making of Modern China*. New York: Columbia University Press, 2005.

van Walt van Praag, Michael C. *The Status of Tibet: History, Rights, and Prospects in International Law*. Boulder, CO: Westview Press, 1987.

INTERNET RESOURCES AND WAYS TO GET INVOLVED

DALAILAMA.COM
The Office of His Holiness the Dalai Lama. The definitive place for the Dalai Lama's words, biographical information, and schedule of upcoming events. Stay tuned to what's happening with the Dalai Lama and get inspired by the work and words of this great man. Use this site to stay informed and support the Dalai Lama's vision for peace and justice in the world.

PHAYUL.COM
A central resource on the Web for news and information about Tibet and the activities of support organizations around the world. Includes an online Tibetan radio station playing Tibetan music and a rich audio and video section with recorded speeches, video clips, etc.